The Great Stat

TEXAS

Fundamental Concepts in Texas Government & Politics

Kendall Hunt
publishing company

E. Michael Young

Cover image © Shutterstock, Inc.

www.kendallhunt.com
Send all inquiries to:
4050 Westmark Drive
Dubuque, IA 52004-1840

Text alone ISBN: 978-1-5249-4928-0
Text with KHQ ISBN: 978-1-5249-4849-8

Printed in the United States of America

To my grandmother, Dorothy P. Young.
The first person to talk with me about politics.

CONTENTS

UNIT TWO
Texas Constitutions within the Federal System 67

UNIT THREE
Three Branches of Texas Government 127

PREFACE

With the *Great State of Texas: Fundamental Concepts in Texas Government & Politics*, I tried to do something unique: write a textbook students would actually read!

Students today read in a different way than their instructors. Instead of patiently reading through a whole article or chapter, they scan or search for the information they need. Professors hate it when a student says, "is this going to be on the test" or "is this important?", but students don't want to waste their time on non-essential information.

This textbook solves this problem by providing the essential concepts of Texas government in short, concise chapters. My students will no longer read the traditional textbook with 50 to 60-page chapters. But they will read the brief chapters in *The Great State of Texas* that provide the essential information in an easy-to-read format.

And the text provides other features for Millennials and Generation Z students that fit with their learning style:

- Each chapter, focusing on one topic, can be read in one sitting.
- Important terms are bolded and clearly defined.
- The text is segmented into short, easy to perceive sections.
- The textbook provides photos and graphs to help students remember and visualize important concepts.

And professors and teachers love *The Great State of Texas*. Whether they teach a freshmen college course, an AP high school class, or a home school group, instructors prefer the unique features of this textbook:

- Each chapter, covering a single topic, corresponds to one lecture or class period.
- The book is **politically balanced**, fairly describing the conservative and liberal perspectives.
- Essay questions and terms are provided at the end of each chapter.
- And the textbook provides a strong **historical perspective** that helps the student understand the proper context of Texas politics and government.

My great wish is that this textbook will help spark an interest in students to read more about the rich history and lively politics of *The Great State of Texas*.

NOTE TO INSTRUCTORS

This textbook, *The Great State of Texas,* covers the subject matter and learning outcomes proscribed by the THECB for a college-level course in Texas government.

Learning Outcomes

Upon successful completion of this course, students will:

1. Explain the origin and development of the Texas Constitution.
2. Demonstrate an understanding of state and local political systems and their relationship with the federal government.
3. Describe separation of powers and checks and balances in both theory and practice in Texas.
4. Demonstrate knowledge of the legislative, executive, and judicial branches of Texas government.
5. Evaluate the role of public opinion, interest groups, and political parties in Texas.
6. Analyze the state and local election process.
7. Describe the rights and responsibilities of citizens.
8. Analyze issues, policies, and political culture of Texas.

Core Curriculum

The Higher Education Coordinating Board (THECB) mandates that the core curriculum must ensure that students will develop the essential knowledge and skills they need to be successful in college, in a career, in their communities, and in life. Through the Texas Core Curriculum, students will gain a foundation of knowledge of human cultures and the physical and natural world, develop principles of personal and social responsibility for living in a diverse world, and advance intellectual and practical skills that are essential for all learning.

Students enrolled in GOVT 2306 core curriculum courses will complete assessments designed to measure the following core objectives:

Critical Thinking Skills—to include creative thinking, innovation, inquiry, and analysis, evaluation and synthesis of information.

Communication Skills—to include effective development, interpretation, and expression of ideas through written, oral, and visual communication.

Personal Responsibility—to include the ability to connect choices, actions, and consequences to ethical decision-making.

Social Responsibility—to include the ability to connect choices, actions, and consequences to ethical decision-making.

Student assessment of proficiencies mandated by THECB may include testing, projects, or assignments.

Suggestions for Assessing the THECB Core Curriculum

The THECB requires that all Texas Government course be assessed in four core curriculum areas: critical thinking (CT), communication skills (CS), social responsibility (SR), and personal responsibility (PR).

We suggest that the best way to measure students in these skills is through short essay questions with appropriate topics.

In order to write a good essay, a student needs to utilize good written communication and critical thinking skills. These skills can be graded using a **rubric** that lists a set of criteria to be measured.

Criteria for good communication skills: use proper grammar, explain points clearly, define terms, provide context, give examples, and summarize.

Criteria for good critical thinking skills: organize in a logical manner, make a thesis statement, support the thesis with evidence, analyze data and ideas, and make a convincing overall argument that arrives at a conclusion.

An instructor can measure all four core curriculum skills by assigning **short essay questions** that deal with social and personal responsibility:

1. What is your personal responsibility to vote? (measures CT, CS, SR, and PR) (Chapter 14)
2. What is your personal responsibility to get informed about Texas politics in order to be a knowledgeable voter? (CT, CS, SR, and PR) (Chapter 14)
3. What interest group would you consider joining in order to get involved with an issue you are concerned with? (CT, CS, SR, and PR) (Chapter 18)
4. What can you do to get involved in local government and improve your community? (CT, CS, SR, and PR) (Chapter 8)
5. What government policies would you support that provide for the general welfare? (CT, CS, SR, and PR) (Chapter 5)
6. What is the importance of law in society, and when would you consider breaking the law? (CT, CS, SR, and PR) (Chapter 13)
7. What percentage of your income would you pay in taxes to support government and government programs? (CT, CS, SR, and PR) (Chapter 17)

UNIT ONE

Political History of Texas

Texas Flag

CHAPTER 1

Six Flags over Texas

TOPICS

- Pre-Spanish History
- Texas as a Territory
- The Republic of Texas
- Texas Statehood
- Confederacy and Return to Union

LEARNING OBJECTIVES

When you finish reading this chapter, you will be able to:

1. Describe the history of Texas as a European territory.
2. Discuss how Texas won its independence from Mexico.
3. Explain why Texas was an independent nation before it became a state.
4. Discuss how the Civil War impacted Texas politically.

Just as people are a result of their upbringing and life experiences, countries and states are also a product of their history. For this reason, the first few chapters of this book are devoted to Texas history. Texas's political culture, constitutions, laws, and political institutions have been shaped by the unique history of the Great State of Texas.

PRE-SPANISH HISTORY

Several Native American groups had lived in Texas for thousands of years before the arrival of Europeans.

Native Indians: During the Ice Age, around twenty-five to ten thousand years ago, Asian tribal groups migrated to America across the Bering Land Bridge following migratory herds. Coming down into North America, these groups hunted mega-fauna, such as the mammoth and the giant bison. Then about seven to eight thousand years ago a period of global warming killed off the big game and changed the climate in Texas, making it warmer in the summer, colder in the winter, and producing less rainfall.

Eventually, several American Indian tribes settled in Texas, each developing their unique culture and way of life. Along the Gulf Coastal Plains, from east to west, lived the Atakapans, the Karankawas, and the Coahuiltecans. These were semi-migratory tribes that lived by hunting, fishing, and gathering along the wetlands and grasslands of the coast. Reminding us that mosquitoes have always been a nuisance in Texas, some of these groups rubbed alligator fat on their bodies to repel insects.

From central Texas to the High Plains of the panhandle lived the Apache. They practiced some agriculture but mostly lived by hunting the American bison, commonly called buffalo. The Apache used every part of the buffalo: eating the meat, using the hides for clothing and shelter, and

The Comanche Indians were skilled horsemen.

crafting the sinews and bones into tools and weapons. After the Spanish brought horses, the Apache became skilled horsemen. Another group renowned for their horsemanship was the Comanche, which migrated to northern Texas from the Great Plains in the 1700s. This war-like group was especially feared by other Indian tribes and European settlers.

The most civilized Texas tribe was the **Caddo**, *which lived in the Piney Woods of East Texas.* The Caddo Indians lived in sophisticated villages with large beehive homes and farmed maize along with a variety of other vegetables. Many Caddo villages featured earthen mounds used for religious and civic ceremonies. The Caddo Mounds State Historic Site, located in Alto, Texas, contains two mounds of what was once a Caddo Village established around 800 AD. The Caddo developed extensive trade networks, a refined pottery and textile culture, and a sophisticated oral tradition. The Caddo word for "friends" or "allies" was *tejas*. Early Spanish explorers and settlers used this word as a name for Texas, and thus today the Texas motto is "Friendship."

Caddo Indians

The most civilized Texas tribe, which lived in the Piney Woods of East Texas.

TEXAS AS A TERRITORY

Eventually, six flags would fly over the territory of Texas. The first two were the flags of Spain and France. After Mexico became independent from Spain, the Mexican flag would also fly over Texas.

The Spanish flag flew over Texas for 300 years.
© Globe Turner / Shutterstock.com

Spanish Explorers: The first flag to fly over Texas was carried by Spanish explorers. In 1519, Alonso Alvarez de Pineda, seeking a water route to Asia, explored the coastal area of Texas by ship. The first Spaniard to set foot on Texas soil was Cabeza de Vaca. In 1528, his expedition landed on the coast of Texas near Galveston. De Vaca suffered greatly in Texas, spending several years as a slave of the Karankawa. Remarkably, he survived and after returning to Spain wrote the first book about Texas, *La Relacion*, which provides fascinating details of Indian life before the influence of European cultures.

When De Vaca was in Mexico, some of his tall tales seemed to indicate to his listeners that the legendary Seven Cities of Cibola (gold-laden cities of enormous wealth) must be in or north of Texas. In 1540, Francisco Vasquez de Coronado set out to find the riches of Cibola. His expedition followed the Rio Grande north then crossed the panhandle of Texas. Coronado went as far north as present-day Kansas, but never found any treasure. Because these expeditions failed to discover any gold or silver, Spain lost interest in Texas and the Southwest for the next hundred and fifty years.

France: The second flag to fly over Texas was that of France. Robert de La Salle, an intrepid if mentally unstable French adventurer, explored Canada, the Great Lakes region, and the Mississippi River all the way down to New Orleans, thus claiming the Mississippi River basin, including East Texas, for France. In 1684, La Salle led an expedition of two ships and 300 settlers to set up a colony at the mouth of the Mississippi. Sailing hundreds of miles off course, La Salle landed in Texas and built Fort St. Louis in present-day Victoria, about 30 miles up the Guadalupe River from the Gulf of Mexico.

Certain that he was near the Mississippi, La Salle led his men on a wild goose chase all over Texas, from the Rio Grande to East Texas. After surviving several mutinies by his own men, La Salle was killed by Karankawas Indians near present-day Huntsville. All but a few of the original 300 members of his expedition died. Besides the fact that he built the first and only French fort in Texas, the significance of La Salle's expedition is that it led Spain to return to Texas. Fearful that the French would establish a colony in Texas, Spain launched a manhunt to capture all the members of La Salle's expedition, and then Spain returned to Texas to protect its territory against any future French ambitions.

Return of Spain: When Spain returned to Texas in the late 1600s, it developed the mission and presidio system as a way to hold and protect their land claims. Eventually, the Spanish would build 26 **missions** in Texas, *outposts established by the Spanish Catholic Church to convert native Indians, but that also served as agricultural, industrial, social, governmental, and religious centers.* **Presidios** *were walled fortresses with soldiers who were responsible for defending a particular area, including the local mission.* These served as a buffer against future French encroachment on Spanish territory and to fight against hostel Indians. The safety provided by the presidios encouraged some Europeans living in Mexico to settle in Texas. **Tejanos** *is the term used to describe people of Spanish or Mexican ancestry living in Texas.*

As part of the Spanish Empire for centuries, Texas was impacted by Spain in many ways. Many Texas rivers and geographical features have Spanish names, as do numerous cities and counties. More importantly for our discussion of Texas government, Spanish law has had a lasting influence on the Texas legal code and Constitution. Under Spanish law, women enjoyed more property rights than women under English law, debtors

Missions

Outposts in the territory of Texas established by the Spanish Catholic Church to convert Native Indians, but that also served as agricultural, industrial, social, governmental, and religious centers.

Presidios

Spanish walled fortresses with soldiers in the territory of Texas that were responsible for defending a particular area, including the local missions.

Tejanos

People of Spanish or Mexican ancestry living in Texas.

Conception Mission in San Antonio, built in 1731.
© NeonLight / Shutterstock.com

Homestead protection

Legal protections that guard somebody from being forced to sell their primary residence in order to pay a debt.

Empresario

An agent hired by Spain and then Mexico to recruit and develop a colony in Texas.

were safeguarded against imprisonment, and homesteads were protected. **Homestead protection** *means that somebody cannot be forced to sell their primary residence in order to pay a debt.* And unlike English law in which waterways were part of private property, under Spanish practice water belonged to all the residents to share. Today, the state of Texas retains title to all lakes, rivers, streams, and aquifers.

The Republic of Mexico: The Mexican flag became the third flag to fly over Texas when, in 1821, Mexico won its independence from Spain. After centuries of Spanish rule, only a few thousand *Tejanos* resided in the vast territory of Texas. In order to populate and build up the territory, Spain hired Moses Austin to settle Anglo families in Texas. Mexico renewed the contract with his son Stephen, who took over the project after his father suddenly died. Austin was the first Mexican **empresario**, *an agent hired to recruit and develop a colony*. Because he settled the first 300 families of Texas (known as the Old Three Hundred), Stephen F. Austin is often called the "Father of Texas."

Stephen F. Austin settled the "Old 300" between 1824 and 1828.
The New York Public Library / Art Resource, NY

The empresario system successfully increased the population of Texas, but it soon caused other problems for Mexico. Most of the American settlers came from the southern states with the intention of growing cotton, and thus they brought their slaves with them. Ten years after Mexican independence, the Texas population consisted of 10,000 Anglos, 1,000 slaves, 4,000 Tejanos, and perhaps 20,000 Native Indians. In order to get a homestead, Anglo settlers had to agree to convert to Catholicism, learn Spanish, and become Mexican citizens, but few settlers took these stipulations seriously. When Mexico banned slavery, the settlers found a legal loophole to get around the prohibition.

In 1824 Mexico ratified its new constitution, creating a republic with a federal system of state governments. Texas was combined with the state of Coahuila to create the Mexican state of Coahuila y Texas, with its capital in far-off Saltillo. In 1830, seeing that Texas was being taken over by Americans, Mexico banned further immigration and prohibited slavery. But by this time, the Anglo settlers had built up many grievances against the Mexican government. In 1833, Sam Houston, the former governor of Tennessee who came to Texas to start a new life, headed a convention that produced a list of suggested reforms. The Texians, as they called themselves, asked for Texas statehood (as part of Mexico), for Mexico to end the tariff on American imports, to suspend the ban on immigration, and to terminate the prohibition on slavery. Stephen F. Austin delivered this petition to Mexico City.

The Texas Revolution: From here things went from bad to worse. Austin was imprisoned in Mexico City on charges of treason. Santa Anna became dictator of Mexico, suspending the Constitution of 1824 and centralizing the government. Santa Anna took a hard line with Texas and ordered Mexican troops to confiscate the cannon at Gonzales. In defiance, the residents raised a flag with an image of the cannon that read, "COME AND TAKE IT." When they actually defeated the Mexican troops that came for the small cannon, Texians started to think independence was possible.

Raising the "Come and Take It" flag was an act of defiance by the Texians of Gonzales.

While the Alamo was under siege, Texas declared independence.
© Sean Pavone / Shutterstock.com

Then Santa Anna himself led some 2,500 troops into Texas. In February 1836, he fought the Texians at the Alamo, a former Spanish mission and presidio. Under the command of William B. Travis, 183 men held out before they were overwhelmed by superior numbers. All the men were killed and Santa Anna ordered that their bodies be piled up and burned. During the siege of the Alamo, on March 4, 1836, a convention at Washington-on-the Brazos voted that Texas separate from Mexico and drafted the Texas Declaration of Independence.

After the fall of the Alamo, Mexican troops headed for Gonzales and surrounded James Fannin's troops as they attempted to evacuate the town. Seeing the situation as hopeless, Fannin surrendered and the Mexicans hacked 350 prisoners to death and burned their bodies. Sam Houston was selected as Commander in Chief of the army of Texas. After the defeats at the Alamo and Gonzales, Houston knew that Texas could not afford to lose another battle. Although many called him a coward for not fighting, Houston wisely shadowed Santa Anna's army as it moved eastward, waiting for a propitious moment to attack. That moment came on April 21, 1836, when Santa Anna made camp on the shores of the San Jacinto River. Houston launched an attack and utterly defeated Santa Anna's troops in 18 minutes. After the *Battle of San Jacinto*, Santa Anna was captured and forced to sign a treaty, recognizing Texas's independence.

THE REPUBLIC OF TEXAS

The flag of the Republic of Texas was the fourth flag to fly over Texas. For nearly ten years, from 1836 to 1845, Texas was an independent nation, but due to political instability and lack of financial recourses, it was never able to truly coalesce into a real country.

Texas becomes a Nation: After winning the Texas Revolution, the people of Texas had no intention of being an independent country. They wanted to be part of the United States. But in 1836, Andrew Jackson had his hands full. After the Nullification Crisis, the Bank War, and the Indian Removal, Jackson could not take on another controversy. Adding Texas to the Union would have intensified the debate on slavery between the North and South because Texas would have become a slave state, perhaps several slave states. Also, the move likely would start a war with Mexico because they never accepted Texas independence. So, for ten years *Texas was an independent country*, the ***Republic of Texas***.

The hero of the Battle of San Jacinto, **Sam Houston**, *was elected the first and third president of the Republic of Texas.* His petition to join the Union was rejected by the US Congress. In the early days of the Texas Republic, there were no political parties, conflicts revolved around pro-Houston and anti-Houston factions. Sam Houston advocated peaceful relations with the Indians, paying down the debt, reducing tensions with Mexico, and eventually achieving Texas statehood.

Republic of Texas

Texas was an independent nation from 1836–1845.

Sam Houston

The hero of the Battle of San Jacinto, he was elected the first and third president of the Republic of Texas. In 1859, he became the seventh Governor of Texas.

The flag of the Republic of Texas flew over Texas from 1836 to 1845.

The faction opposed to Houston was led by David G. Burnet, who once challenged Houston to a duel (Houston refused by saying "he never fights downhill") and Mirabeau B. Lamar, the second president of the Republic of Texas. Lamar attempted to build up Texas's small navy and army and fought aggressively with the Indians, saying they must be brought to "total extinction or total expulsion." He had no intention of Texas becoming a state but instead dreamed of the Republic of Texas becoming a great nation, perhaps spreading all the way to California. But his dream was crushed in 1841 when Mexico captured his army and marched the prisoners all the way to Mexico City.

There are several reasons why the Republic of Texas failed to develop into an independent nation. Although the population exploded to just over 100,000 in ten short years, Texas did not have a taxable population large enough to fund a government and a military. And due to intense political infighting, the government could barely function. Also, Texas wasn't able to achieve diplomatic recognition from Mexico or support from European nations. In the end, the citizens of Texas always wanted to be part of the United States, and they got their wish in 1846.

TEXAS STATEHOOD

The flag of the United States of America became the fifth flag to fly over Texas, but the early years of Texas statehood were marked by growing division in the nation over the issue of slavery.

Texas Joins the Union: Right after the Texas Revolution, Texans voted for annexation. But political divisions in America made this impossible. It was not until December 29, 1845, that Texas became the twenty-eighth state in the Union. This was accomplished after the pro-annexation presidential candidate, James K. Polk, won the election. Some members of Congress were afraid that Texas statehood would rekindle the slavery debate and start a war with Mexico, but the public was caught up in *Manifest Destiny* (the idea that America was destined to occupy the North American continent) and they were glad to add Texas to the Union.

Sam Houston, the first president of the Republic of Texas, had always wanted Texas to join the Union.

The Texas Articles of Annexation of 1845 contained two unique features: (a) When Texas became a state, it would retain ownership of its public lands. This was because Congress refused to accept the land in exchange for Texas's $10 million debt. Today this land provides Texas with hundreds of millions of dollars in state revenue, some of which helps finance the public colleges of

Texas. And, (b) the articles also granted Texas the privilege of creating up to four additional states. Southern pro-slavery interests wanted more slave states and thus more US Senators. Contrary to popular belief, the articles did not allow Texas the right to secede from the Union.

The Mexican–American War: As many people feared, Texas statehood did result in war with Mexico. The Mexican-American War lasted from 1846 to 1848. Although it was more difficult than many predicted, America won the war, and both sides signed the Treaty of Guadalupe Hidalgo. The United States paid $15 million (equivalent to $420 million today), assumed the $3.25 million debt Mexico had owed before the war, and gained the southwest territory (what is now Texas, New Mexico, California, Arizona, and Utah). The treaty also established the Rio Grande as the border between Texas and Mexico, but it was still unclear how far north Texas extended.

Texas Gets its Current Shape in 1850: You may have seen old maps of Texas which depicted the state's territory going all the way up into the territories of New Mexico and Utah. Well, as part of the Compromise of 1850, the US government purchased this land from Texas for $10 million, finally eradicated the debts left over from the Republic of Texas. This land purchase by the federal government cut out the Northwest corner of Texas, giving it its current shape.

Adelsverein Society

An organization that tried to establish a Germany colony in Texas in the mid-1800s.

Texas from 1845–1860: During this period, the population of Texas significantly increased as more settlers came in from other parts of America and Europe. In the 1840s and 1850s, some 25,000 people emigrated from Germany, settling mostly in the Hill Country of central Texas. They were sponsored by the **Adelsverein Society**, *which tried to establish a German colony in Texas*. At this time most Texans were farmers and Texas grew into the fifth largest cotton producer of the southern states. About one-third of Texas farmers owned at least one slave. The cotton/slave labor economy explains Texas's connection with the pro-slavery South. Most of the political disputes of early Texas statehood revolved around the issue of slavery and whether Texas should join the southern rebellion.

Sam Houston served in the US Senate representing Texas from 1848 to 1859. Although he did not engage in the debate on the morality of slavery, he consistently remained a strong Unionist. In response to pro-southern forces in Texas that advocated seceding from the Union, Houston warned that such a rebellion would be an "unequal contest" in which the southern states would "go down in a sea of blood and smoking ruin." In an attempt to impose calm and reason on Texas, Houston ran for governor in 1859 and won, but he would fail to keep Texas out of the War Between the States.

CONFEDERACY AND RETURN TO UNION

When Texas joined the Confederacy in 1861, the Confederate flag was the sixth flag to fly over Texas. But after the South lost the Civil War, Texas returned under the flag of the United States of America.

Secession: After Abraham Lincoln was elected in 1860, a Texas convention, dominated by pro-secessionist Democrats, voted to leave the Union. Governor San Houston called the convention illegal. The Texas legislature, however, upheld it as legitimate. After Houston refused to sign an oath to the Confederacy, he was removed from office. Twice Lincoln had offered to send Houston 50,000 federal troops to keep Texas in the Union, but Houston refused because he did not want to start a civil conflict in Texas. Then Houston retired to Huntsville and never returned to public office.

On February 1, 1861, a constitutional convention overwhelmingly voted for Texas to secede from the Union. It published a "Declaration of Causes," which stated that the people of Texas originally joined the Union with the intention of "holding, maintaining, and protecting the institution of slavery . . . which her people intended should continue in all future time." But when a "great sectional party" (Lincoln's Republican Party) was elected, it threatened the "beneficial and patriarchal system of African slavery" and thus Texas was forced to secede from the Union. So, Texas made it clear that it was joining the Confederacy to defend the institution of slavery.

Civil War 1861–1865: Perhaps 60,000 to 70,000 Texans served in the Civil War, with about 12,000 to 15,000 losing their lives. Although few battles were fought on Texas territory, Texas supplied a large number of troops to various Confederate armies. Texans fought in most of the major battles in the eastern theater, including Antietam and Gettysburg.

In the West, Texas was responsible for defending the western territory and the Mexican border and for shipping cotton to European markets through Mexico. No major Civil War battle took place in Texas, but there were skirmishes along the Gulf Coast, a naval battle at Galveston, and fighting along the Red River, resulting in the taking of thousands of Union prisoners which were held in Camp Ford in Tyler, Texas. Since Texas territory was not invaded, the people of Texas suffered fewer hardships than those in the battleground states.

Nearly 15,000 Texans lost their lives in the Civil War.

Texas Rejoins the Union: The Civil War ended on April 9, 1865, when Robert E. Lee surrendered to Ulysses S. Grant in the small town of Appomattox Courthouse. Because participants had not heard that the war had ended," the last Civil War battle actually took place a month later near Brownsville, Texas (known as the Battle of Palmito Ranch). After the Civil War, with the defeat of the Confederate states, Texas rejoined the Union and the American flag once again flew over Texas.

Like many southern states after the Civil War, Texas found itself in debt and occupied by their former enemy, Union soldiers and Republicans. Near anarchy reigned in Texas for a period of time after the fall of the Confederacy. Order was restored when Union troops occupied Texas. And on June 19, 1865, slaves were informed that they were now free when Union General Gordon Granger issues General Order #3. This date is now celebrated by African Americans as **Juneteenth**, *a holiday celebrating the abolition of slavery in Texas*. Slavery officially ended in America in December of 1865, when the Thirteenth Amendment was ratified.

Juneteenth

A holiday celebrating the abolition of slavery in Texas held on June 19.

Slaves in Texas found out they were freed on June 19, 1865.

NOTES

Randolph B. Campbell. *Gone to Texas: A History of the Lone Star State*. Oxford: Oxford University Press, 2003.

James L. Haley. *Passionate Nation: The Epic History of Texas*. New York: Free Press, 2006.

ESSAY QUESTIONS

1. Why didn't Texas immediately become a state after independence from Mexico?
2. What were some of the influences of Spain on Texas?
3. What were the unique features of the terms of annexation by which Texas became a state?

TERMS

Adelsverein Society:____________________

Caddo Indians:____________________

Empresario:____________________

Homestead protection: ____________________

Missions:____________________

Presidios:____________________

Republic of Texas:____________________

Sam Houston:____________________

Tejanos:____________________

Juneteenth:____________________

TEXAS FUN & FACTS SHEET 1

How to Speak Texan

1. **Drop the G from the end of most words:** Instead of saying "eating," "going," or "fixing," a Texan will say "eatin," "goin," or "fixin."

   We've been fishin' all night.

2. **Use Y'all:** A true Texan will never say "you guys" or "all of you," but instead will always use "y'all."

   Hey, Bubba Joe and Sue Ann, are y'all fixin' to go to the rodeo?

3. **Ain't:** Like y'all, Texans like contractions. Another popular one is "ain't," instead of "am not."

   I ain't never goin' to New York.

4. **All sodas are called "coke":** The only exception is Dr Pepper, which was invented in Texas before Coca-Cola.

   I need a coke. What kind? 7-Up.

5. **Use "fixin' to" as much as possible:** Never say that you "plan on doing" something. If a Texan is going to do something, he is "fixin' to" do it.

   I'm fixin' to get a new pair of cowboy boots.

6. **The Texas swear word is "Dang!"** If a Texan is disappointed with a situation, he will say DANG!

   Dang! Somebody hit my truck.

7. **Use a little Texas/Spanish lingo:** Texans pronounce Spanish words their own unique way.

   Gracias (grassy - ass), Amigo (ahh – me – go),
   Manana (mahn – ya – nah), and cerveza (ser – vay – sah).

8. **Howdy:** Only a Yankee would say hello or hi. A True Texan greets you with "Howdy!"

CHAPTER 2

Texas Political History I

TOPICS

- Reconstruction
- Post-Civil War Conservative Democrats
- The Populist Era
- The Progressive Era
- WWI, the 1920s, and the Return of the Fergusons
- The Great Depression

LEARNING OBJECTIVES

When you finish reading this chapter, you will be able to:

1. Describe the significance of E. J. Davis.
2. Compare the Populist and Progressive Movements.
3. Discuss the political career of James Ferguson.
4. Explain the political developments in Texas during the Great Depression.

This chapter covers the political history of Texas from Reconstruction to the Great Depression. During this time, Texas was a one-party state in which one political party dominated the Great State of Texas. During Reconstruction, the Republican Party, propped up by the Republicans in Congress, ruled Texas. But after the end of Reconstruction in 1875, Texas politics was once again dominated by the Democratic Party. Typical of the southern Democratic Party of this era, Texas Democrats resisted social change, advocated small government, and appealed to the grit and self-reliance of the Texas farmer. Texas was a rural state with few cities, and no politician could be successful without winning the support of small-town folk and family famers.

RECONSTRUCTION

Reconstruction (1865–1875) is the term given to the tumultuous period following the Civil War. During this time, America struggled to solve many difficult political and social problems resulting from the Civil War: By what terms should the former Confederate states be accepted back into the Union? What political status would the 4 million newly freed slaves have in society? And how much government assistance should be afforded to the freedmen? On all these issues Texas fought bitterly with the policies of the federal government.

Presidential and Congressional Reconstruction: Before the end of the Civil War, Abraham Lincoln outlined rather easy terms by which the former Confederate state could return to the Union. After Lincoln died, Vice President Andrew Johnson, upon taking the presidency, implemented the plan known as *Presidential Reconstruction*. Basically, rebel states could rejoin the Union by recognizing the *Thirteenth Amendment*, which prohibited slavery in America, and pledging loyalty to the United States. But the North quickly became dissatisfied with this plan.

The former Confederate states quickly rejoined the Union and elected the very same secessionists and pro-slavery leaders that helped start the war in

During Reconstruction, the nation fought over what political rights the freed slaves should be granted.

the first place. And southern states adopted **black codes,** *laws that denied blacks the right to vote, serve on juries, marry a white person, make their own labor decisions, and many other ordinances that treated Black Americans as second-class citizens.* Outraged that Confederate leaders so quickly returned to power and denied blacks their rights, Republicans in the US Congress adopted the *Fourteenth Amendment*, which states that freedmen are US citizens and the states must treat all citizens equally under the law. Then Congress crafted a new reconstruction plan.

Black codes

Laws that denied blacks the right to vote, serve on juries, marry a white person, make their own labor decisions, and many other ordinances that treated Black Americans as second-class citizens.

Under *Congressional Reconstruction*, the South was divided into five military zones. Texas was under the authority of General Philip Sheridan. He replaced hundreds of officials and judges elected under Presidential Reconstruction with Republicans and moderate Democrats with no Confederate ties. And Texas had to adopt a new constitution. Presided over by Edmund J. Davis, the convention of 1869 produced what critics called the "radical constitution." It allowed all adult males, white or black, to vote and hold office. It centralized power under a strong governor with an extended four-year term. And it gave the governor the power to appoint many officials, including all state-wide offices and judgeships.

Scalawag

A derogatory term used during Reconstruction to describe southern Republicans.

The Governorship of E. J. Davis (1870–1874): The voters of Texas, which under the new voter registration rules included blacks but excluded many former Confederates, approved the new constitution and elected Republican E. J. Davis for governor. Davis was a Texan and a radical Republican who had fought for the Union in the Civil War. After the election, Texas was re-admitted to the Union and military authority was dissolved.

Governor Davis used the augmented powers of the "radical constitution" to reform Texas. He filled hundreds of offices and judgeships with Republicans, including Black Americans. To restore law and order and protect the freed slaves against physical violence, Davis created a state militia and a state police force, 40 percent of which were black. And he established a free public school system in Texas. The Republican-controlled state legislature approved the public school system, placing it under centralized authority, and establishing the first college in Texas, the Texas Agriculture and Mechanical College (Texas A & M), which was paid for by land grants.

Edmund J. Davis was the much hated Republican Governor of Texas during Reconstruction.

Texans, however, deeply resented the governorship of Davis. Many Texans felt that the Davis Administration was imposed on a defeated people and they hated the Republican's pro-black policies. *They called southern Republicans* **"scalawags."**

During Reconstruction, white supremacist groups used violence to scare African Americans away from political participation.

And they called *northern "Yankees" who came to the South to get government jobs, such as teachers, railroad workers, and officials in the Freedmen's Bureau,* **"Carpetbaggers."** White supremacist groups, similar to the Ku Klux Klan, killed, beat, and intimidated thousands of blacks and the white scalawags that attempted to help them vote or run for political office.

Then in the 1873 election, when ex-Confederates were allowed to vote, the Democrats won in a landslide and Richard Coke was elected governor. But due to a legal technicality, the Davis Supreme Court declared the election invalid. Davis locked himself in the capitol building and surrounded himself with state police, refusing to relinquish office until the issue was resolved. He asked President Grant to send federal troops to help him, but Grant refused. Then the legislature broke into the capitol building, formed a quorum, and declared the election valid. Finally, Davis left the building.

Carpetbagger

A derogatory term for northerners who came to the South during Reconstruction to get jobs.

For many decades, E. J. Davis was vilified by politicians, journalists, and historians. They depicted his governorship as a tyranny of unlimited power and corruption. Because he raised property taxes to fund the new public school system, they accused him of imposing punitive taxes. And because he tried to protect the rights of Black Americans, he was called a "Black Republican." Today, historians have a more balanced view of Davis. It is true that he probably tried to change Texas society too fast, but now he is considered a hero by many rather than a villain.

The End of Republicanism: In 1874, Texas once again became a one-party state but this time controlled by the Democrats. Governor Coke called for a convention to rewrite the Texas Constitution. The convention consisted of 75 Democrats, 15 Republicans, and 40 members belonging to the Grange (a Populist, pro-farmers party). The 1876 Constitution, often called the "redeemer constitution," cut expenditures, decentralized state government, returned the governorship to a two-year term, and severely restricted the appointment power of the governor. Although heavily amended, this is the constitution used today in Texas.

John H. Reagan

He was a postmaster general of the Confederacy, a member of the US House of Representatives, and the first Railroad Commissioner.

The legacy of the Davis administration had two long-lasting effects on Texas. First, because the "radical constitution" used by Davis centralized powers under a strong governor, the 1876 "redeemer constitution" went far in the other direction to weaken the governorship and radically *decentralize* Texas state government. And second, because the Republican governorship of Davis was so vilified, it created a rhetorical tool for Democrats to defeat Republicans, helping them to dominate the state for generations.

POST-CIVIL WAR CONSERVATIVE DEMOCRATS

After the Democrats returned to power and drafted the 1876 Constitution, the Republican Party became a minority and thus powerless party. Still led by E. J. Davis, the Republicans received support mostly from blacks and German Americans, but its numbers were too small to challenge the Democrats except in a few of counties. During this period, the Democrats governed on the principle of very limited government.

John H. Reagan was the first Texas Railroad Commissioner.
Library of Congress

Conservative Democrats: From 1874 to 1890, Texas was ruled by a series of conservative Democratic governors: Richard Coke, Richard B. Hubbard, Oran M. Roberts, and John Ireland. They held traditional political views, believing that government should do little beyond protecting private property, maintaining law and order, limiting spending, and keeping taxes low. The two major accomplishments of this era, the establishment of the University of Texas at Austin and the construction of the capitol building, were paid for by land grants, not by raising taxes, which the people of Texas adamantly opposed.

John H. Reagan: One of the most well regarded Texas politicians of this era was **John H. Reagan**, who *became*

Postmaster General of the Confederacy, a member of the US House of Representatives, and the first Railroad Commissioner. Born in Tennessee, Reagan came to Texas at the age of nineteen. At first working as a surveyor in Kaufman County, he then studied law on his own and passed the bar in 1848. From 1852–1857, he served as district judge in Palestine. In 1857, he was elected to the US Congress. Reagan was a moderate who supported the Union and resigned when Texas seceded. During the Civil War, he served as Postmaster General of the Confederacy. His office was the best run Confederate department, actually making a profit!

In 1865, Reagan was imprisoned in Boston with Confederate Vice President Alexander Stephens and spent 22 months in solitary confinement. He wrote an open letter to Texas urging cooperation with the Union, renunciation of secession, the abolition of slavery, and allowing freedmen to vote. He warned of military rule if Texas did not follow his advice. For this he was hated by Texans. He was released a year after he wrote this letter. Over time, people realized he was right. His reputation grew as a wise statesman, and later in life he was often called "Old Roman" or the "Texas Cincinnatus."

Populist Movement (1880s to 1896)

A political revolt by the farmers against the ruling class, business interests, and intellectual elite.

After the Civil War, Reagan had a long and distinguished career in public service. He helped remove E. J. Davis from office. He served in the US Congress from 1875 to 1887. And he was a leading delegate at the constitution convention of 1875, which produced our current Texas constitution. In 1887, though just elected to the US Senate, he served as the first Railroad Commissioner of Texas, appointed by his friend Jim Hogg. As commissioner, he regulated the Texas railroads until 1903. Before he retired, Reagan founded the Texas State Historical Association. In Palestine, there is a statue of John H. Reagan in Reagan Park.

POPULIST ERA

Conservative Democrats stayed in power, in part, by reminding voters of the horrendous decade under the rule of the Black Republicans. Large farmers, merchants, railroad owners and managers, bankers, and other segments of the population were content with the policies of conservative Democrats, but small famers and poor rural folk began to feel that very limited government did little to help improve their lives. This is when a new type of politician emerged: a populist, one that could relate to the needs and fears of the common man. The **Populist Movement** (1880s to 1896) *was a political revolt by the farmers against the ruling class, business interests, and intellectual elites.*

Farmers' Groups: Although Texas as a state was producing more and more agricultural products, many small farmers were losing money. And a growing number of Texas farmers were *sharecroppers* or *tenants*: farmers who did not own their land but paid rent with a percentage of their harvest, normally one-fourth to one-half of their crop. Small farmers did not understand the macroeconomic trends that were taking place at that time. With advancing agricultural science and mechanization, large farming businesses could out-produce small farmers and make a bigger profit. The stark reality was that America no longer needed so many famers. (At this time 40 percent of Texans were farmers, and today less than 3 percent are full-time farmers.)

In the 1880s, nearly 50 percent of Texas farmers were tenants.

During this period of transition from the family farmer to big ag business, two organizations, the *Grange* and the *Farmers' Alliance*, gained political clout as they won the support of poor farmers. These organizations suggested many reforms, such as cooperates, railroad regulation, easy credit, and public storage facilities for grain. They also advocated that the federal government convert to a currency backed by silver (not gold) to increasing the money supply. It was thought that if the government created more inflation, then farm prices would go up. (But they failed to understand that *all* other prices would also go up, so the farmers still would not come out ahead.)

Populist Party: While the Farmers' Alliance started in Texas, a new party that also catered to the common man was formed in the Midwest. Bringing together disgruntled farmers and union workers, the *People's Party* or Populist Party formed to challenge elites in both the Democratic and Republican parties. The People's Party Platform, written at the national party convention in Omaha in 1892, said that current government policies are breeding two classes in America—"tramps and millionaires." The platform, moving beyond the reforms advocated by the Farmers' Alliance, demanded the free coinage of silver, the eight-hour workday, a progressive income tax, and the government ownership of the railroads, the banks, and the telegraph companies.

At the next presidential election, a young and energetic Democrat ran for president on Populist themes. William Jennings Bryan spellbound the public with his famous "Cross of Gold" speech in which he argued for the silver standard and appealed to the small farmer by skillfully using religious and home-spun phrases. Now the People's Party faced a dilemma. If they supported Bryan and he won the election, then the Populist agenda would be advanced. However, if they "fused" or joined the Democratic Party, then the People's Party would cease to exist. The Texas People's Party decided to endorse Bryan, but he ended up losing the election to Republican William McKinley. And true enough, the People's Party died.

William Jennings Bryan won the support of small farmers with his "Cross of Gold" speech.
Library of Congress

Governor Jim Hogg: The first Populist to become Governor of Texas was Jim Hogg. Known as "Big Jim," **James Stephen Hogg** *was an East Texas lawyer and became the twentieth Governor of Texas by running as a Populist Democrat.* He was born near Rusk, Texas, becoming the first native-born Governor of Texas.

Weighing in at over 300 pounds, he was a commanding presence on and off the stage. On the political stump, he would often chug down a whole pitcher of water in one drink. He named his daughter "Ima Hogg." Early in life, he received only a basic education and worked at and ran a few newspapers. Then he studied law and in 1873 became justice of the peace in Quitman. From 1882 to 1884, Hogg was a Texas district attorney. Hogg practiced law in Tyler, Texas. In 1886 Hogg became state Attorney General on a platform of railroad regulation reform. A Populist, he put an end to railroad pooling and fought big corporations. He won a lawsuit against railroad tycoon Jay Gould. With the support of farmers, ranchers, and small merchants, Hogg won the election of Governor of Texas in 1890.

James Stephen Hogg

An East Texas lawyer, Hogg became the twentieth Governor of Texas running as a Populist Democrat.

Railroad Commission

It no longer regulates the railroad industry but instead regulates Texas's vast oil and natural gas industries, making it one of the most powerful state agencies in the nation.

Two years later, running on the Populist platform, Hogg won a second term as governor. The major issue of the campaign was railroad regulation. In 1891 he created the three-member railroad commission, appointing his friend John H. Reagan as Commissioner. Special interests fought the creation of the commission for two years in the courts. The courts finally determined the commission was valid. Today the **Railroad Commission** *no longer regulates the railroad industry but instead regulates Texas's vast oil and natural gas industries, making it one of the most powerful state agencies in the nation.*

PROGRESSIVE ERA

While the Populist Movement sought to help poor farmers in the South and Midwest, the Progressive Movement had a national scope and was led by more educated, urban leaders. The **Progressive Movement** (1900–1920) *sought to use government as a tool to guide the enlightened progress of society, help the common man, and fight business and political corruption.* Progressive Republicans and Democrats initiated many important reforms that changed American politics. They enforced anti-trust laws and broke up the big monopolies, created national parks, protected the consumer, regulated the medicine industry, ended child labor, gave women the right to vote, and implemented prohibition.

Progressive Movement (1900–1920)

A political movement that sought to use government as a tool to guide the enlightened progress of society, help the common man, and fight business and political corruption.

In Texas, however, few Populist and Progressive reforms were implemented. Political leaders adopted a more Populist approach to politicking, but because of the conservative nature of Texas, radical reforms seldom garnered much support. This section will focus on two prominent Progressive Texans, one had a major impact on the nation (Edward M. House) and the other had a major impact on Texas (Jim Ferguson).

Edward M. House: House's father amassed a fortune during the Civil War by running guns and became mayor of Houston. When his father died before he graduated from Cornell University, House returned to Texas to run the family business. Eventually, he sold the cotton plantations and went into banking. He moved to New York in 1902 and anonymously wrote the novel *Philip Dru*, in which the hero fights the rich and becomes a dictator, initiating Progressive reforms.

House returned to Texas and became a political consultant and campaign supervisor. After helping Jim Hogg win the governorship, House advised the next three governors of Texas. Then he moved to national politics and helped Woodrow Wilson win the Democratic nomination for president in 1912. House became close friends with Wilson and helped set up his administration. He was offered the cabinet position of his choice, but instead asked to be an advisor-at-large. He was even provided living quarters within the White House. In 1916, House managed Wilson's successful campaign for reelection.

Although lacking any education or experience in foreign affairs, House became very involved in diplomacy during WWI. After the sinking of the Lusitania, he saw the conflict as between autocracy and democracy, urging Wilson to support England and France against Germany. House assembled "the Inquiry," a group of scholars that formed the basis of Wilson's famous "14 Point Plan." House also helped orchestrate the constitution for the League of Nations. From 1917–1919, he was Wilson's chief negotiator at the Paris Peace Conference. But after the Treaty of Versailles was signed, he urged Wilson to compromise with Senator Henry Cabot Lodge, which Wilson refused to do, and the US Senate failed to ratify the treaty. At this point, their relationship began to falter. When Wilson returned home from Paris in 1919, he dismissed House. They never spoke again and House retired from politics.

The Rise of Farmer Jim: A controversial and powerful force in Texas politics, **James Ferguson** *was the twenty-sixth Governor of Texas (1915–1917), and served two non-consecutive terms as first gentleman of Texas.* Ferguson grew up on a family farm and for a few years worked as a migrant worker in several states. An intelligent man, he studied law and got accepted to the Texas bar in 1897. Later he started several businesses in real estate and banking, and in 1907 he founded Temple State Bank. Although he had never held elected office, he adopted the name "Farmer Jim" and ran for governor on the platform of helping the small tenant farmers who lived "at the forks of the creek." His energy and folksy manner served him well on the political stump and he won the governorship in 1914.

James Ferguson

He was the twenty-sixth Governor of Texas (1915–1917), and served two non-consecutive terms as first gentleman of Texas.

Wet

A supporter of the legalization of alcohol.

At a time when most Progressives were *dry* (supporting prohibition), Ferguson came out as **wet** (*supported the legalization of alcohol*). But in other regards he was a moderate Progressive Democrat, supporting legislature that attempted to alleviate the problems of tenant farmers, prisons, schools, and the courts. After winning reelection in 1916, he focused on

James and Miriam Ferguson dominated Texas politics for a generation.

building highways and reforming education. Then he got into a quarrel with the board of University of Texas. Angry that they refused to fire some professors that Ferguson found objectionable, and disapproving of the new president, Ferguson vindictively cut off funds to the whole university with a line item veto. This caused a tremendous backlash from people who supported the college.

In July of 1917, a Travis County grand jury indicted Ferguson on nine charges of embezzlement and misuse of public funds. Then the state legislature called for a special session to consider impeachment. Surprisingly, Ferguson approved the special session. Within a few weeks the Texas House of Representatives voted for twenty-one articles of impeachment, including accepting bribes from alcohol companies, tampering with state officials, and refusing to disclose the source of a $150,000 loan. By a two-thirds vote, the Texas Senate removed him from office and banned him from ever holding public office in the state of Texas.

WWI, THE 1920S, AND THE RETURN OF THE FERGUSONS

In the years before and after WWI, the population of Texas grew. People moved to Texas because of its warm climate. Also several federal military bases were established in Texas to guard against a Mexican attack (this was due to the Zimmerman Note, in which Germany promised that if Mexico joined the fight against America, after the WWI Mexico would be rewarded with the southwest territory, including Texas). Nationally, the 1920s was an era of tremendous innovation and prosperity as new industries flourished: autos, radios, the movies, electric appliances, and synthetic chemicals, to just name a few. In Texas, it was a boom time for the oil industry. Oil was discovered in the Permian Basin and for the first time Texas led the nation in oil production.

Texas was one of the first states to give women the right to vote.
© Tony Baggett / Shutterstock.com

Politically, the post-WWI era marked the end of Progressive reforms, with the exception of the ratification of the Eighteenth Amendment (Prohibition) and the Nineteenth Amendment (woman's suffrage). The 1920s also saw a rise of the new KKK, gaining a majority in the Texas state legislature. Fortunately, Ma Ferguson was successful in fighting the Klan.

Prohibition and Woman's Suffrage: Before the end of the decade, Texas voted to approve the last two major Progressive reforms. Alcohol was seen as something that undermined the basic American values of temperance, self-control, and industry. Prohibitionists also claimed that alcohol was detrimental to the health and well-being of the individual and the family. In 1918 Texas ratified the Eighteenth Amendment, making the manufacture, sale, and consumption of alcohol illegal. Texas was also a leader in the woman's suffrage movement. In 1918, the Texas Equal Suffrage Association (founded in 1903) was successful at persuading the state legislature to pass a law giving women the right to vote in the primary. Then in 1919 Texas was the ninth state to ratify the Nineteenth Amendment, giving women the right to vote in all elections.

The Klan: *In the 1860s, during Reconstruction, the original* **Ku Klux Klan** *used violence to intimidate blacks from voting and participating in politics.* In the 1920s, the KKK was reborn in the face of post-WWI social changes. The new Klan was a patriotic, Protestant, fraternal organization that was devoted to anti-black, anti-Jew, anti-Catholic, and anti-Progressive causes. The Klan supported native-born rule and the return to a traditional way of life. It used intimidation and violence to frighten groups it perceived as a threat to America. From 1921–1925, the Klan played a major role in Texas politics as perhaps 80,000 Texans were members of the "invisible empire."

Ku Klux Klan

During Reconstruction, this white supremacist group used violence to intimidate blacks from voting and participating in politics.

The Return of the Fergusons: The strongest anti-Klan candidate in the gubernatorial election of 1924 was **Miriam "Ma" Ferguson**, *wife of the impeached and convicted Farmer Jim, who was the first woman Governor of Texas.* As part of his impeachment, James Ferguson (who by this time started calling himself "Pa" Ferguson) was banned from holding office in Texas. So, to get around this his wife ran for governor, but people knew that he would really be running things. They ran on the platform of "two governors for the price of one" and their campaign slogan was "Me for Ma, and I aint got a darn thing against Pa."

Miriam Ferguson

The first woman Governor of Texas and wife of James Ferguson, the impeached Governor of Texas.

Once again the Fergusons appealed to the poor folk and the tenant farmer (in the 1920s tenancy rose to 60 percent). The Fergusons ran against Felix D. Robertson, a known Klansman. Pa argued that Robertson would be under the directive of the "Grand Gizzard," and Ma Ferguson won the election. Once in office, they pushed a bill through the legislature prohibiting the wearing of a mask in public—a very effective anti-Klan law. But they were criticized for their lenient pardoning policy. They released over 2,000 convicts and rumors arose that Pa was accepting bribes from family members of prisoners. In 1926 Ma was defeated in her reelection bid to Attorney General Dan Moody, also a reformer and anti-Klan candidate.

THE GREAT DEPRESSION

In 1929, the economy collapsed, ushering in a decade-long period of job loss and bankruptcy known as the Great Depression. By 1932, unemployment in America reached 30 percent. At first, Texas was not affected as badly as some other parts of the nation. The Texas oil industry remained strong. And although Texas farmers were poor, at least they could grow their own food and feed their families. But then things got bad for Texas as oil prices collapsed and a multi-year drought (called the Dust Bowl) hit northern Texas.

The New Deal: In 1932 Franklin D. Roosevelt ran for president and defeated Herbert Hoover. He promised a "new deal" for America to combat the Depression by focusing on three Rs: relief, recovery, and reform. Many New Deal programs had a big impact on Texas. About 50,000 young men worked for the Civilian Conservation Corps (CCC), improving the parks and forests. Nearly 240,000 men worked for the Civil Works Administration (CWA) and other public works agencies, building such things as the Riverwalk in San Antonio. The most important New Deal program was Social Security, which had three parts: an old–age pension, unemployment insurance, and welfare (aid to poor families and the handicapped). These programs were very popular in Texas.

During the Great Depression, the CWA built the Riverwalk in San Antonio.

Ma Ferguson Returns: In the same year Franklin Roosevelt was elected president, the Fergusons returned to the governor's mansion for the third time. In 1932 Ma won the governorship on a platform of economy in government. She hired a private firm to suggest a plan of reorganization. They recommended reorganizing the state bureaucracy into twenty departments. And they also recommended reorganizing the college and school systems. Most of these reforms, however, were never implemented and they did little to alleviate the suffering during the Great Depression. Having served two non-consecutive terms, Ma did not run for reelection and the Fergusons retired from politics.

James Nance Garner: On the national level, the best known Texas politician during the Great Depression was "Cactus Jack" Garner. **James Nance Garner** *became the first vice president from Texas.* He was born in South Texas and attended Vanderbilt University for one semester and then studied law. He was elected County Judge in 1896. He then served two terms as a Texas representative and picked the official state flower—the prickly pear cactus. In 1902, he was elected to the US House of Representatives, winning fourteen consecutive terms. In 1931, he was elected Speaker of the House. He was liked by members of both parties in Congress, in part because he held what he called the "Board of Education," drinking parties in the backrooms during Prohibition.

James Nance Garner

He was the Speaker of the House of Representatives and the first Vice President of the United States from Texas (1933–1941).

In 1932, Garner ran for the Democratic presidential nomination. Franklin Roosevelt did not have a majority of the delegates, so he cut a deal with Garner and selected him as vice president. Garner served two terms as FDR's vice president, from 1933–1941. As VP, he was given little to do. Garner is famous for saying that the vice presidency is "not worth a bucket of warm piss." During his second term, his relationship with FDR soured as he opposed FDR's Court Scheme, supported a balanced budget, and opposed a third term for any president. After Garner unsuccessfully challenged FDR for the Democratic nomination in 1940, FDR chose another vice president and Garner returned to South Texas. He died at 98 in 1967.

NOTES

Randolph B. Campbell. *Gone to Texas: A History of the Lone Star State.* Oxford: Oxford University Press, 2003.

Mike Kingston, Sam Attlesey, & Mary G. Crawford. *Political History of Texas.* Austin, Texas: Eakin Press, 1992.

Carl H. Moneyhon. *Edmund J. Davis: Civil War General, Republican Leader, Reconstruction Governor.* Fort Worth, Texas: TCU Press, 2010.

ESSAY QUESTIONS

1. Why was Governor E. J. Davis so hated in Texas?
2. Compare the Populist and Progressive movements.
3. Discuss the pros and cons of the Fergusons.

TERMS

Black Codes: ______________________________

Carpetbagger: ______________________________

James Ferguson: ______________________________

James Nance Garner: ______________________________

James Stephen Hogg: ______________________________

John H. Reagan: ______________________________

Ku Klux Klan: ______________________________

Miriam Ferguson: ______________________________

Populist Movement: ______________________________

Progressives Movement: ______________________________

Railroad Commission: ______________________________

Scalawags: ______________________________

Wet: ______________________________

MEXICO, TEXAS, GUATIMALA & WEST INDIES.

Texas Republic, North America, Central America, 1870

CHAPTER 3

Texas Political History II

TOPICS

- The World War II Era
- The Booming 1950s
- The Turbulent 1960s
- The Realignment of the 1970s and 1980s
- The 1990s to Present, Republican Ascendency

LEARNING OBJECTIVES

When you finish reading this chapter, you will be able to:

1. Describe the unique nature of Texas Populist leaders.
2. Discuss when Texas industrialization and urbanization took place.
3. Explain why Texas Democrats started to vote for Republicans on the national ticket.
4. Discuss when Texas became a one-party Republican state.

This chapter covers the political history of Texas from World War II to the present. During this time, Texas, along with the rest of the southern states, experienced a major electoral realignment in which the southern states turned from Democratic to Republican. If you look at an electoral map of the 1924 election, you will see that conservative Republican Calvin Coolidge won all the northern states from the Northeast to the West Coast, and the Democratic candidate won all the southern states from Virginia to Texas. Then look at an electoral map of the 2000 election in which the situation reversed. Now the Republican George W. Bush won all the southern states and retained the Midwest, while the Democrat won the Northeast and the West Coast. How did this reversal take place?

What happened is that the two political parties became ideological pure. In 1960, when John Kennedy beat Richard Nixon, the most liberal people in the country were Democrats (residing in the liberal cities such as Massachusetts and San Francisco), and the most conservative people in the country were Democrats (residing in southern states). As the national Democratic Party shifted leftward, embracing more centralized government, expanding the welfare state, legalizing abortion, supporting civil rights legislation, secularizing the public schools, increasing taxes, and demonizing traditional American values, they lost the support of conservatives in the South, the Midwest, and in small towns in general. Today the parties are more ideologically consistent: the Republican Party is the conservative party, and Democrat Party is the liberal party.

Populist politician

Often possessing a colorful personality and the ability to communicate with everyday folks, this type of politician runs as a representative of the common man in a fight against the economic and culture elite.

THE WORLD WAR II ERA

In the 1940s, the vast Texas terrain was still spotted by small towns, yeoman farmers, and isolated ranches. The most successful politicians of this era were colorful characters who could entertain small town folk with a story and at the same time appeal to their traditional values. Two politicians who exemplified these traits were W. Lee O'Daniel and Lyndon Baines Johnson. Both were "men of the people" who knew how to win votes of small town folks by exhibiting showmanship and Texas style. O'Daniel would serve as governor and then US senator for Texas before and during WWII. And Johnson would win a seat in the US Senate in a controversial election in 1948. Both men represented the type of politicians popular with rural Texans.

W. Lee O'Daniel, a prototypical Texas Populist, used country music to appeal to the common man.
Joseph Scherschel/Contributor/Getty

Texas Populist: O'Daniel is the perfect example of a Populist politician. *Often possessing a colorful personality and the ability to communicate with everyday folks, a* **Populist politician** *runs as a representative of the common man in a fight against the economic and culture elite.* In essence, the Populist says that government hasn't been working for you, the great masses, but instead has been rigged by the elites to give them more wealth and power. The Populist promises to change that and make government work for the common folk. Generally speaking, all successful politicians, from Franklin Roosevelt to

Ronald Reagan to Donald Trump, use some degree of populism in their campaigns.

Pass the Biscuits Pappy: W. Lee "Pappy" O'Daniel was a man with no political experience, but his big personality and down-home style rhetoric made him well-liked by small town folks in Texas. O'Daniel was a successful flower salesman and the host of a very popular radio show. In the 1938 gubernatorial race he used the campaign slogan "pass the biscuits, Pappy" and toured Texas on a flatbed truck with his band, the Light Crust Doughboys, led by Bob Wills (later of the famous Texas Playboys). O'Daniel ran on the platform of the Ten Commandments, the Golden Rule, and an old-age pension. His campaign simply consisted of driving from town to town and playing country music. He admitted he knew nothing about government and that he had never even voted before, but the people loved him and he won the election!

O'Daniel became governor in 1938 and won reelection in 1940 even though he was not successful in leading any legislation. To celebrate his reelection, he invited everybody to Austin for a Texas-style BBQ. He personally shot dozens of buffalo to supply the meat. Then before his term was up, he picked 87-year-old Andrew Jackson Houston—the last surviving descendant of Sam Houston—to fill a vacant seat in the US Senate. The plan was for Houston to hold the seat until O'Daniel could run. Houston died eighteen days later.

After Houston died, Pappy ran in the special election for that senate seat and won. He beat out twenty-nine other Democratic candidates, including the young Lyndon B. Johnson. In 1942 he won reelection to a full six-year term. Just as he never accomplished much in Austin, Pappy didn't do much in Washington either. O'Daniel was a prototypical Texan Populist of that era. He was a bigger-than-life personality who related to the common man but was better at winning elections than actually governing.

Johnson Wins Contested Election: In 1948, Lyndon B. Johnson ran for the US Senate against former Governor Coke R. Stevens in the Democratic primary. Showing tremendous energy, Johnson rented a helicopter dubbed the "Johnson City Windmill" and hopped all over the state. This was the closest election in state history. Four days after the election, it was announced that Stevens had won by only 362 votes. But when the amended results came in from rural counties in South Texas, Johnson won the election by eighty-seven votes. "Box 13" in Jim Wells County,

Johnson was a Populist who could relate to the common man. He became the first president from Texas.

dominated by the political boss George Parr, "the Duke of Duval," found 203 uncounted ballots, 202 of which were for LBJ! Johnson easily beat Republican Jack Porter in the general election and would eventually become one of the most powerful men in the US Senate.

THE BOOMING 1950s

In the 1950s, Texas started to become an economic powerhouse as it matured from a cotton and oil state, to a diversified economy with many important urban centers. And in the 1950s, several Texas politicians gained national prominence.

Population Growth and Urbanization: During the Depression Era of the 1930s, the Texas population stagnated. But after WWII, with Texas's booming economy, population growth once again took off. According to the 1930 US census, the population of Texas was 5,825,000. But by the end of the 1950s, it rose 60 percent to 9,577,000. By 1970, Texas reached a population of over 11 million, becoming the fourth largest state in the Union. In that year, 12 percent of the population was African American and 18 percent was Latino.

During this period of dramatic population growth, an important landmark was reached in the Lone Star State: Texas transitioned from a rural to an urban state. By 1970, eight out of ten Texans lived in a town of over 2,500 residents. And Texas became the home of many of the largest cities in America: Houston had a population of 1,232,000; Dallas 844,000; and San Antonio 654,000.

Oil: One reason that the Texas population grew during the 1950s was the continual growth of the oil industry. Since the tapping of the famous gusher Spindletop in Beaumont in 1901, oil had been an important part of the Texas economy. For the next decade, most of the oil wells in Texas were located in the southeast portion of the state around Beaumont, and Texas became the sixth largest oil producing state in the nation. Then in the 1920s oil was discovered along the Permian Basin in the Panhandle and West Texas. Boom towns like Armirillo, Midland, and Odessa attracted tens of thousands of people seemingly overnight. By 1928 Texas led all other states in oil production, drilling nearly 20 percent of the world's oil supply.

During the Great Depression, oil was discovered in East Texas. Kilgore gained 10,000 residents in one year. But the overproduction of oil severely lowered prices. The price of a barrel of oil dropped from $1.27 in 1927 to sixty-five cents a barrel in 1932, briefly going as low as two cents a barrel! In an attempt to raise prices by reducing oil production, Governor Ross

Sterling ordered the oil companies of East Texas to stop drilling. When they ignored him, the governor sent in national guardsmen to close down the oil fields. Eventually the legislature passed a law granting the Railroad Commission the authority to set production limits.

By 1928, Texas was the nation's number one oil producer.
© chippix / Shutterstock.com

During WWII Texas oil helped fuel the American armed forces and win the war. For a while German submarines were successful at destroying American oil tankers coming out of the Gulf of Mexico, so the federal government built the first major oil pipelines connecting Texas to New Jersey and New York. After the war, Texas production steadily increased. During the 1970s, when most of the nation was in a recession, Texas oil kept the Texas economy strong. Actually, 1972 was a record year, still unbroken, for Texas crude oil production, hitting 1.3 million barrels a day.

Industrialization: More than anything else, oil and gas contributed to the urbanization and industrialization of Texas, turning it from a rural, agricultural state, to an urban, industrial one. Oil improved the Texas economy by spurring all kinds of oil-related industries, including petrochemicals, refineries, pipelines, storage tanks, drilling equipment, trucking, office buildings, insurance, and banking.

After WWII, many non-oil related industries developed in Texas. In 1947 Texas had 7,128 manufacturing companies, and by 1973 it had 14,431 companies, producing over $15 billion in goods. Aided by easy access to energy, cheap transportation, affordable land, and access to the Gulf of Mexico, many famous companies opened up plants in Texas: Hughes Tool Company at Houston, Reynolds Aluminum at Corpus Christi, Dow Chemicals in Brazoria County, Shell Oil at Deer Park, DuPont at Orange, Texaco at Port Author, and Ford in Dallas, just to name a few.

Two notable Texas companies led the American technology revolution. Texas Instruments, founded in Dallas in 1951, developed the silicon circuit board and the "computer chip," which operated all the electronic devices that were becoming so popular, such as televisions, radios, phonographs, calculators, and computers. And in 1962, Ross Perot started Electronic Data Systems, which led the world in using computers to manage data to help run complex businesses.

In the 1950s, Texas Instruments developed the world's first silicon transistor and integrated circuits, which it used to invent the hand-held calculator and transistor radio.

1950s Politics: In the 1950s, Texas Democrats split into two factions. Liberal Democrats, led by Ralph Yarborough, supported Harry Truman's Fair Deal (an extension of FDR's New Deal), civil rights, unionization, tax increases, and school reform. Conservative Democrats, on the other hand, disliked Truman, supported state's rights, opposed unionization, feared communism, and resisted civil rights reforms. In this battle, the conservative Democrats would win under the shrewd leadership of **Allen Shivers**. *The first man to win three terms as Governor of Texas, Shivers led the conservative wing of the Texas Democrat Party, who voted for Republicans on the national ticket and conservative Democrats on the state and local tickets.*

Before the 1952 gubernatorial primary between Shivers and Yarborough, an important federal-state's rights issue developed that was critical to Texas's oil industry and tax revenue, known as the **tidelands controversy**. *After oil was discovered in the Gulf of Mexico, Texas and the US government fought over the extent of Texas's jurisdictional boundary. Texas claimed three leagues from shore (ten miles), but the federal government said Texas can only claim three miles.* Hundreds of millions of dollars were at stake. This issue became entangled with the 1952 presidential race. Democrat candidate Adlai Stevenson supported the federal government's position in the tidelands controversy. Republican candidate Dwight "Ike" Eisenhower, who was born in Texas but raised in Kansas, was sympathetic to Texas on the issue. After Ike became president, the tidelands issue was eventually settled in favor of Texas.

Allen Shivers

The first man to win three terms as Governor of Texas, in the 1950s Shivers led the conservative wing of the Texas Democrat Party.

Tidelands controversy

After oil was discovered in the Gulf of Mexico in the 1950s, Texas and the US government fought over the extent of Texas's jurisdictional boundary. Texas claimed three leagues from shore (ten miles), but the federal government said Texas can only claim three miles.

The tidewater controversy and the presidential election crystallized a split in the Texas Democratic Party. Shivers cited the tidewater controversy as an example of the overbearing power of the federal government. And the liberal Democratic candidate Adlai Stevenson symbolized the leftward direction of the national Democrat Party. Conservative Texas Democrats, known as "Shivercrats," ended up voting for Republican Eisenhower for president and Shivers for governor in 1952. Liberal "Loyalist Democrats" voted for Stevenson for president and Yarborough for governor.

Yarborough and many local liberal Democrats lost, but eventually Yarborough would serve in the US Senate from 1956 to 1971.

Sam Rayburn: Before we conclude the 1950s, we should mention one more Texas politician that played a major role in national politics. Sam Rayburn became one of the most powerful and esteemed Speakers of the House in congressional history. After graduating from University of Texas Law School, he passed the bar in 1908. A year later, Rayburn was elected to the US House of Representatives. During his second term, he was elected Speaker at the young age of twenty-nine! **Sam Rayburn**, a *highly respected member of Congress, would serve in Congress for forty-nine years, holding the speakership three times: 1911, 1947–49, and 1953–55.* During periods of Republican control, he served as House Minority Leader.

U.S. 6c POSTAGE
DWIGHT D. EISENHOWER

Dwight Eisenhower was the first Republican that Texans voted for president. He was born in Texas but raised in Kansas.

Rayburn was a very effective leader in Congress and the Democratic Party for decades. He was a protégé of Nance Garner and a close friend and mentor of Lyndon Johnson. Rayburn helped elevate the young LBJ to Senate Majority Leader. Like LBJ, Rayburn did not sign the "Southern Manifesto," a 1956 letter expressing opposition to racial integration that was signed by 99 percent of southern congressmen. A man of spotless integrity, Rayburn refused to do any legal work related to congressional legislature. After decades of enormous power, he died with only $15,000 in savings—quite a testament to his honesty and honor.

THE TURBULENT 1960s

The 1960s was a turbulent period in American history. Many young people who opposed the Vietnam War protested in the streets and took over college campuses. The counterculture movement celebrated drugs, free love, and rejected the values of the American middle class. Led by Martin Luther King, Jr., the 1950s civil rights movement was peaceful. But by the sixties the Black Panthers took over and declared "black power." Dozens of race riots set fire to some of the major cities in America. For the most part, Texas remained calm during this decade. Instead of protesting the Vietnam War, Texas men enlisted. The state of Texas contributed the second most soldiers to Vietnam, and according to surveys 97 percent say they were glad they served.

Sam Rayburn

A highly respected member of Congress, he would serve in Congress for forty-nine years, holding the speakership three times: 1911, 1947–49, and 1953–55.

LBJ: Lyndon B. Johnson was the iconic Texas figure in the 1960s. *Growing up in a small town in central Texas and attending Southwest Teachers College (now Texas State University, San Marcus), Johnson rose to become the Majority Leader of the US Senate, Vice President, and President of the United States.* After LBJ lost his bid to win the Democratic nomination for president in 1960, he accepted John F. Kennedy's offer to run on the ticket as the vice presidential candidate.

Kennedy, a wealthy Massachusetts elite, needed LBJ to deliver votes from southern Democrats, especially Texas's twenty-four electoral votes. To cover his bases, LBJ ran simultaneously for vice president and for reelection to the senate. He won both, and thus a special election was needed to fill the vacant senate seat. Surprisingly, John Tower won—the first Republican since Reconstruction to represent Texas in the US Senate.

After Kennedy and LBJ won the election, there were accusations of voter fraud in Illinois and Texas. If Republican Richard Nixon won those two states, he would have been president. In Texas, Nixon lost by only 46,000 votes. Some argued that Johnson's political machine in South Texas manufactured enough votes to give Kennedy the victory, as with the infamous Box 13. Although cases of fraud were discovered, historians are unsure whether Nixon actually won the state. Nixon, however, refused a recount. He later said that if he won the recount it would be too disruptive to the country to overturn a presidential election, and if he lost the recount the press would label him a "sore loser."

Lyndon B. Johnson

Growing up in a small town in central Texas, Johnson rose to become the Majority Leader of the US Senate, Vice President, and President of the United States (1963–1969).

Johnson served as vice president for little over 1,000 days before tragedy struck the nation. On November 22, 1963, Kennedy was assassinated by Lee Harvey Oswald as his motorcade drove through Dallas. Oswald was a communist who hated JFK's anti-Castro policies (Fidel Castro was the communist dictator of Cuba). But the press blamed conservatives in Dallas for JFK's assassination. The other Texan in the car with Kennedy was Governor John B. Connelly, who received bullet wounds in the chest, wrist, and leg. A moderate Democrat and former Secretary of Navy, Connelly was a very popular three-term governor.

After Johnson became president, his first task was to bring to fruition the civil rights initiates that Kennedy proposed. LBJ guided through Congress and signed the Civil Rights Act of 1964, which outlawed discrimination based on race and ended segregation in public facilities. Then after winning a landslide victory against conservative Republican Barry Goldwater, LBJ signed the Voting Rights Act of 1965, making it a federal crime for states to discriminate at the voting booth.

When Lee Harvey Oswald assassinated John F. Kennedy in Dealey Plaza in Dallas, Lyndon B. Johnson became president.
© William A. Mueller (mere artist) / Shutterstock.com

After winning the presidency on his own right, Johnson, an admirer of Franklin Roosevelt, wanted to expand the New Deal. In 1964, LBJ launched *a massive government program to fight poverty, called "the* **Great Society**,*" which expanded the welfare state by offering dozens of programs including food stamps, public housing, Head Start, Medicare, and Medicaid.* Unfortunately for LBJ, the Vietnam War ended up overshadowing his presidency. Johnson escalated the war (sending over 500,000 troops in 1968), but never formulated a winning strategy. The massive public demonstrations against the war hurt LBJ personally, and he declared that he would not seek reelection in 1968. In that year, Richard Nixon came back and won the presidency over Democrat Herbert Humphrey.

Great Society

A federal government program started by Lyndon Johnson, which expanded the welfare state by offering dozens of programs including food stamps, public housing, Head Start, Medicare, and Medicaid.

THE REALIGNMENT OF THE 1970s AND 1980s

In 1970, Texas remained a one-party state controlled by the Democrats, with Republicans only holding one US Senate seat, three seats in the US House of Representatives, a few seats in the Texas state house, and no state wide offices. But the tide was turning. In 1978, a Republican (William P. Clements) would win the governorship. And with the leadership of Ronald Reagan, the southern states started becoming solidly Republican.

The 1970s: In 1971, the "Sharpstown scandal" weakened the Democrat Party in Texas. It started when the US Security and Exchange Commission (SEC) filed a suit against several Texas officials accusing them of fraud and bribery, all Democrats, including the speaker and the governor. They also filed a suit against Frank Sharp, the owner of Sharpstown State Bank. In the wake of the scandal, many "reform" candidates were elected, including Dolph Briscoe for governor. This was the first time a Democrat did not win the majority of votes over the Republican (he won a mere plurality). Briscoe, however, gained popularity and won reelection in 1974.

Ann Richards

The first genuine female Governor of Texas.

Also in 1974, state legislatures served as delegates to a Texas constitutional convention but failed to present a new constitution to the voters because they split on a *right to work* provision (union membership cannot be a requirement for employment). They were, however, successful at changing the term of the governor from two to four years. The second governor to serve a four-year term was William P. Clements. Winning a historic gubernatorial election in 1978, Clements became the first Republican Governor of Texas since Reconstruction. This victory for Texas Republicans revealed that many Texans were changing their registration from Democrat to Republican.

The 1980s: In 1980, Ronald Reagan (with Texan George H. W. Bush as vice president) won the presidency with 55 percent of the Texas vote. Reagan led a conservative revival in America, and in 1984 he won a forty-nine-state landslide. From this point on, Texans would vote for every Republican presidential candidate. In 1982, however, Democrat attorney general Mark White defeated Clements with the support of teachers, to whom he promised to raise their pay. In 1986, Clements triumphantly returned to the governor's mansion. Two years later, Republicans won seats on the bench and to many powerful state commissions, and George H. W. Bush was elected President of the United States. Republicans were gaining strength in Texas.

George H. W. Bush first ran for elected office in 1966 when he became a US Congressman representing the Houston area. In 1988 he became the second US President from Texas.

THE 1990s TO PRESENT, REPUBLICAN ASCENDENCY

In the first half 1990s, Texas could be defined as a true two-party state, with Democrats and Republicans winning state-wide offices. In 1990, Democrat **Ann Richards** *became the first genuine female Governor of Texas* (Miriam Ferguson was recognized as a puppet of her husband,

James Ferguson). In 1993, Republican **Kay Bailey Hutchison** *was elected the first woman US Senator representing Texas.* The following year, Republican George W. Bush became governor. Exemplifying the coexistence of the two parties, Bush worked closely with Democrat Bob Bullock, the Lieutenant Governor, who presided over the Democratic controlled state senate.

But before the end of the decade, Texas would return to one-party status, this time controlled by the Republicans. In 1996, Phil Gramm won reelection to the US Senate, giving both senate seats to Republicans. In that same year, Republicans won the majority in the state senate for the first time since Reconstruction. Truly, *1998 was the watershed year* for the GOP. This was the year that Republicans achieved true dominance of the state by winning the governorship (George W. Bush's second term), all state-wide elective offices, and majorities in the state house and senate.

Kay Bailey Hutchison

Elected the first woman US Senator representing Texas

George W. Bush

The third President of the United States from Texas. He is the son of President H. W. Bush

George W. Bush: In 2000, **George W. Bush** *became the third President of the United States from Texas. He is the son of President H. W. Bush*, and grandson of influential US Senator Prescott Bush of Connecticut. In 1992, President George H. W. Bush lost his reelection bid because Texas billionaire Ross Perot ran a third party campaign, drawing Republican votes away Bush and giving the victory to Bill Clinton. So, it was a family triumph for a Bush to return to the White House, although the election was controversial. In the 2000 election, Democrat Al Gore won the popular vote, but Bush won the Electoral College only after the Supreme

George W. Bush was the owner of the Texas Rangers baseball team before he became Governor of Texas and the third US President from Texas.

Court awarded Florida's twenty-five electoral votes to Bush after a partial recount was determined unconstitutional.

George W. Bush grew up in West Texas where his father owned an oil exploration business. Bush earned a Bachelor's degree in history from Yale, and a Master's in business from Harvard. After Bush sold his oil company, he became a part owner of the Rangers baseball team. Bush was president for less than nine months when America was attacked by terrorists on September 11, 2001. As a result, he launched a war on Afghanistan, which continued through the Obama administration. More controversially, he went to war against Iraq because Saddam Hussein aided terrorists and was suspected of having weapons of mass destruction (WMD). After Bush won reelection in 2004, his presidency became less popular when WMDs were not found and the wars dragged on. Bush retired to Dallas, where he opened up a presidential library at the Southern Methodist University.

Rick Perry: While Bush was president, **Rick Perry**, *Bush's former Lieutenant Governor, served as the forty-seventh Governor of Texas from 2000 to 2015, the longest serving governor in Texas history.* In 2001, Perry proposed the *Trans-Texas Corridor*, a $150 billion project that would have built multi-lane highways and rails through Texas. Instead of raising taxes to pay for the project, Perry proposed that private contractors build the system and get revenue through tolls. The project became unpopular and was dropped in 2010.

Rick Perry

The forty-seventh Governor of Texas, he served from 2000 to 2015, the longest serving governor in Texas history.

Competitive federalism

The ideas that states compete with each other to attract businesses and people to their states by offering incentives.

Despite his failure with the Trans-Texas Corridor, Perry became a popular, conservative governor who won reelection in 2002, 2006, and 2010. Perry gained national prominence in the years after the Great Recession of 2008 because Texas's economy rebounded so quickly. From 2000 to 2015, Texas created 2.1 million jobs, about 30 percent of all the jobs created in America during that time. Rick Perry claimed that this was due to Texas's low taxes and low regulation environment. Perry also aggressively courted companies to relocate to Texas, offering financial incentives through the Texas Enterprise Fund. Perry became an advocate of **competitive federalism**: *the ideas that states compete with each other to attract businesses and people to their states by offering incentives.* Perry unsuccessfully ran for president in 2012 and 2016.

Texas Today: Today, Texas remains a red state in which the Republicans are dominate. The 2017, the Texas legislature retained a large majority of Republicans in both chambers. In the state senate, there were twenty Republicans and eleven Democrats. And in the state house, there were

Rick Perry was the longest serving governor in Texas history.
© Christopher Hlloran / Shutterstock.com

ninety-nine Republicans and forty-eight Democrats. Republicans currently control all the state-wide offices. In 2014, Republican Gregg Abbot became Governor of Texas, winning against Democrat Wendy Davis, who was a prominent advocate of abortion. Before Abbot became governor, he was Attorney General. In this capacity, he won a Supreme Court case, *Van Orden v. Perry*, which allowed Texas to keep a monument of the Ten Commandments on the grounds of the capitol.

Currently, the two Texas senate seats are occupied by Republicans. A former member of the Texas Supreme Court, John Cornyn was elected to the senate in 2002. He currently serves as the Senate Majority Whip, a powerful leadership position in the senate. The junior senator representing Texas is Ted Cruz. He served as Solicitor General of Texas from 2003 to 2008, when he argued nine cases before the US Supreme Court. In 2012 he was elected to the senate as Tea Party conservative. In 2013, Cruz gained national recognition when he made a twenty-one-hour filibuster speaking against President Barack Obama's healthcare plan. Since then he has been a harsh critic of establishment Republicans who he called too timid to effectively lead an opposition to Obama. In 2016, Cruz lost the Republican nomination for president to Donald Trump.

NOTES

Randolph B. Campbell. *Gone to Texas: A History of the Lone Star State*. Oxford: Oxford University Press, 2003.

Mike Kingston, Sam Attlesey & Mary G. Crawford. *Political History of Texas*. Austin, Texas: Eakin Press, 1992.

Archie P. McDonald. *Texas: A Compact History*. Abilene, Texas: State House Press, 2006.

ESSAY QUESTIONS

1. In what way was W. Lee O'Daniel a typical Texas Populist?
2. Discuss the significance of Allen Shivers and the voting patterns of Shivercrats in national and local elections.
3. When and why did Texas become a Republican, one-party state?

TERMS

Allen Shivers: ______________________________

Ann Richards: ______________________________

Competitive federalism: ______________________________

George W. Bush: ______________________________

Kay Bailey Hutchison: ______________________________

Lyndon B. Johnson: ______________________________

Populist politician ______________________________

Rick Perry: ______________________________

Sam Rayburn: ______________________________

Great Society: ______________________________

Tidelands Controversy: ______________________________

TEXAS FUN & FACTS SHEET 2

List of Official Texas Designations

Texas State Flower: Bluebonnet

State Tree: Pecan

State Bird: Northern Mockingbird

State Song: Texas, Our Texas

State Mammal Small: Armadillo

State Mammal Large: Texas Longhorn

State Dog: Blue Lacy

State Dish: Chili Con Carne

State Fiber: Cotton

State Fish: Guadalupe Bass

State Dance: Square Dance

State Fruit: Texas Red Grapefruit

State Gem: Texas Blue Topaz

State Insect: Monarch Butterfly

State Instrument: Guitar

State Pepper: Jalapeno

State Plant: Prickly Pear Cactus

State Reptile: Texas Horned Lizard

State Shrub: Crape Myrtle

State Snack: Tortilla Chips and Salsa

State Sport: Rodeo

State Team Sport: Football

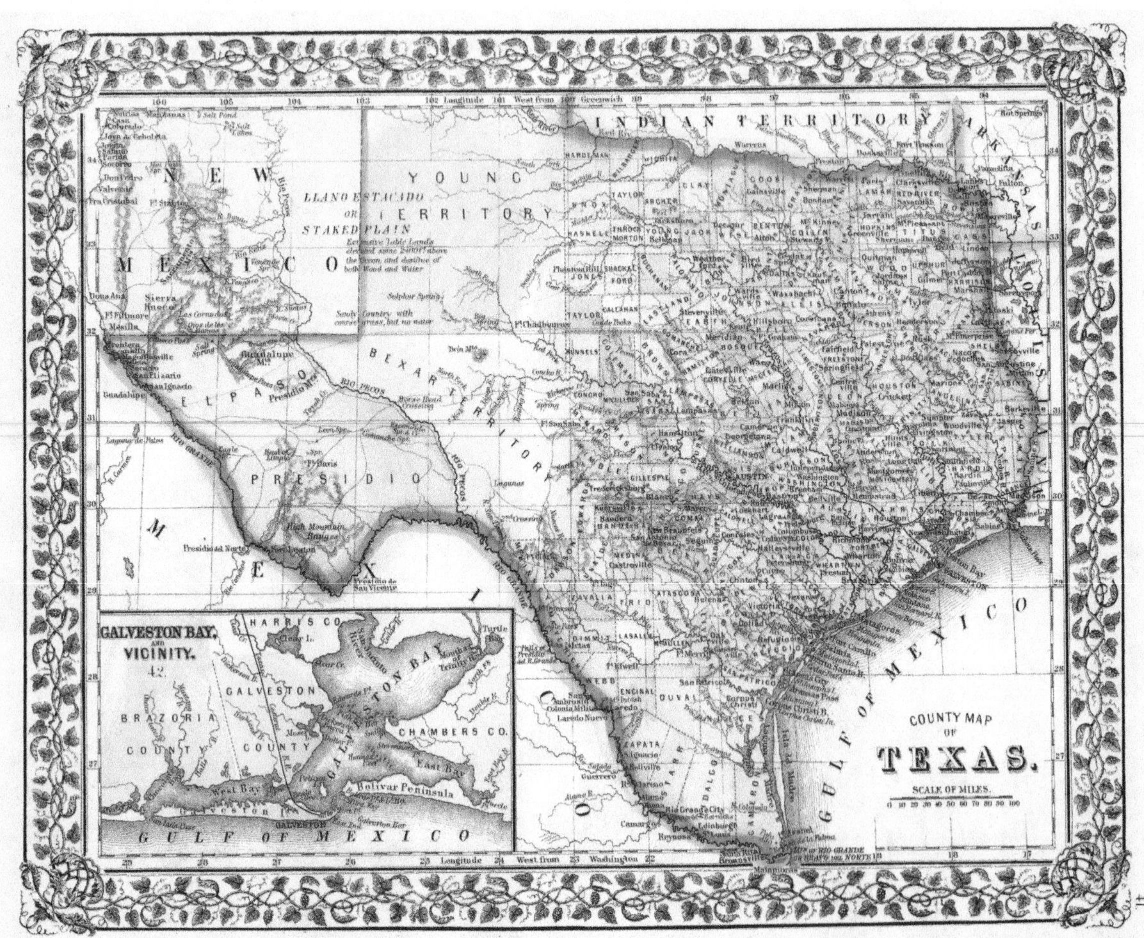

Texas with Indian Territories, 1870

CHAPTER 4

Texas Political Culture and Demographics

TOPICS

- Seven Regions of Texas
- Demographics
- The Texas Economy
- Texas Political Culture

LEARNING OBJECTIVES

When you finish reading this chapter, you will be able to:

1. Describe the unique economic and cultural characteristics of the different regions of Texas.
2. Outline the key demographic features of Texas.
3. Explain the historic and current sectors of the Texas economy.
4. Describe the major political subcultures in Texas.

This chapter will provide a geographic, demographic, economic, and political overview of the Lone Star State. What will emerge from this overview is a picture of the tremendous diversity and dynamic energy of the state of Texas and its people. Around the world Texas has a reputation for its magnitude—"Everything is big in Texas!"—and indeed the acreage, population, and economy of Texas are one of the largest in the world. This is one reason why this textbook is titled *The Great State of Texas.*

SEVEN REGIONS OF TEXAS

In land mass (167 million acres), Texas is the second largest state in the Union, following only Alaska. But Texas is more ecologically diverse than Alaska and consists of several distinct regions. Compare the Piney Woods of East Texas to the sandy deserts of West Texas, and compare the Hill Country of Central Texas to the grasslands of the Gulf Coast. And beyond geographical differences, each region has a unique history and culture. This is why there is no such thing as a "typical Texan," you must understand the region from where a Texan comes. There are different ways to divide Texas, but for our purposes we will discuss *seven* distinct ecological, cultural, and economic regions of Texas.

East Texas

Also known as the Piney Woods, a region marked by its thick pine and oak forests, receiving the most rain than any other region of Texas. It can trace its historical roots to the Old South.

East Texas (the Piney Woods): *Marked by its thick pine and oak forests,* **East Texas** *receives the most rain than any other region of Texas. This region can trace its historical roots to the Old South.* In the old days, cotton was king in East Texas, but now cotton has been replaced by cattle, poultry, and timber. In 1931 a major oil field was discovered in Rusk, Gregg, and Smith counties, which contributed greatly to the economic growth of the region. Many towns are still dominated by the old families which made their money in oil, real estate, banking, and merchandising.

East Texas is considered to be the westernmost part of the Deep South and is right in the middle of the Bible Belt, and so this region is politically very conservative. Once they reach adulthood, young people often migrate out

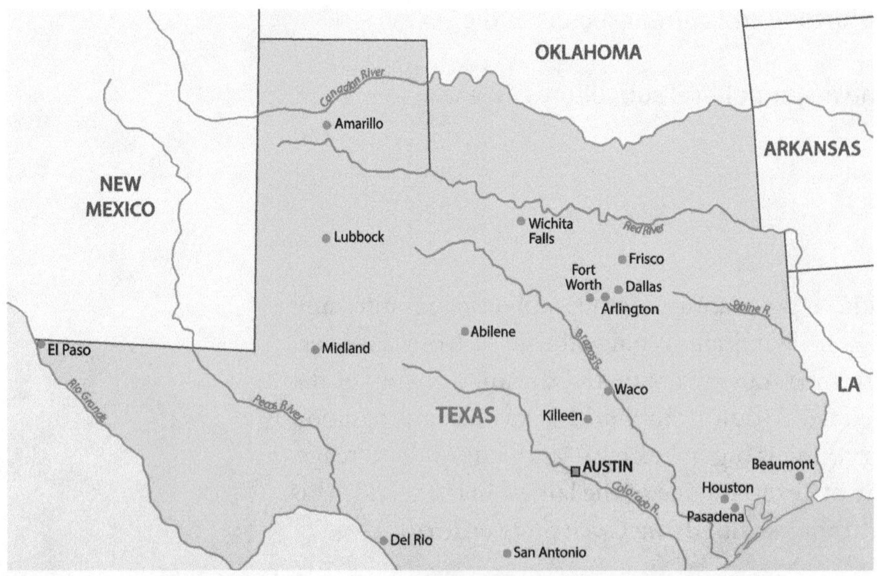

Texas is a huge state with a land mass of 167 million acres and seven distinct regions.

of East Texas and head toward the big cities. As a result, East Texas has one of the oldest populations in Texas and thus has developed into a retirement and healthcare region.

The High Plains: The High Plains region of Texas consists of the twenty-six counties of the northern block or "Panhandle" of Texas. Geographically, the High Plains are an immense, flat plain covered with thick layers of alluvial material. The Spanish explorer Coronado named it the *Llano Estacado* or "Staked Plains." Economically, the Panhandle is part of the vast, Midwestern parries that are so well suited to the farming of grains, corn, and cotton. The agriculture economy is dependent on water from the *Ogallala Aquifer*, one of the world's largest aquifers, extending from North Texas to South Dakota. The Panhandle has also developed into a livestock, oil, and wind power (Texas is the top wind power state in the nation) region. Amarillo is the largest city in the High Plains. Dominated by the Midwestern sensibility and Protestant churches, the region tends to be conservative politically and socially.

The Gulf Coast: This region goes along the coast of the Gulf of Mexico from Corpus Christi, through Houston, to Beaumont. In 1901, an oil well named Spindletop was drilled near Beaumont. This changed Texas and the Gulf Coast region became a petrochemical center, filled with oil refineries. It also became one of the most important shipping centers in the nation. The Port of Houston is the busiest port in the United States based on foreign tonnage. Since the 1970s, with great oil reserves being shipped out of its port, the Houston economy has boomed and the population

The Port of Houston is the busiest in the US.
© Sheila Fitzgerald / Shutterstock.com

exploded. Today Houston is the largest city in Texas with a vibrant economy of petrochemicals, manufacturing, retail, shipping, fishing, high tech, and aerospace (NASA). This diversity helps explain how Houston is able to weather the boom and bust cycles of the oil and gas industries.

Border—South Texas: This area goes along the Rio Grande River (the border of Mexico) from Brownsville to El Paso. The "Valley" and the "Winter Garden" areas are major producers of vegetables and citrus. This was the first area settled by the Spanish. Anglo Americans did not dominate the region until after Texas independence in 1836. There still exists large ranches owned by the same families for several generations; however, corporate ranchers have moved in. This region is nearly bi-national. Hundreds of thousands of immigrants stream across this region and into America. Many people go back and forth from Mexico and mostly speak Spanish. The Roman Catholic Church is the dominate church in the area. El Paso is the fifth largest city in Texas. It is a military, industrial, and commercial center with many ties to Mexico.

Metroplex

This region stretches from Dallas to Fort Worth and includes Arlington. Traditionally it has been the banking and commercial center of Texas.

Metroplex of North Texas: *This region is dominated by the cities of Dallas and Fort Worth, known as the* **Metroplex**. *Dallas is the banking and commercial center of Texas.* When the railroads came down from the North, Dallas became a hub. Fort Worth is a banking and commercial center for West Texas. In 1900, Swift meatpacking created a plant in Fort Worth. The

The city of Dallas is at the heart of the Dallas-Fort Worth-Arlington Metroplex, which has a population of 7 million.

population in this region exploded after WWII. Many international corporations have their headquarters here. Today, it has a diversified economy: banking, manufacturing, telecommunications, defense, aerospace, electronics, computers, plastics, energy, and food. Taken together, the Dallas-Fort Worth-Arlington Metroplex has a population of 7 million, making it the largest urban area in Texas, and one of the fastest growing areas in the country.

Central Corridor: This region goes from College Station in the East, to San Antonio in the South, and to Waco in the North, with Austin in the center. The **Central Corridor** *is the governmental and educational core of Texas.* This region contains Texas A & M, UT Austin, and Baylor. The center piece is the capital of the state of Texas, Austin, with its many government offices. Austin is one of the fastest growing cities in the nation. Not only is it the government center of Texas, but now Austin is becoming the Texas "Silicon Valley." Many of the top high tech companies in America have offices in Austin, including Dell Computer. This region also has many military bases in and around San Antonio and Waco, including Fort Hood (the largest military base in the world). Today, people are coming from all over the United States to live in Austin and the Central Corridor.

Central Corridor

This region goes from College Station in the East, to San Antonio in the South, and to Waco in the North, with Austin in the center. This is the governmental and educational core of Texas.

West Texas: The last of the seven regions is West Texas. The defeat of the Comanche in the 1870s opened up this dry and craggy region for Anglo Americans. There are few African Americans in West Texas, but more Mexicans are moving there. The western part of the Bible Belt starts here, making this region socially and politically conservative. Historically, the economy was based on the ranching of cattle, sheep, and goats. This region includes the southern portion of the Llano Estacado. These rugged plains were often depicted in the old cowboy movies. Another important geographical formation in West Texas is the *Permian Basin*: the largest petroleum basin in the United States, which includes the oil drilling cities of Midland, Snyder, and Odessa. The Permian Basin produced 30 billion barrels of oil since it was first drilled in the 1920s, making Texas one of the largest oil producing regions in the world.

DEMOGRAPHICS

As we learned in the last section, Texas covers a vast territory and consists of several distinct regions. This section will provide some basic demographic information about the Great State of Texas as a whole. Much of the statistics in this chapter came from the *Texas Almanac*, which is published every year by the Texas State Historical Association. The *Texas Almanac* provides a treasure trove of information about Texas.

Population: With 254 counties and 1,216 incorporated cities, Texas is the second largest state by population. According to a 2015 US Census report, Texas has a population of 27 million people (California has 38 million people). One of the fastest growing states in America, the population of Texas has been increasing by about 500,000 a year. This reflects mostly migration from other states and countries.

Urban Growth: The popular image of Texas is rural, with cowboys, rolling tumbleweeds, and farms and ranches. But the reality is that Texas has several of the biggest cities in America. Actually, Texas contains six of the top twenty American cities: Houston, the largest city in Texas, has 2.3 million residents, San Antonio (1.4 million), Dallas (1.3 million), Austin (900,000), Fort Worth (800,000), and El Paso (nearly 700,000). If an urban area is defined as a town with a population over 50,000, then nearly 85 percent of Texans live in urban areas. So, Texans are no longer rural folk living in small towns and employed in agriculture.

Religion: According to a 2014 Pew Survey, 77 percent of Texans identity as Christian: Evangelical Protestant (31 percent), Roman Catholic (23 percent), Mainline Protestant (13 percent), and Black Church (6 percent). Less than 4 percent of Texans identify as Jewish, Hindu, Sikhs, Buddhists, and Muslim, combined. However, Texas has the largest Muslim population than any other state at 422,000. People who claim no religion

Seventy-seven percent of Texans identify as Christian, and Texas has the most "mega churches" in the nation.

make up 13 percent of the population. Texas is home to some of America's largest churches in America, often called "mega churches." A mega church is defined as one with over 2,000 weekly attendants. It is estimated that Texas has 206 mega churches.

Income: Ranked by income, Texas is the twenty-sixth state in America. The median household income in Texas in 2014 was $49,427.

Age: Ranked by median age, Texas is the second youngest state in the Union. The average Texan is only 33.60 years old.

Race or Ethnicity: According to a 2015 Census report, the following is the racial makeup of Texas: White (45 percent), Hispanic (37 percent), Black (12 percent), Asian (3.8 percent), and American Indian (0.1 percent). Accurate statics are difficult to come by because many Hispanics identify as "white." Since 2004, Texas has been a **"majority-minority"** *state: all minority groups combined represent the majority of the state's population, while the white population is in the minority.* As a result of continuous immigration from Mexico and Latin America, and the fact the Hispanics tend to have more children, the Hispanic segment of the population is the fastest growing.

Majority-minority

When all minority groups combined represent the majority of the state's population, while the white population is in the minority.

Demographics and Politics: Currently, Texas is solidly Republican. In the 2016 presidential election, Republican Donald Trump beat Democrat Hillary Clinton in 227 of the state's 245 counties. Although the political culture of Texas is conservative, many political scientists predict that Texas may become Democratic in a few decades. This is due to its demographics. Ethnic minorities, urban dwellers, and younger people tend to vote for the Democratic Party, and Texas's population is growing in these areas.

THE TEXAS ECONOMY

The Great State of Texas, with all its natural resources and ability to attract people with big ambitions, has grown to be one of the most vibrant economies in the world. Texas is a diversified economy, which includes energy, agriculture, trade, business services, and manufacturing. Diversification helps explain why Texas recovered from the Great Recession of 2008 faster than any other state. At $1.6 trillion, Texas has the second highest Gross Domestic Product (GDP) in the nation, after California. If Texas were an independent nation, it would have the ninth largest economy in the world, ahead of Canada, Korea, and Russia.

Land: In many ways, Texas was founded on the attraction of inexpensive land and all the opportunities that represented to people who wanted to forge a new life. The Spanish and then the Mexican governments granted liberal land grants. Each family could get a league or a *Sitio*, equivalent of about 4,428 acres, for a nominal fee. A single person could get 1,500 acres. After Texas independence, millions of Americans, mostly from the southern states, came to Texas to buy cheap land and start a farm or a ranch.

Cotton: *From 1820 to 1860s,* **King Cotton** *dominated the Texan economy and formed the epicenter of social and political power. This staple crop was the number one crash crop for export.* At this time cotton production was strongest in East Texas. Before the Civil War, Texas was the eighth top cotton producer among the states. By 1890, Texas led all the states in cotton production. Cotton is the raw material used to make cloth and textiles, a very profitable industry in the nineteenth century.

King Cotton

The era before the Civil War when cotton was the number one crash crop for export. Cotton plantations dominated the Texan economy and formed the epicenter of social and political power.

Cattle Ranches: In the 1800s, cattle ranches spotted the southern and eastern regions of Texas. After the Civil War, as the American population expanded and people developed a taste for beef, cattle became big business. With the invention of the refrigerated railcar, the great cattle drives became obsolete. Cattle were simply shipped to Chicago and other northern metropolitan areas via rail. One of the symbols of Texas is the Longhorn cow, known for its tremendous horns which reach over five feet from

The Texas Longhorn descends from Spanish cattle and is known for its high drought-stress tolerance.

tip to tip (the record is nine feet). The Longhorn is a direct descendant to the cattle that Christopher Columbus brought to the New World, and it is known for its drought resistant ability.

Agriculture Today: With 248,000 farms and ranches covering 130.2 million acres, the Great State of Texas leads the nation in cattle, cotton, hay, sheep, goats, and mohair production. Texas sells billions of dollars worth of agriculture products to other countries and other parts of the US. According to the Texas Department of Agriculture, the top ten commodities with their cash receipts in 2012 was: cattle ($11 billion), cotton ($2.2 billion), milk ($1.8 billion), broilers—chickens ($1.7 billion), greenhouse and nursery ($1.3 billion), corn ($1.2 billion), grain sorghum ($594 million), wheat ($538 million), forestry ($520 million), vegetables ($439 million), and eggs ($439 million). Contrary to popular opinion, nearly 99 percent of Texas farms are family owned, and 14 percent of Texans work in an agriculture related job.

Oil: Ever since the Spindletop oil field was tapped in Beaumont at the turn of the twentieth century, oil has been major part of the Texas economy. This helped Texas transition from an agricultural economy to an industrial one. And it helped transform Texas from a rural state to one with several major urban centers. In the 1970s and 1980s, oil attracted people from all over the country and the population boomed.

In 2015, Texas produced on average 3.6 million barrels of oil per day, making it by far the largest oil producing state in the nation. If Texas were a nation, it would be tied with Canada as the fifth largest oil producer in the world, after Saudi Arabia, Russia, Iraq, China, and Iran. Many of the world's largest oil companies are headquartered in Texas: Exxon Mobile, Phillips 66, Valero Energy, Conoco Phillips, Enterprise Products Partners, Plains All American Pipeline, Halliburton, and Apache. Oil is a cyclical commodity, producing boom and bust cycles. Each year, fees and taxes on oil and gas production contribute about $4 billion to the state's budget, with much of this revenue going to higher education.

High Tech: Austin, Houston, and Dallas have become high tech leaders of the nation, specializing in computer hardware, software, semiconductors, telecommunication, and other high-tech and scientific industries. Many space agencies, including NASA, are centered in Houston. In 2008, Texas ranked fourth among the fifty states in patents. Some of the top tech companies with their headquarters in Texas include AT&T, Dell, and Texas Instruments.

When Neil Armstrong landed on the moon, he said, "Houston, Tranquility base here. The Eagle has landed."
© Tony Craddock / Shutterstock.com

Service Industry: Today the service sector is the largest sector of the Texas economy. In 2012, the service industry employed 76 percent of the private sector workforce. Some of the top service companies in Texas include Sysco (food wholesale), Waste Management, J. C. Penney, Whole Foods, Tenet Healthcare, Dr Pepper Snapple Group, HEB, GameStop, Michaels, Chuck E. Cheese's, and Neiman Marcus.

Transportation: In such a large state as Texas, the transportation industry plays a vital role in moving people and goods and keeping the economy going. Cars and trucks drive over 300,000 miles of Texas roadways. In 2008, there were forty-four railroad companies in Texas that carried 384 million tons of freight. And the Texas airport system is one of the largest and busiest in the nation. In 2009, over 60 million people flew from one of the twenty-six airports located in Texas. Southwest and American are two notable airlines that have their headquarters in Texas.

Texas Exports: The Port of Houston is the largest port in the US and the sixth largest in the world. Since 2002, Texas has led all states in exports. The top five categories of Texas exports include chemicals, computers and electronics, machinery, petroleum, and transportation equipment.

TEXAS POLITICAL CULTURE

Governor Ann Richards fits in the tradition of a mainstream Texas liberal along with Ralph Yarborough and Lyndon Johnson.
© Nagel Photography / Shutterstock.com

The political values, habits, and beliefs of a people, including what they believe is the proper role and scope of government, is **political culture**. It also reflects what role the people think they should take in government and politics. Political culture is learned and transferred by socialization through the family, schools, churches, popular culture, and other factors.

According to a survey conducted by The Texas Politics Project in October of 2016, 43 percent of Texans identify as conservative (with 16 percent saying they are "extremely conservative"), 38 percent identify as "in the middle," and 19 percent of Texans identify as liberal. So, the vast majority of Texans are moderate to conservative.

Liberalism: Today, the Texas Democratic Party is a liberal political party. The definition of **modern liberalism** *is the belief in the need for a larger central government to ensure greater social justice and equality.* Texans such as Ralph Yarborough, Lyndon Johnson, and Ann Richards were liberals. The Great Society, established by Lyndon Johnson, was one of the most important political achievements of liberalism. It used the federal government to distribute wealth from the rich to the poor through taxation and welfare programs. Liberals place greater emphasis on the importance of class, race, gender, and sexual orientation. They believe in individual social freedom, social change, civil rights, and civil liberties, such as free speech and free thought.

Leftism: Although Leftism has had a spectacularly dismal track record, just look at the Soviet Union, Maoist China, Cuba, Venezuela, and North Korea, in recent years, Leftism seems to be becoming more popular in America, especially on the college campuses. In a 2016 YouGovsurvey poll, 43 percent of respondents under thirty had a positive view of socialism. Today Leftists may call themselves democratic socialists, socialists, members of the Green Party, or members of the left wing of the Democratic Party.

Leftists are animated by a hatred of capitalism and big business. They want to create a society of equal economic outcome by giving the government the ownership of the means of production and highly taxing the rich and big businesses. They understand society as a struggle between the rich and the poor. They disagree with many of America's founding principles, such as limited government, free markets, and private property, because

Political culture

The political values, habits, and beliefs of a people, including what they believe is the proper role and scope of government.

Modern liberalism

The belief in the need for a larger central government to ensure greater social justice and equality.

they think this allowed the privileged classes to exploit the disadvantaged groups. As opposed to traditional American liberals, they tend to not tolerate the free speech of opposition groups.

Conservatism: A conservative believes in limited government, individual freedom and responsibility, traditional social values, law and order, and the virtues of free market capitalism. What is capitalism? *Capitalism* can be defined as an economic system in which individuals freely decide what goods to produce or what services to provide in order to make a profit. Financial success comes from properly understanding how to serve the customer in new or better ways. Free market capitalism is based on the concepts of freedom of choice, private property, reward for hard work and innovation, the sanctity of contracts, and a government that impartially enforces the rules of the marketplace. No system in world history has taken more people out of poverty or improved the standard of living of society as capitalism.

As stated above, Texans have always been conservative, but political scientists can identify several different types of conservatism that have had major impact on the history of Texas politics. These different "political sub-cultures" or ideologies include *traditionalism, individualism, populism, classical liberalism,* and *social conservatism.* And, as you will see, sometimes these conservative "isms" contradict each other.

Traditionalism: Historically, Texas has had a traditionalistic political culture. *The idea that government should maintain the existing social and political order and should be run by the ruling elites is called* **traditionalism.** This attitude predominated in the 1800s when Texas was settled by southerners that established a plantation society. Traditionalistic values maintained the hierarchical social order, with slaves at the bottom and the rich property owners at the top. Some of these values extended into the 1900s in the era of Jim Crow that limited the political rights of blacks, and with the tenant system that limited the economic opportunity of poor white farmers.

Individualism: Another strong aspect of Texas's politics is **individualism**: *the view that government should interfere as little as possible with the private lives of individuals while protecting private property and providing a favorable climate for business.* One political humorist summed up the Texas individualistic political culture this way: "Get off my property before I get my gun!"

The individualistic political culture developed on the western frontier where settlers from the East announced that they have "Gone to Texas" to start a new life. This attitude celebrated the lone cowboy, the rugged

Traditionalism

The idea that government should maintain the existing social and political order and should be run by the ruling elites.

Individualism

The view that government should interfere as little as possible with the private lives of individuals while protecting private property and providing a favorable climate for business.

The lone cowboy is a symbol of Texas's individualistic political culture.

settler families, and the courageous sheriff. Today individualistic culture might honor the successful small businessperson or the star athlete. This attitude values individual effort, self-reliance, and ingenuity. It assumes that an individual can make his or her own success and is not merely a product of his or her environment. Individualism contrasts starkly with the elitism of traditionalism, which assumes a set station in life.

Populism: Another important political subculture of Texas that contrasts with traditionalism is the *Populist political culture*, which believes in the ability of the "common man." It asserts that common folk have a right to exercise control over their government, rather than the wealthy elite or political insiders. Populism has its roots in Jacksonian Democracy, which had a big influence on the Founders of Texas. Following the rugged, frontier spirit of Andrew Jackson, who was born poor but became President of the United States, **Jacksonian democracy** *supported greater voting rights for all white males, trust in the common man, state's rights, strict adherence to the Constitution, and free markets with no government supported tariffs and monopolies.*

Jacksonian democracy

A political ideology that supported greater voting rights for all white males, trust in the common man, strict adherence to the Constitution, and free markets with no government supported tariffs and monopolies. It promoted national strength, while maintaining state's rights.

In the 1900s, Populist rhetoric had a big impact on Texas politicians. Populist Texas politicians, such as "Farmer Jim" Ferguson or "Pappy" O'Daniel, were loved for their larger than life personalities and ability to connect with everyday folk. In the nineteenth century, small Texas farmers voted for populist candidates who were opposed to big ag and big railroads.

Today, Populist candidates rail against the biased media, liberal academia, establishment politicians, and other cultural elites who look down on lives of regular people.

Classical Liberalism: Texas's political culture is part of mainstream political culture of the American Founding, based on the political theory of such Founders as Thomas Jefferson, James Madison, and George Mason. These men were admirers of the British writers John Locke and Adam Smith who established **classical liberalism**: *The belief in God-given rights, limited government, the rule of law, and free markets.* A core concept of classical liberalism is the idea that when the individual has the freedom to pursue his or her own interests, it contributes to the good of the whole society. For example, if a woman has the freedom to start a small business, this contributes to the economic growth and progress of the town she lives in.

Classical liberalism

The belief in God-given rights, limited government, the rule of law, and free markets.

Today, the core principles of classical liberalism are carried on by the *libertarians.* In the 2014 gubernatorial election, 1.41 percent of voters were members of the Libertarian Party. Libertarians emphasize three values: individual liberty, strict adherence to the Constitution, and free markets. They tend to avoid social issues like abortion, and they are opposed to a large, interventionist military. The most prominent libertarian in Texas is Ron Paul, who served in the US Congress for 16 years and ran for president three times.

Ron Paul, who represented the Galveston area in Congress, is an example of a libertarian conservative.

Social Conservatives: Lastly, there is another political culture that describes many Texans. **Social Conservatism** *is the belief held by some conservatives that focus on their Christian identity and support conventional families, the right to practice religion in public, and traditional values.* This type of conservative supports prayer in school and will fight to have textbooks that depict a more positive view of American history. They oppose abortion and euthanasia. They support traditional marriage, as defined as between one man and one woman. They are animated by the strong feeling that morals are crumbling in America. And they feel strongly that traditional Christian holidays, such as Christmas and Easter, ought to be celebrated in public.

Texas Political Subcultures in Conflict: As we can see, Texas is more complicated than most people realize. Most Texans are conservative or moderate, but some Texans are liberal or even accept some Leftist beliefs. And of the people who identify as conservative, there are many different types of conservatives. A Populist conservative might feel hostile to the elitism of traditional conservatism. And a classical liberal or libertarian may not be comfortable with many of the values of a social conservative.

Social Conservatism

The belief held by some conservatives that focus on their Christian identity and support conventional families, the right to practice religion in public, and traditional values.

Let's look at the issue of legalizing marijuana to understand how the various conservative subcultures differ from one another. Traditional and social conservatives would oppose the legalization of marijuana on the grounds that it would morally corrupt young people and introduce something that would have a harmful effect on society. Libertarians, on the other hand, might support it by saying that people should have the freedom to make good and bad choices in life and it is not the role of government to decide such matters. And some Populist politicians would support the decriminalization of marijuana because it is not fair to throw regular people in jail for such a minor offense.

What all this means is that political arguments will continue in Texas not only between liberals and conservatives, but also between conservatives and other types of conservatives. This contributes to the colorful and contentious nature of Texas politics.

NOTES

Texas Almanac. Ed. Elizabeth Cruce Alvarez. Denton: the Texas State Historical Association, 2015. The Texas Handbook online: https://tshaonline.org/handbook.

Ray Stephens. *Texas: A Historical Atlas*. Norman: University of Oklahoma Press, 2010.

ESSAY QUESTIONS

1. Briefly describe the seven regions of Texas.
2. Describe some of the key features of the diverse Texas economy.
3. Compare and contrast modern liberalism with classical liberalism.

TERMS

Central Corridor ______________________________

Classical liberalism: ______________________________

East Texas ______________________________

Individualism: ______________________________

Jacksonian Democracy: ______________________________

King Cotton: ______________________________

Majority-minority: ______________________________

Metroplex: ______________________________

Modern liberalism: ______________________________

Political culture: ______________________________

Social conservatism: ______________________________

Traditionalism: ______________________________

TEXAS FUN & FACTS SHEET 3

Patriot Texas

Pledge to the Texas Flag: "Honor the Texas flag; I pledge allegiance to thee, Texas, one state under God, one and indivisible."

© fotoscool / Shutterstock.com

Official State of Texas Motto: Friendship

State Nickname: The Lone Star State

Texas Independence Day: March 2 (The Texas Declaration of Independence was signed on March 2, 1836)

Preamble to the Texas Constitution: Humbly invoking the blessings of Almighty God, the people of the State of Texas, do ordain and establish this Constitution.

Number of Presidents from Texas: Four, Dwight Eisenhower and Lyndon Johnson were born in Texas. George H. W. Bush was born in Massachusetts, and George H. Bush was born in Connecticut.

Dates of the Republic of Texas: 1836 to 1846

First President of the Republic of Texas: Sam Houston, 1836–1838

Texas becomes the forty-eighth state in the USA: December 29, 1845

First Governor of Texas: James Pinckney Henderson

Number of Texas State Parks: 99

Number of Natural Lakes in Texas: One, Caddo Lake

Number of Reservoirs in Texas: 188 major man-made lakes, with 5,607 square miles of inland water, ranking it first in the 48 contiguous states

Highest Point in Texas: Guadalupe Peak at 2,667 feet above sea level

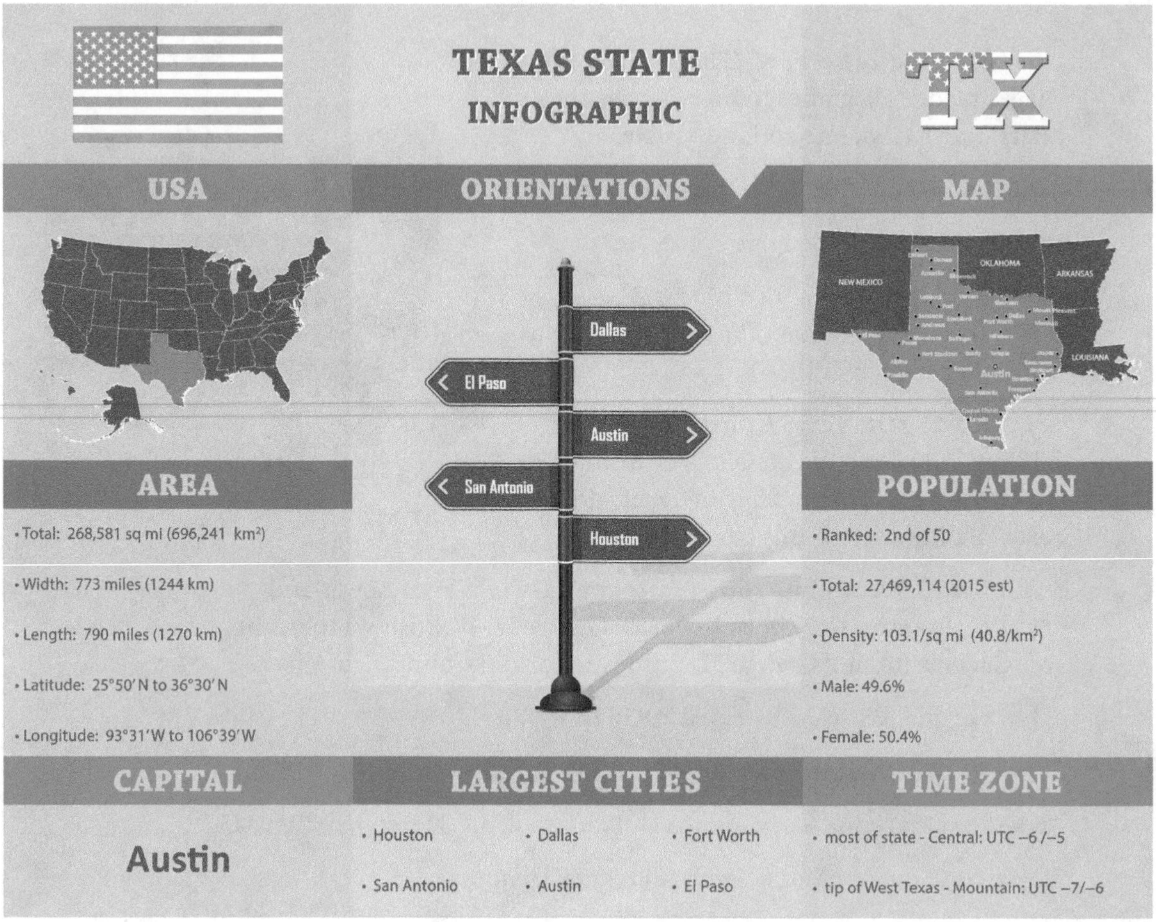

TEXAS STATE INFOGRAPHIC

TX

USA | **ORIENTATIONS** | **MAP**

Dallas
El Paso
Austin
San Antonio
Houston

NEW MEXICO
OKLAHOMA
ARKANSAS
LOUISIANA
Austin

AREA

- Total: 268,581 sq mi (696,241 km²)
- Width: 773 miles (1244 km)
- Length: 790 miles (1270 km)
- Latitude: 25°50′ N to 36°30′ N
- Longitude: 93°31′ W to 106°39′ W

POPULATION

- Ranked: 2nd of 50
- Total: 27,469,114 (2015 est)
- Density: 103.1/sq mi (40.8/km²)
- Male: 49.6%
- Female: 50.4%

CAPITAL

Austin

LARGEST CITIES

- Houston
- Dallas
- Fort Worth
- San Antonio
- Austin
- El Paso

TIME ZONE

- most of state - Central: UTC −6 /−5
- tip of West Texas - Mountain: UTC −7/−6

Texas Infographic Map

UNIT TWO

Texas Constitutions within the Federal System

CHAPTER 5

Texas Declaration of Independence

TOPICS

- Historical Background of Texas Declaration of Independence
- Principles of Texas Declaration
- Annotated Text of the Texas Declaration

LEARNING OBJECTIVES

When you finish reading this chapter, you will be able to:

1. Cite the historical cause of the Texas Revolution.
2. Explain the core ideas that make America and Texas unique.
3. Describe the fundamental principles of a republican form of government as expressed in the Texas Declaration.

Chapter 5 is organized differently than the other chapters in this textbook. This whole chapter consists of the complete texts of the Texas Declaration of Independence along with commentary on the significance of its words and ideas. The reason why we are devoting so much space to this document is that not only did it establish Texas as an independent government, but more importantly the Texas Declaration of Independence proclaims the founding principles on which the United States and the Great State of Texas were established.

During Santa Anna's siege of the Alamo, Texas wrote its Declaration of Independence.

HISTORICAL BACKGROUND OF THE TEXAS DECLARATION OF INDEPENDENCE

On March 1, 1836, a convention consisting of forty-four delegates met in an unfinished building at Washington-on-the Brazos, the temporary capital of Texas. The meeting was urgently called because at that moment the Alamo was under attack by the Mexican army led by General Santa Anna. After years of debate, it was finally apparent that Texas must declare independence from Mexico.

The convention president, Richard Ellis, appointed George C. Childress, James Gaines, Edward Conrad, Collin McKinney, and Bailey Hardman to a committee to write a declaration outlining the case for Texas independence. Historians think that Childress was the primary author. And since the declaration was submitted to the convention the very next day, on March 2, it is assumed that Childress had already prepared it before he arrived. After the convention unanimously approved the declaration, it also wrote the Constitution of the Republic of Texas and appointed Sam Houston as commander of the military.

The Texas Declaration borrowed many ideas written by Thomas Jefferson in the US Declaration of Independence.

PRINCIPLES OF THE TEXAS DECLARATION

Along with a list of grievances, the Texas Declaration of Independence contains statements on the nature of government, constitutional principles, and political values. It was written only sixty years after the US Declaration of Independence, authored by Thomas Jefferson, and it freely borrows phrases and ideas from America's founding document. The ideas represented in the Declaration form the *Founding Principles* on which the Republic is established.

The Idea of America: America is different than other countries because America is an idea. When you think of Germany or Japan or Russia, you may conjure up their unique histories and cultures, but you do not think of any set of principles. This is not true of America. America is an idea, and the idea of America is expressed in the Declaration of Independence and the Texas Declaration of Independence. When people decide to come to America, they come because they believe in the idea of America.

E Pluribus Unum

This motto of America is Latin for "from many one." It means that individuals of all sorts of backgrounds and ethnicities and religions come together to form one American nation.

The unique set of ideas and values, sometimes called American Exceptionalism, are what bind Americans together as one people. This concept is contained in the phrase **E Pluribus Unum,** *from many one*. This motto of America is so important that it is engraved on every US coin. *E Pluribus Unum means that individuals of all sorts of backgrounds and ethnicities and religions come together to form one nation*. The idea of America is the glue that joins together the diverse mix of Americans that have come from all over the world to fulfill their "American Dream."

THE TEXT OF THE TEXAS DECLARATION

This section contains the complete text of the Texas Declaration of Independence along with explanations of the significance of key words and phrases.

"The Unanimous Declaration of Independence made by the Delegates of the People of Texas in General Convention at the town of Washington on the 2nd day of March 1836.

"When a government has ceased to protect the lives, liberty and property of the people, from whom its legitimate powers are derived, and for the advancement of whose happiness it was instituted, and so far from being a guarantee for the enjoyment of those inestimable and inalienable rights, becomes an instrument in the hands of evil rulers for their oppression."

Inalienable rights

God-given, inherent rights that were not granted by government, so government cannot take them away.

Inalienable Rights: The US Declaration of Independence says that human beings are "endowed by their Creator with certain unalienable rights." This is the first principle of our Founding. It means that every person possesses God-given rights simply by virtue of being a human being, and that each human has equal rights. **Inalienable rights** *are inherent rights that were not granted by government, so government cannot take them away.* This principle places rights outside of government.

Protect Lives, Liberty, and Property: Since each human is endowed with certain inalienable rights, the proper purpose of government is to protect those rights. The phrase "protect the lives, liberty, and property of the people" comes from John Locke. He said that a government that can arbitrarily execute

A motto of the United States, E Pluribus Unum means "from many one." People with different backgrounds come together to form one nation.
© rorem / Shutterstock.com

a person, or take away his or her freedom and property without following the law, is illegitimate. Locke placed special importance on property rights. One's money, investments, and property are a result of a lifetime of work, sweat, and toil. If government can just come along and confiscate your property, then in reality your life and labor belong to the government and you have no freedom at all.

Pursuit of Happiness: The statement that governments are "instituted" for the "advancement of happiness" succinctly describes government built around the principle of liberty. In America, the individual is free to pursue her own happiness, chase her own dreams, and make her own life decisions, without undue government interference. The type of "happiness" the Founders described was the Aristotelian concept of happiness that comes from a good life lived to its full potential.

...

> "When the Federal Republican Constitution of their country, which they have sworn to support, no longer has a substantial existence, and the whole nature of their government has been forcibly changed, without their consent, from a restricted federative republic, composed of sovereign states, to a consolidated central military despotism, in which every interest is disregarded but that of the army and the priesthood, both the eternal enemies of civil liberty, the everready minions of power, and the usual instruments of tyrants."

Popular sovereignty

The people are the ultimate rulers and the government serves the people.

State sovereignty

In a decentralized federal system, the power of the national government is limited and the states have independent power to take care of many of its own affairs.

Consent of the Governed: A government that does not have the consent of the people is a tyranny. The American and Texas Republic is based on the principle of the "consent of the governed," otherwise known as **popular sovereignty**, *meaning that the people are the ultimate rulers and the government serves the people.* No constitution or constitutional amendment is valid unless it wins the consent of the people, and government officials are elected to serve the people.

State Sovereignty: As we will learn in more detail in Chapter 7, the United States of America is a federal government consisting of fifty states, including Texas. *In a decentralized federal system, the power of the national government is limited and the states have independent power to take care of many of its own affairs. This is known as* **state sovereignty**. This system of state's rights and local government is more democratic and efficient than one based on the monopoly of the national government.

. . .

"When, long after the spirit of the constitution has departed, moderation is at length so far lost by those in power, that even the semblance of freedom is removed, and the forms themselves of the constitution discontinued, and so far from their petitions and remonstrances being regarded, the agents who bear them are thrown into dungeons, and mercenary armies sent forth to force a new government upon them at the point of the bayonet."

Virtue of Government Officials: "Moderation" is one of the virtues of the *Protestant Ethic* (hard work, thrift, and moderation) that played such a central role in early American culture. The Framers believed that no matter how good the laws and constitution of the land are, that government will crumble without the virtue of government officials. The best way to ensure good government is for the people to elect virtuous leaders.

Freedom: Individual freedom or **liberty** *is an inalienable right central to human existence that allows a person to pursue their own happiness as long as they do not hurt other people.* The Texas Declaration of Independence and the Texas Constitution protects individual freedom, which includes *personal freedom*: the right of the individual to be free in thought and beliefs, to be free to travel, and to be free to make personal decisions without government interference; *political freedom*: the right to vote, participate in government, assemble into groups, gain access to truthful information (a free press), and be treated equally under the law; and *economic freedom*: the right to own property, start a business, choose a career, engage in economic activity, and make all decisions regarding one's own labor and employment.

Liberty

An inalienable right central to human existence that allows a person to pursue their own happiness as long as they do not hurt other people.

. . .

"When, in consequence of such acts of malfeasance and abdication on the part of the government, anarchy prevails, and civil society is dissolved into its original elements. In such a crisis, the first law of nature, the right of self-preservation, the inherent and inalienable rights of the people to appeal to first principles, and take their political affairs into their own hands in extreme cases, enjoins it as a right towards themselves, and a sacred obligation to their posterity, to abolish such government, and create another in its stead, calculated to rescue them from impending dangers, and to secure their future welfare and happiness."

Nations, as well as individuals, are amenable for their acts to the public opinion of mankind. A statement of a part of our grievances is therefore submitted to an impartial world, in justification of the hazardous but unavoidable step now taken, of severing our political connection with the Mexican people, and assuming an independent attitude among the nations of the earth."

No other book than John Locke's *The Second Treatise on Government* had a bigger influence on the Founding Generation.

General Welfare: This idea goes back to Aristotle, who said that *good governments provide for the* **general welfare** *or common good of the people*, while tyrannical government only serves the interest of the rulers.

Right of Rebellion: The right to rebel is the central premise of the Declaration. This is another idea that goes back to John Locke, who in *The Second Treatise on Government* said that the people have the right of revolution if the government does not protect individual rights and fails to provide for the safety and happiness of its citizens.

Extreme Cases: The purpose of the Texas Declaration of Independence was to explain to mankind that Texas was justified in its rebellion. A large part of the declaration lists the grievances and wrongs committed by the Mexican government. As Jefferson wrote in the US Declaration, rebellion is not justified for "light and transient causes . . . [but only by] a long train of abuses and usurpations." For minor government wrongs, the proper remedy is the ballot box and free elections. But for "extreme cases," the proper remedy is rebellion.

. . .

"The Mexican government, by its colonization laws, invited and induced the Anglo-American population of Texas to colonize its wilderness under the pledged faith of a written constitution, that they should continue to enjoy that constitutional liberty and republican government to which they had been habituated in the land of their birth, the United States of America."

General welfare

Governments provide for the common good of the people.

Rugged Individualism: America and Texas was built by the men, women, and children who through hard work and determination ventured into the wilderness and build a better life for themselves. The "American Dream" is the belief that in a free society in which the individual is allowed to reap the benefits of his or her hard work and innovation, not only will the individual become prosperous, but the whole country will collectively prosper. The quintessential American is the president that was born in a log cabin (Abraham Lincoln), the immigrant that came to America with a few dollars and became the richest man in the world (Andrew Carnegie), and the geek that dropped out of college to start his own computer company (Bill Gates).

Limited government

The idea that through such mechanisms as written powers and checks and balances government must be limited in order to protect the liberty of the people.

Written Constitution: Since the Mayflower Compact, Americans believed in written constitutions that spell out the explicit powers of government. This is an important part of the principle of **limited government**: *the idea that through such mechanisms as written powers and checks and balances, government must be limited in order to protect the liberty of the people.* The Framers strongly believed that if you give an individual or a group of people power without limits, they will eventually abuse their authority and try to grab more and more power.

Over the last hundred years, history has proven that the Founders were right about their principle of limited government. In the name of creating more equality for the people, several socialist and communist regimes have concentrated unlimited power in a central government and ruined the lives of tens of millions of people. Leftist leaders such as Stalin of Russia or Mao of China censored the press, spied on the people with secret police, executed dissidents for criticizing the government, outlawed religion, and held show trials to discredit political opponents. It is estimated that unrestricted socialist regimes in Germany, China, Russia, Cambodia, and North Korea have killed over 100 million people in the last century.

The communist government of the Soviet Union under Stalin had no limits, thus millions of people were subjugated and killed.

...

"In this expectation they have been cruelly disappointed, inasmuch as the Mexican nation has acquiesced in the late changes made in the government by General Antonio Lopez de Santa Anna, who having overturned the constitution of his country, now offers us the cruel alternative, either to abandon our homes, acquired by so many privations, or submit to the most intolerable of all tyranny, the combined despotism of the sword and the priesthood."

Civilian Control of the Military: It is an important American doctrine that civilians must control the military and that military leaders are excluded from political power, otherwise the government could easily turn into a military dictatorship. This is why the US Secretary of Defense, even if he is a former general, would never wear a military uniform in public.

Separation of Church and State: When Texas was a Mexican territory, colonists were forced to convert to Catholicism and priests had political power. These things violate the American principle of the separation of church and state. The Texas Constitution guarantees the freedom of religion and forbids a religious test to hold elected office. A government run by the church is called a theocracy, as they have today in Iran. The Framers knew that when government is run by religious leaders it tends to corrupt the church and erode public faith in religious institutions.

...

"It has sacrificed our welfare to the state of Coahuila, by which our interests have been continually depressed through a jealous and partial course of legislation, carried on at a far distant seat of government, by a hostile majority, in an unknown tongue, and this too, notwithstanding we have petitioned in the humblest terms for the establishment of a separate state government, and have, in accordance with the provisions of the national constitution, presented to the general Congress a republican constitution, which was, without just cause, contemptuously rejected."

It incarcerated in a dungeon, for a long time, one of our citizens, for no other cause but a zealous endeavor to procure the acceptance of our constitution, and the establishment of a state government.

It has failed and refused to secure, on a firm basis, the right of trial by jury, that palladium of civil liberty, and only safe guarantee for the life, liberty, and property of the citizen."

Republican Form of Government: The American and Texas Founders distrusted democracy, but instead established a republic. A republican form of government stresses individual rights and rejects monarchy and aristocracy, which are based on inherited power. Instead, a republic is a meritocracy, a system in which an individual's success is based on his or her own hard work, talents, and competence. In a **republic**, *the people vote for representatives to make laws for the common good, not to benefit a privileged class or faction.*

Minority Rights: The Framers feared a democracy, which is based on majority rule. In a democracy, whatever the majority decides, regardless of established law, is right. In the heat of the moment, a democracy can devolve into mob rule and individual or minority rights can be discarded. Instead, the Founders established a constitutional republic, with a Bill of Rights, that protects minority rights. For example, even if the majority of Americans wanted to outlaw Quakers, a religion hated by many in the 1700s, the Bill of Rights protects this minority religion.

Republic

The people vote for representatives to make laws for the common good, not to benefit a privileged class or faction.

Legal Rights: Before the Texas Revolution, Stephen F. Austin travelled to Mexico City to deliver a petition written by the Convention of 1832 to the Mexican government. Suspecting that Austin was trying to incite insurrection, the Mexican government threw Austin in jail, where he was confined for two years with no trial. This sort of action violates the right

The right of habeas corpus is a fundamental right that goes back to the Magna Carta.

to a writ of ***habeas corpus***, *which states that a person cannot be imprisoned without being told what the charges are and must have a trial in a reasonable period of time.* The Texas Constitution protects individuals against the government abuse of the legal system with many provisions, most important of which are the right of habeas corpus and the right to a *jury of one's peers.*

...

"It has failed to establish any public system of education, although possessed of almost boundless resources, (the public domain,) and although it is an axiom in political science, that unless a people are educated and enlightened, it is idle to expect the continuance of civil liberty, or the *capacity for* self government.

It has suffered the military commandants, stationed among us, to exercise arbitrary acts of oppression and tyranny, thus trampling upon the most sacred rights of the citizens, and rendering the military superior to the civil power."

George Mason, the author of the Virginia Declaration of Rights, had a big influence on the Bill of Rights and the Texas Declaration.

Necessity of a Republican Education: George Mason, the author of the Virginia Declaration of Rights, wrote that "no free government, or the blessings of liberty, can be preserved to any people but by a firm adherence to justice, moderation, temperance, frugality, and virtue, and by *frequent recurrence to fundamental principles.*" The Framers strongly believed the Republic would not last long unless the people were educated about the principles of which our government is founded. This is the purpose of this chapter.

Habeas corpus

A person cannot be imprisoned without being told what the charges are and must have a trial in a reasonable period of time.

...

"It has dissolved, by force of arms, the state Congress of Coahuila and Texas, and obliged our representatives to fly for their lives from the seat of government, thus depriving us of the fundamental political right of representation.

It has demanded the surrender of a number of our citizens, and ordered military detachments to seize and carry them into the Interior for trial, in contempt of the civil authorities, and in defiance of the laws and the constitution.

> It has made piratical attacks upon our commerce, by commissioning foreign desperadoes, and authorizing them to seize our vessels, and convey the property of our citizens to far distant ports for confiscation."

Rule of Law: John Adams said that "we are a nation of laws, not men." In contrast to a monarchy, which is based on the general power of the king, a constitutional republic is based on the rule of law. Government officials must follow the written and established laws of the land. Without the strict adherence to the rule of law, liberty cannot be safeguarded.

Free Markets: The Founders embraced the economic teachings of Adam Smith, which were described in his book the *Wealth of Nations* published in 1776, the year of the Declaration of Independence. Smith described modern **capitalism** *that is based on competition, property rights, and free commerce without undue government interference. Capitalism fosters progress because it rewards hard work and innovation.* No other system in world history has done more to eradicate poverty and lifted the standard of living as capitalism.

Capitalism

The economic system based on competition, property rights, and free commerce without undue government interference. Capitalism fosters progress because it rewards hard work and innovation.

...

> "It denies us the right of worshipping the Almighty according to the dictates of our own conscience, by the support of a national religion, calculated to promote the temporal interest of its human functionaries, rather than the glory of the true and living God.
>
> It has demanded us to deliver up our arms, which are essential to our defence, the rightful property of freemen, and formidable only to tyrannical governments."

Freedom of Religion: Freedom of religion and freedom of conscience is an inalienable right that cannot be violated by the government. People have the right to practice their own religion or no religion without government interference.

Right to Bear Arms: The right to bear arms is an essential right in a free society based on individual liberty and autonomy. The right to bear arms provides the individual with the ability to defend his or her life, family, and property. Also, the Founders considered it an important check on

The Texas pioneers needed guns to protect their property and family.

government. One of the first things dictators do is take away arms from the citizens, thus stripping them of any power to defend themselves against tyrannical government.

...

> "It has invaded our country both by sea and by land, with intent to lay waste our territory, and drive us from our homes; and has now a large mercenary army advancing, to carry on against us a war of extermination.
>
> It has, through its emissaries, incited the merciless savage, with the tomahawk and scalping knife, to massacre the inhabitants of our defenseless frontiers.
>
> It hath been, during the whole time of our connection with it, the contemptible sport and victim of successive military revolutions, and hath continually exhibited every characteristic of a weak, corrupt, and tyrannical government."

Primary Purpose of Government is Protect the Nation: When humans lived in the wilderness they had maximum freedom but lived in a dangerous and precarious world. "Might makes right" was the only rule. Eventually people formed governments to protect the safety of the people. The Founders believed that the primary responsibility of government is to provide law and order and to protect the country against hostile foreign forces. Only after the people are safe can society start working on promoting happiness and general welfare.

. . .

"These, and other grievances, were patiently borne by the people of Texas, untill they reached that point at which forbearance ceases to be a virtue. We then took up arms in defence of the national constitution. We appealed to our Mexican brethren for assistance. Our appeal has been made in vain. Though months have elapsed, no sympathetic response has yet been heard from the Interior. We are, therefore, forced to the melancholy conclusion, that the Mexican people have acquiesced in the destruction of their liberty, and the substitution therfor of a military government; that they are unfit to be free, and incapable of self government."

The necessity of self-preservation, therefore, now decrees our eternal political separation.

We, therefore, the delegates with plenary powers of the people of Texas, in solemn convention assembled, appealing to a candid world for the necessities of our condition, do hereby resolve and declare, that our political connection with the Mexican nation has forever ended, and that the people of Texas do now constitute a free, Sovereign, and independent republic, and are fully invested with all the rights and attributes which properly belong to independent nations; and, conscious of the rectitude of our intentions, we fearlessly and confidently commit the issue to the decision of the Supreme arbiter of the destinies of nations."

We the People: In sum, the Founders established a constitutional republic that would protect individual liberty while providing for the safety and happiness of the people. In a representative government, the people vote for the best leaders to make the laws and to run the government. At a time in world history when governments were ruled by kings, this was a brave experiment in self-government. In the words of Abraham Lincoln, it was a "government of the people, by the people, [and] for the people."

In God We Trust: Although it is a nation "of the people," the Founders strongly believed that the people need God for guidance. The Founding Generation believed that not only do our rights come from God, but that there is no objective morality without God. They also strongly believed that God, or a "Supreme arbiter," judged all individuals and nations. Reflecting our Puritan origins, the Founders believed that God planned a special destiny for America as an example of a moral democracy and a force for good in the world. If America did the right thing, it would prosper, but if it did wrong it would be punished. For example, in Lincoln's Second Inaugural Address, he said that the Civil War was God's punishment for slavery.

Public Rectitude: The Founders were worried that the people may not be able to maintain the virtue necessary for self-government without religion. In a vast country so filled with abundance, they worried that people might eventually devote their lives to the selfish pursuit of pleasure. In George Washington's Farewell Address he said, "Of all the dispositions and habits which lead to political prosperity, religion and morality are indispensable supports. . . . And let us with caution indulge the supposition that morality can be maintained without religion." In other words, for self-government to flourish, people need to love their neighbor and figure out ways they can contribute to the common good. As John Kennedy said, "Ask not what your country can do for you; ask what you can do for your country."

ESSAY QUESTIONS

1. Describe the three types of freedom.
2. Describe how adherence to limited government would have prevented the mass-murdering regimes that existed in the 1900s.
3. What do you think are the most important principles of self-government?

TERMS

Capitalism: ____________________

E Pluribus Unum: ____________________

General welfare: ____________________

Habeas corpus: ____________________

Inalienable rights: ___

Liberty: ___

Limited government: ___

Popular sovereignty: ___

Republic: ___

State sovereignty: ___

CHAPTER 6

Texas Constitutions

TOPICS

- History of Texas Constitutions
- Features of the Current Texas Constitution
- Principles of the Texas Constitution

LEARNING OBJECTIVES

When you finish reading this chapter, you will be able to:

1. Describe the main feature of the early constitutions of Texas.
2. Describe how the Civil War influenced Texas government.
3. Outline the main sections of the current Texas Constitution.
4. Explain the major principles of the Texas Constitution.

As we learned in Chapter 4, Texas's political culture embodies elements of traditionalism, individualism, populism, and classical liberalism. When a constitution was imposed on Texas from without, such as the Mexican constitutions and the Reconstruction constitution, it did not reflect the political values of the people of Texas. But when Texas was finally allowed to write its own constitutions, such as in 1845 and 1876, it reflected the political values of the people of Texas, and it included the principles of limited government and decentralization.

HISTORY OF TEXAS CONSTITUTIONS

The federal government, as well as the fifty state governments, has a **Constitution**: *the basic document that provides the structure, powers, and limits of government.* Like all constitutions, the Texas Constitution reflects the political culture and history of the state. Texas has operated under eight different constitutions, and all of them reflect the historical and political dynamics of the era.

Constitution

The basic document that provides the structure, powers, and limits of government.

Republic of Mexico (1824): This was the first constitution to govern Anglos in Texas, adopted soon after Mexico secured independence from Spain in 1821. This constitution was federalist in construction, making a clear break from Spain's centralized government—today there are thirty-one states in Mexico. But instead of establishing a Mexican state of Texas alone, the Mexican Constitution combined Texas with Coahuila, creating Coahuila y Texas. This was the source of much conflict with the Texan settlers because the capital city of Saltillo was hundreds of miles south of Texas, thus making local administrative issues difficult to manage.

Coahuila y Texas State (1827): In 1827, the state of Coahuila y Texas framed a provincial constitution. It had a unicameral legislature and no bill of rights. Texas sent two representatives to this legislature. But Texas disregarded the provisions that declared Catholicism the official state religion and that prohibited slavery. When General Santa Anna became a

In 1824, Mexico wrote a federal constitution that included the state of Coahuila y Texas.

dictator, he suspended the Mexican Constitution, including the 1827 state constitution. This suspension of federalism was one of the disputes that sparked the Texas Revolution.

Republic of Texas Constitution (1836): This constitution was quickly written primarily by George Childress and Sam Houston in Washington-on-the-Brazos during the Battle of the Alamo. They copied sections of the US Constitution and constitutions from other southern states. It provided a clear separation of church and state: there was no official state religion and no clergymen could hold public office. It strengthened property rights. It legalized slavery and forbade a master from freeing his slaves without permission from the legislature. Blacks and Indians could not be citizens. Recalling the abuses of Santa Anna, it limited the president to one three-year term. And the president was prohibited from raising an army without legislative consent. This constitution existed during the ten-year period when Texas was an independent nation.

State Constitution of 1845: Written in preparation for the acceptance of Texas into the United States in 1845, this conservative constitution limited government power in many ways. The elected governor served a two-year term. The state legislature had two chambers and met biannually (every other year). The executive branch was plural—most statewide offices, including Lieutenant Governor, were elected by the people, not appointed by the governor. This constitution also reflected populist hostility towards banks and corporations. It required two-thirds of the legislature to approve a corporation, and it outlawed bank corporations altogether.

The Texas Constitution of 1845 also retained many influences of Spanish law: exempting homesteads from foreclosure, protecting a wife's property rights, and providing for communal property (women were giving half of the property accumulated during the marriage).

Confederate Constitution of 1861: This was written after Texas joined the Confederacy. It only made four significant changes to the 1845 constitution: it increased the debt ceiling, it prohibited the emancipation of slaves, it allowed secession from the Union, and it included a provision to join the Confederacy.

Rejoining the Union in 1866: After the Civil War, when the Confederacy was defeated, Texas once again had to rewrite its constitution. They thought this constitution would get them back into the Union under Andrew Johnson's mild Reconstruction Plan. It nullified secession, abolished slavery, repudiated the right of future secession, and renounced Confederate war debt. It also included *black codes*, laws treating Black

Americans as second-class citizens. But under the new Reconstruction Act passed by Radical Republicans, military leadership took over Texas and this constitution was overturned by Congress.

Sam Houston helped write the Constitution of the Republic of Texas.
© Everett Historical / Shutterstock.com

Reconstruction Constitution of 1869: With most whites barred from or refusing to vote, in 1868 a constitutional convention was formed to gain reacceptance into the Union under the Republican's Reconstruction Plan. Most native Texans hated this new constitution, calling it the "radical constitution" or the "carpetbagger's constitution."

The new government centralized power under the governor (E. J. Davis): he was given a four-year term, and his power to select state officials and judges was greatly augmented. It created a public school system under a centralized administration. Local county courts were abolished. The Texas legislature met every year. And it gave African Americans the right to vote while it disenfranchised former rebels.

Redemption Constitution of 1876 (current): Reconstruction in Texas came to an end in 1875 when the Republicans were kicked out of office and Democrats regained control of the state. A constitutional convention was called, which was attended by ninety Democrats, forty members of the Grange Party (a third party that supported small farmers), and fifteen Republicans. The leaders of the convention were ex-Confederate leaders, members of old Texas families, and large landowners. The constitution they produced was ratified by the people of Texas in 1876. In large part, it returned government to the conservative values that permeated the 1845 constitution.

The best way to understand the 1876 constitution, the current constitution of Texas, is that it was an attempt to reverse the centralized government imposed under Reconstruction. It severely weakened the state government, cut salaries, lowered the debt ceiling, and reduced property taxes. The governor's salary was also cut and his term was reduced to two years. Many officials, such as the Attorney General and state judges, were elected by the people, not appointed by the governor. The legislative sessions went back to one short session every two years. And local county governments were restored and strengthened.

FEATURES OF THE CURRENT TEXAS CONSTITUTION

The 1876 Constitution is the basis of the current constitution of Texas, but it is buried under nearly 500 amendments that have been added over the last 140 years. With over 87,000 words, the Texas Constitution is the second longest state constitution. This has made it the subject of criticism by some political scientists. They argue that constitutions should be the basic framework of government, but the Texas Constitution is far too detailed, ungainly, and repetitive. Some have called for a new constitutional convention, if for no other purpose than to edit down the current constitution. Most Texans, however, are afraid of what a new constitutional convention would produce and have refused to vote for a convention every time it is proposed.

The Texas Constitution is organized into seventeen Articles. The following is a thumbnail sketch of the basic features of the major articles of the Texas Constitution.

Preamble: The Texas Preamble consists of only one sentence: "Humbly invoking the blessings of Almighty God, the people of the State of Texas, do ordain and establish this Constitution."

Article 1: Bill of Rights: The Texas Bill of Rights is contained in the very first article of the constitution. It comprises many of the individual liberties in the US Bill of Rights, such as freedom of religion, freedom of speech, and protection of people accused of a crime. But the Texas Bill of

In Texas, one's primary residence cannot be confiscated due to debt. This is called homestead protection.

Rights also contains some rights not listed in the US Constitution. In 1973 Texas adopted an amendment prohibiting discrimination based on sex. It forbids committing the mentally ill for long periods of time without a jury trial. And it prohibits the suspension of habeas corpus under *any* circumstances. In contrast, the US Constitution allows the suspension of habeas corpus during "rebellion or invasion."

Many provisions in the Texas Bill of Rights strengthen property rights and protect the poor against undue government intrusion. It forbids imprisonments for debt, and it protects *homesteads* (your primary residence cannot be confiscated due to debt). It prohibits garnishment of wages except for child support. And a 2010 amendment protects private property against broad *eminent domain* confiscation by the government. **Eminent domain** *is the right of the government to expropriate private property for public purposes, such as to build highways or schools, with fair monetary compensation to the land owner.*

Article 2, Three Separate Departments: This article expresses the principle of **separation of powers:** *the government is divided into three branches: executive, legislative, and judicial.* And each branch has its primary power. The legislative branch makes law, the executive branch administers the law, and the judicial branch interprets the law.

Article 2, however, fails to clearly explain the principle of checks and balances. It says that each branch "shall be confided to a separate body of magistracy...and no collection of persons . . . being of one of these departments, shall exercise any power properly attached to one of these departments." This is not how the principle of *separation of powers* and *checks and balances* is designed to work.

In order to limit government power and to prevent one branch from becoming too powerful, the Framers created three branches of government, but it gave each branch some power over the other branches. This is known as the principle of **checks and balances.** For example, the legislature will pass a law, but the governor can veto this law, and the Texas Supreme Court can nullify it by declaring it unconstitutional. In other words, it is not the complete separation that makes checks and balances work. Rather, checks and balances works only when the three branches share some power with each other.

Article 3, Legislative Branch: Article III, by far the longest, deals with the legislative branch. It created a **bicameral legislature,** *with two chambers*: today there are 31 senators and 150 representatives. Senators serve a four-year term; representatives serve a two-year term. Texas legislators have one of the lowest salaries in the US. And they meet in a **biannual**

Eminent domain

The power of the government to expropriate private property for public purposes, such as to build highways or schools, with fair monetary compensation to the land owner.

Separation of powers

The government is divided into three branches: executive, legislative, and judicial.

Checks and balances

In order to limit government power and to prevent one branch from becoming too powerful, the Framers created three branches of government, giving each branch some power over the other branches.

Bicameral legislature

A legislature divided into two chambers, the Senate and the House.

Biannual session

The legislature meets every other year.

The Texas legislature meets every other year for 140 days.

session, *every other year* for 140 days. The Texas legislation cannot call itself into session or extend a session. Only the governor can call a special thirty-day session. The one exception is for impeachment.

And the Texas Constitution sets many procedural limits on the legislature. A bill must be read out loud on three separate days, unless 4/5 suspends this. And Article III establishes strict limits on public debt. Also, Article III is unique in that it sets public policy on several issues, such as cattle brands, water funds, and student loans.

Plural executive

An executive branch in which many powerful state officials are elected by the people and are independent from the governor.

Article 4, Executive Branch: The executive branch consists of the governor, Lieutenant Governor, Comptroller of public accounts, land commissioner, and Attorney General—all elected separately. This establishes a **plural executive**: *many powerful state officials are elected by the people and are independent from the governor.* This fragmented executive branch was designed to limit the power of the governor. Today, the governor serves a four-year term with no term limits. Compared to most states, his power is limited. The Texas governor has no formal cabinet. Many factions of government, like agriculture, energy, and education, are controlled by independent boards and commissions. And the governor has very weak appointment and removal powers.

However, the governor's veto is the one tool that gives him power over the legislative branch. And the governor has *line-item veto* power: he can strike out individual spending provisions, while keeping other parts of the budget intact. This, in essence, gives the Texas governor leverage over every agency in state government.

Article 5, the Courts: Article V creates a limited and fragmented court system. Texas is the only state other than Oklahoma that has two final courts of appeal: the *Supreme Court*, for civil cases, and the *Court of Criminal Appeals*, for criminal cases. And judges are chosen by partisan elections, in which they campaign for votes as Democrats or Republicans. Most judges serve four- to six-year terms.

Article 6, Suffrage: Article VI denies the right to vote to people under 18, certain felons, and the mentally incompetent. Texas does not have the initiative, referendum, and recall measures that give the people more power in most other states. Some Texas cities, however, have a limited initiative and referendum. In addition to voting for public offices, the voters of Texas must approve four things: amendments, state income taxes, legislative salaries, and convening a constitutional convention.

Article 7, Education: Article VII established the public school system for Texas. It states that "it shall be the duty of the legislature to establish . . . an efficient system of public free schools." It also established the *Permanent University Fund* to finance the University of Texas at Austin and Texas A&M University with proceeds from public lands.

The Texas Constitution of 1876 put aside land to help finance the University of Texas.

Article 9, County Governments: The state constitution decentralizes power by assigning many functions to local government, especially the counties.

Article 17, Amendments: This article establishes a procedure for amending the state constitution. The **Amendment Procedure**: *a proposed must pass both houses of the legislature by a two-thirds votes and be ratified by a majority of the voters in a general or special election.* This is significantly easier than the amendment procedure for the US Constitution. This accounts for why Texans have amended their constitution more than twice the average for the other states.

Amendment Procedure

For an amendment to be added to the Texas Constitution, a proposal must pass both houses of the legislature by a two-thirds vote and be ratified by a majority of the voters in a general or special election.

PRINCIPLES OF THE TEXAS CONSTITUTION

Texas has a conservative constitution that limits government power while it protects individual liberty. Some of the features of the Texas Constitution follow traditional American constitutional principles, while others are unique to Texas:

A. Traditional American Constitutional Principles:

Republican Form of Government: Article I, section 2 of the Texas Constitution states that "the faith of the people of Texas stands pledged to the preservation of a republican form of government." In a *republic*, representatives and government officials are elected by the people.

Separation of Powers: The Framers of the US Constitution sought to create a strong central government to establish order, but they were afraid that eventually government officials would abuse their power and infringe on individual and state's rights. To guard against this abuse, the Framers established the *separation of powers*: government is divided into three branches: executive, legislative, and judicial.

Checks and Balances: And the three branches have *checks and balances*: each branch has some power over other branches, allowing it to restrain the other branches. This brilliant scheme allowed for greater central power but created an internal check designed to prevent the growth and abuse of government power.

The three branches of government are able to check each other because they share power.
© JPL Designs / Shutterstock.com

B. Unique aspects of the Texas Constitution:

Decentralization: The government of Texas is highly **decentralized,** *power is transferred from a central government to independent agencies and commissions and local bodies.* This is designed to thwart abuse of state government power.

Plural Executive: The executive branch is divided up into several departments, the heads of which are elected by the people. Moreover, many executive branch functions are administered by independent commissions and agencies, such as the Railroad Commission and the Texas Land Office, which are also elected by the people.

Biannual Legislature: The Texas Constitution creates a part-time legislature. They are in session only 140 days every other year.

Elected Judges: Contrary to federal judges, who are appointed by the president for life, Texas judges run for election. This holds judges accountable to the public.

Balanced Budget: Unlike the federal government, which is currently burdened by a $20 trillion national debt, several provisions of the Texas Constitution mandate a **balanced budget**: *lawmakers are forbidden from spending more money than is brought in by tax revenue.*

Individual Rights: The Texas Bill of Rights protects freedom of speech, freedom of religion, and equal protection under the law, but it also places special protections on property rights, such as homestead protection and limits on eminent domain.

Popular Sovereignty: The Texas Bill of Rights states that "all political power is inherent in the people, and all free governments are founded on their authority, and instituted for their benefit." Many of the unique features of the Texas Constitution, such as decentralization, a plural executive, and elected judges, are based on the principle of popular sovereignty and rule of the people.

Decentralized

In decentralized government, power is transferred from a central government to independent agencies and commissions and local bodies.

Balanced budget

Lawmakers are forbidden from spending more money than is brought in by tax revenue.

NOTES

Handbook of Texas: https://tshaonline.org/handbook/online

Texas Constitution & Statutes: http://www.statutes.legis.state.tx.us/

ESSAY QUESTIONS

1. Describe the main features of the 1845 constitution, including the influence of Spanish law.
2. Outline the unique aspects of the current Texas Constitution.

TERMS

Amendment procedure: ______________________________

Balanced budget: ______________________________

Biannual session: ______________________________

Bicameral legislature: ______________________________

Checks and balances: ______________________________

Constitution: ______________________________

Decentralized: ______________________________

Eminent domain: ______________________________

Plural executive: ______________________________

Separation of powers: ______________________________

TEXAS FUN & FACTS SHEET 4

Famous Texans

© neftali / Shutterstock.com

Business
Red Adair
May Kay Ash
Michael Dell
Howard Hughes
T. Boone Pickens, Jr.
Ross Perot

Musicians
Buddy Holly
Janis Joplin
Scott Joplin
Willie Nelson
Roy Orbison
Kris Kristofferson
ZZ Top

Movies
Joan Crawford
Jayne Mansfield
Sissy Spacek

TV
Carol Burnett
Walter Cronkite
Larry Hagman
Dan Rather
Gene Roddenberry

Politics
Sam Houston
Lyndon B. Johnson
George H. W. Bush
George W. Bush
Sam Rayburn

Sports
Earl Campbell
Tom Landry
Don Meridith
Nolan Ryan
Willie Shoemaker
Roger Staubach

CHAPTER 7

National and State Constitutional Powers

TOPICS

- Federalism
- How the Federal System Works
- From Dual Federalism to Cooperative Federalism
- The Supreme Court and Federalism
- Public Policy and Growth of the National Government
- Politics of Federalism

LEARNING OBJECTIVES

When you finish reading this chapter, you will be able to:

1. Describe how the Framers intended federalism to work.
2. List the traditional powers of the states.
3. Explain how through history the national government has grown over the states.
4. Compare the liberal and conservative positions on current political issues related to federalism.

This chapter describes the constitutional principle of federalism, which balances power between the national government in Washington, DC, and the state governments, such as Texas. First we will describe how the Framers envisioned federalism to work, and then we will show how it has changed over the years. The system of federalism can be complicated, and thus many political fights have revolved around the question of what exactly are the powers of the national government and what are "states' rights"? This chapter seeks to clarify these questions.

FEDERALISM

Federal system

Power and responsibility is divided between the national government and the state governments.

Unitary system

All functions and power are controlled by one central government.

Besides the checks and balances of three branches of government, the Founders sought to limited centralized power another way, with a **federal system**: *power and responsibility is divided between the national government and the state governments.* When the Founders wrote the US Constitution, they created a system that allowed the states to keep many of their powers and responsibilities. This made sense because the states existed before the national government was established, and they did not give up all their power when they joined the Union.

Unitary System: The concept of federalism was one of the unique features of the US Constitution, differentiating it from the British system which was a **unitary system**: *all functions and power are controlled by one central government.* Under a unitary system, there may be different regional governments and municipalities, but they are all ultimately controlled by the central government. In the last 225 years, many countries have rejected a unitary system and adopted a federal system similar to America's, such as Mexico, Canada, and Russia.

Advantages of Federalism: The Framers thought there were many advantages to a decentralized, federal system of government. James Madison, in the *Federalist Papers*, said that federalism creates "laboratories of democracy." Each state can experiment and try its own laws and policies. If these reforms are successful, then other states can adopt them. Madison also said that federalism is much more efficient because state and local government can take care of local matters (such as road construction) much quicker than relying on a massive national bureaucracy.

Lastly, America is a large country consisting of several different regions, each with a different culture and history. A law that might make sense in California may not work for the people of Texas. It is better to allow local people to make laws that fit with their unique ideology and culture.

James Madison said that federalism turns the states into "laboratories of democracy," meaning they are free to make their own laws.

HOW THE FEDERAL SYSTEM WORKS

The US Constitution created three zones of authority: powers assigned to the national government, powers assigned to the state governments, and powers shared by both the national and state governments (concurrent powers).

National Powers: What powers are assigned to the national government? The Constitution, especially in Article I, Section 8, gives the US Congress several *enumerated power:* powers explicitly listed in the Constitution. These include things like the power to tax, to borrow, to print money, to make foreign policy, to raise and support armies, to declare war, to regulate interstate and foreign commerce, to establish federal courts, to create rules for naturalization, and to establish post offices.

Some of these powers are *exclusive powers*, meaning that only the national government can exercise these powers. Article I, Section 10 of the US Constitution says that the states are forbidden from doing certain things, such as printing money, declaring war, making foreign treaties, or taxing imports.

The national government also has **implied powers** *under the Necessary and Proper Clause of the Constitution, which grants the national government certain unspecified powers.* The Necessary and Proper Clause, found at the end of *Article I, Section 8,* states that the national government has the power "to make all Laws which shall be necessary and proper for carrying into Execution the foregoing powers (the enumerated powers)." This is often called the "elastic clause" because it can be stretched to fit the needs of Congress.

Implied powers

Under the Necessary and Proper Clause of the Constitution, the national government has certain unspecified powers.

Police powers

The traditional powers of the state, which include criminal law, laws effecting public health and safety, and laws regulating public morality.

State Powers: The Constitution places several explicit limitations on state power. States cannot pass *bills of attainder* (legislative punishment), *post ex post facto laws* (retroactive laws), or grant titles of nobility. States cannot impair contracts. Also, each state must grant *full faith and credit* to the other states, meaning each state must recognize the laws, records, and judicial rulings of other states. For example, if a married couple moves to another state, the new state must recognize the marriage. And if a criminal escapes to another state, that state must return him or her to the original state.

The Constitution places several restrictions on the states, but they still retained their traditional powers. So, what are the *traditional powers of the state*? Historically, state governments played a primary role in what is called **police powers**: *the responsibility to make criminal law, laws effecting public health and safety, and laws regulating public morality.* Traditionally

Traditional state powers include the responsibility to make criminal law and laws effecting public health and safety.

the states primarily controlled public education, road construction, general welfare, family law, commerce within a state, property rights, regulation of banks and corporations, and land laws.

When the states joined the Union, the delegates at the constitutional convention assumed that the states would retain all their powers, except those exclusively assigned to the national government. To make this concept clear, the Tenth Amendment was added to the Constitution. The **Tenth Amendment** states that "*The powers not delegated to the United States by the Constitution, nor prohibited by it to the states, are reserved to the states respectively, or to the people.*" So, the states have powers not listed in the US Constitution.

Tenth Amendment

It states that "The powers not delegated to the United States by the Constitution, nor prohibited by it to the states, are reserved to the states respectively, or to the people."

Concurrent Powers: The third zone of power created by the US Constitution allows the national and states governments to share some powers. This is called *concurrent powers*. As long as the states don't use these powers to destroy or interfere with national powers, the states enjoy the concurrent powers to do such things as levy taxes, borrow money, maintain law and order, and establish courts.

FROM DUAL FEDERALISM TO COOPERATIVE FEDERALISM

The Framers created the federal system in order to decentralize power and maintain state control over local matters. But as time went on, to the consternation of "*states' rights*" advocates, the national government grew in power and the states lost sole control of many of its traditional powers. Political scientists use two terms in describing this transformation: they say America transitioned from *Dual Federalism* to *Cooperative Federalism*.

Dual Federalism: From 1789 to 1932, the country functioned on the model of **Dual Federalism**: *the national government operated only on its limited enumerated powers while the states retained their sovereign powers, and the two layers of government had separate functions and responsibilities.* For example, the national government had primary responsibility for things like national defense, foreign policy, monetary policy, and interstate commerce, while the states were responsible for things like education, public safety and welfare, criminal law, labor law, and infrastructure (building roads, canals, bridges, and ports). States' rights advocates supported dual federalism because it gave the states more freedom and independence.

Dual federalism

The national government operated only on its limited enumerated powers while the states retained their sovereign powers, and the two layers of government had separate functions and responsibilities.

Cooperative Federalism: But after 1933, with the implementation of the New Deal, the national government started taking over more and more powers away from the states. This was done to help solve several national problems, such as poverty, racial discrimination, labor laws, corporate regulation, and education. Although the states' rights advocates in Texas and other states fought this, America turned to a model of **Cooperative Federalism**: *the national government and the state governments cooperate and work together to serve the public.* For example, education had always been a local power, but today the federal government is involved in education in many ways, such as by providing Pell Grants and student loans for college students.

Cooperative federalism

The national government and the state governments cooperate and work together to serve the public.

THE SUPREME COURT AND FEDERALISM

The Supreme Court helped lay the legal foundation for the transition from Dual Federalism to Cooperative Federalism. When the Supreme Court decides a case, the opinion establishes a particular interpretation of the Constitution for Congress and the states to follow. In two landmark Supreme Court cases, *McCulloch v. Maryland* (1819) and *Gibbons v. Odgen* (1824), the Supreme Court interpreted three clauses of the Constitution in such a way as to support a stronger national government: the Necessary and Proper Clause, the Supremacy Clause, and the Commerce Clause.

Necessary and Proper Clause: In *McCulloch v. Maryland*, a case dealing with the US central bank, the Supreme Court established a broad interpretation of the Necessary and Proper Clause that influenced the nation for centuries.

During George Washington's first term, Congress established the Bank of the United States (BUS), the nation's first central bank. Secretary of State Thomas Jefferson was opposed to the BUS on the grounds that nothing in the Constitution explicitly said that the national government could establish a central bank. But Secretary of Treasury Alexander Hamilton opposed Jefferson and broadly interpreted the Necessary and Proper Clause. He said that Article I, Section 8 gives Congress the power to "collect taxes," "to borrow money," and "to coin money." And since Congress needs a central bank to do all these things, it is perfectly proper for Congress to create the BUS.

In *McCulloch*, Chief Justice John Marshall agreed with Hamilton and ruled that under the Necessary and Proper Clause it was constitutional for Congress to create a central bank. As long as Congress is carrying out an enumerated power, it can pass laws and create institutions not explicitly stated in the Constitution. By broadly interpreting the Necessary and Proper Clause, Marshall made it more difficult for the states in the future to limit the power of the federal government.

Chief Justice John Marshall often interpreted the Constitution in such a way as to strengthen the national government.

Supremacy Clause: In *McCulloch*, the Supreme Court also established the principle of national supremacy over the states. Article 6 of the US Constitutions contains the *Supremacy Clause*, which states that the Constitution is the "supreme law of the land." The *McCulloch* case involved a Maryland law that taxed branches of the BUS in an attempt to drive them from the state. John Marshall ruled that the states cannot use taxes to try to destroy something created by Congress. This established the principle that if state law is in conflict with national law (in areas where the national government has primary responsibility), national law is supreme over state law.

Interstate Commerce Clause: Although the Necessary and Proper Clause and the Supremacy Clause has been used to justify growing national power, nothing has diminished state power more than a broad interpretation of the *Commerce Clause*: "Congress shall have the power to . . . regulate commerce with foreign nations and among the several states." In the eighteenth century most people understood "commerce" to mean "trade," as in the phrase "foreign trade." In *Gibbons v. Odgen* (1824), however, John Marshall broadly interpreted "commerce" to mean all "economic activity." Moreover, Marshall wrote that Congress' power to regulate commerce between the states "may be exercised to the utmost."

This broad interpretation of the Commerce Clause has led to the vast expansion of the national government's power to regulate nearly all aspects of modern life. This is because today practically every item you purchase has been made in whole or in part in another state or country, and nearly every activity you do can be said to influence the economic activity of other states. For example, in *Wickard v. Filburn* (1942), the Supreme Court ruled that a farmer could not feed his livestock with wheat that he grew on his own farm because it interfered with the interstate commerce of wheat.

PUBLIC POLICY AND GROWTH OF THE NATIONAL GOVERNMENT

Over the last century and a half, many public policy debates affected federalism either directly or indirectly. To deal with money in politics, the Seventeenth Amendment was added to the Constitution. And to provide more money to the national government, the Sixteenth Amendment was adopted. But two political issues in particular, civil rights and poverty, contributed the most to the expansion of federal power and turned America from Dual Federalism (with strong states' rights) to Cooperative Federalism (with strong national powers).

Civil Rights: One reason the national government grew in power over the states is due to the failure of many southern states to establish racial equality under the law. During and shortly after the Civil War, three important amendments were added to the Constitution to protect the rights of the freed slaves: the *Thirteenth Amendment* prohibited slavery in America, the *Fourteenth Amendment* required that "the states" treat all US citizens equally under the law (the Equal Protection Clause), and the *Fifteenth Amendment* ordered that "the states" shall not deny somebody the right to vote on account of race or ethnicity. The former slave states, however, ignored these amendments and established *Jim Crow* laws that separated blacks from whites and made it more difficult for blacks to vote.

For nearly a hundred years, however, the federal government did little or nothing to enforce the Civil War amendments. Not until 1954, in *Brown v. the Board of Education*, did the Supreme Court rule that segregation violated the Equal Protection Clause. And not until the *Civil Rights Act of 1964* did the federal government enforce the Fourteenth Amendment and prosecute states for discriminating against blacks. And not until the Voting Rights Act of 1965, did the federal government enforce the Fifteenth Amendment and prosecute states for making it more difficult for blacks to vote. So, another reason for the diminution of states' rights was the southern states failure to uphold civil rights.

Seventeenth Amendment: Another blow to states' rights was the adoption of the Seventeenth Amendment, but in this case the justification seemed less clear cut than it was for civil rights. In 1913, the **Seventeenth Amendment** was ratified, *allowing the voters of the state to select the state's two US Senators, rather than the state legislatures as stipulated in the original Constitution.* This took place during the Progressive Era when politicians and reporters argued that there was too much money in politics and the state legislatures were corrupt. They argued that popular election of senators would reduce political corruption.

Seventeenth Amendment

Ratified in 1913, this amendment allows the voters of the state to select the state's two US Senators, rather than the state legislatures as stipulated in the original Constitution.

But looking back over the last hundred years, there is no evidence that the Seventeenth Amendment has reduced corruption and money in politics. Instead, it undermined a major feature of the federal system. The Framers wanted the representatives of the states to have a seat at the table in Congress. The Framers understood that the representatives of the state legislators would serve as a major check on the expansion of federal power. Indeed, since the adoption of the Seventeenth Amendment, the size of the federal government has grown tremendously.

Sixteenth Amendment: A year before the ratification of the Seventeenth Amendment, progressives were successful at giving the national government a way to gain enormous power over the state: access to more money. In 1913, the *Sixteenth Amendment was ratified, creating the personal income tax.* Now the national government has the power to raise enormous revenues, far more than the states, by directly taxing the income of each American. Since power is money, this is another major way the federal government has grown in strength over the states.

The Welfare State: Now that the national government had more money, it was able to launch massive government efforts to fight poverty. Traditionally, the states had the primary role in helping the poor, but during the Great Depression it was determined that a national effort was needed. In the 1930s, Franklin Roosevelt created the New Deal. The most important part of the New Deal was the Social Security Act, which created

Since the passage of the Sixteenth Amendment creating the income tax, the federal government has had much more money than the state governments.

unemployment insurance, a pension for the elderly, and aid to poor families. The New Deal allowed the capitalistic system to continue, but created a "safety net" for Americans so that if they lost their job, became blind, or were old and poor, the federal government would help them.

In the 1960s, Lyndon Johnson created the Great Society. This went beyond the "safety net" and created the modern welfare state in America. The **welfare state** *is a national government system designed to promote the welfare of the people by enacting laws to alleviate poverty and providing such things as food stamps, healthcare, education, and housing.* Ironically, when the Great Society was implemented the poverty rate in America was 13 percent. After spending trillions of dollars over the last 50 years, the poverty rate remains 13 percent. Another unintended consequence of the welfare state is the skyrocketing of the national debt. Although America is the richest country in the world, it has a national debt of $20 trillion dollars (as of 2017). The main cause of the debt is paying for programs created by the welfare state.

Welfare state

A government system designed to promote the welfare of the people by enacting laws to alleviate poverty and providing such things as food stamps, healthcare, education, and housing.

Categorical grants

Federal monetary grants to the states for specific purposes, which comes with federal rules and regulations.

Much of the money given by the federal government to the states comes in the form of **categorical grants**: *federal monetary grants to the states for specific purposes, which comes with federal rules and regulations.* If the states accept this money, they must agree to follow the mandates of the national government. For example, if states accept federal money for road

Governor Rick Perry advocated block grants as a way to give the states more freedom to finance state programs.

construction, they must set their alcohol drinking age at twenty-one. This is why today all fifty states have the same drinking age, when in the past each state set its own drinking age (in 1985, Texas's drinking age was nineteen). To a large degree, categorical grants are a distribution of money from the richer states to the poorer states.

One critic of categorical grants was Rick Perry, the Governor of Texas from 2000 to 2015. Like other states' rights conservatives, Perry blamed the establishment of the welfare state for creating a culture of dependence. In 2010 he wrote a book titled *Fed Up* which critiques the history of the expansion of the federal government. Among other suggested reforms, Perry called for a replacement of categorical grants with **block grants**: *federal money that is transferred to the states with no strings attached to be used for general purpose.* Block grants were initiated by Richard Nixon and expanded by Ronald Reagan in the 1980s. Conservatives like block grants because they still provide income distribution from the wealthy states to the poorer states, but block grants afford the states with the freedom to run their own programs.

Block grants

Federal money that is transferred to the states with no strings attached to be used for general purpose.

POLITICS OF FEDERALISM

Many of the most contentious political fights in American history have revolved around issues related to federalism. Of course, the biggest fight was the Civil War. The southern states argued that the Constitution allowed the states to retain their traditional power of controlling labor and protecting private property (slaves). But by 1865, most northerners believed slavery was not a states' rights issue but a human rights issue: slavery violated the Fifth Amendment's rights of life and liberty. This conflict between the national and state governments did not end until after 620,000 Americans died.

Today federalism is still a major part of the political debate in America. In general, conservative Republicans advocate decentralization and a return of more power to the states. They argue that state and local governments can better serve the people, while a bloated federal bureaucracy wastes too much money and gives too much power to Washington politicians. Liberal Democrats, on the other hand, advocate more centralization and more power to the national government. They argue that in order to help create more equality and social justice, the national government needs to implement uniform laws and programs to benefit the whole country.

On a slew of issues, such as abortion, gun control, education (common core), gay marriage, and transgender bathroom, Texas takes the position that these areas fall under the control of traditional state powers. And on issues related to immigration, such as the border wall or sanctuary cities, Texas argues that the national government should set the policy because

Hispanics have protested against Governor Gregg Abbott's position on sanctuary cities and the border wall.

© a katz / Shutterstock.com

Article I, section 8 of the US Constitution expressly gives the federal government power in naturalization and immigration. Let's look more closely at two of these issues; gay marriage and sanctuary cities.

When gay marriage became the topic of intense national debate, Texas argued that family law had always been under the purview of the states, indeed marriage certificates were issued by state and local governments. To make Texas's position clear on the issue, in 2005 Texans voted to add an amendment to the Texas Constitution defining marriage as "a union between one man and one woman." But ten years later the Supreme Court ruled, in *Obergefell v. Hodges*, that there will be one national policy in the United States with regard to gay marriage, and it ruled that states must recognize gay marriage due to the guarantees provided by the Equal Protection Clause.

On April 30, 2017, Governor Greg Abbott signed into law S.B. 4, popularly known as the "sanctuary cities law." The law stipulates that local law enforcement officials must cooperate when Immigration and Customs Enforcement (ICE) agent's requests that criminal illegal immigrants be held in jail for up to forty-eight hours until an ICE agent can pick them up and possibly deport them. If local police chiefs, sheriffs, jail administrators, or constables refuse to comply with federal agents, they can be fined, removed from office, and held liable for civil action. For example, if a criminal is set free before ICE agents arrive and that criminal murders somebody, the local official that let the prisoner go can be sued. Normally, liberals oppose state's rights positions, but in this case they oppose the law on grounds that it may cause illegal aliens to fear local police.

NOTES

Michael Les Benedict. *Blessings of Liberty: A Concise History of the Supreme Court.* Boston: Wadsworth, 2006.

Adam Freedman. *The Naked Constitution: What the Founders Said and Why it Still Matters.* New York: Broadside Books, 2012.

Rick Perry. *Fed Up!: Our fight to Save America from Washington.* New York: Little, Brown and Company, 2010.

ESSAY QUESTIONS

1. What are "police powers" and the traditional areas where the states had primary power? Do you think the states should retain primary authority in these areas?
2. Explain how the states' failure to protect civil rights and deal with poverty led to the expansion of national governmental power.
3. Describe the liberal (centralized) and conservative (decentralized) position on one of the following topics with regards to federalism: gay marriage, transgender bathrooms, sanctuary cities, abortion, or gun control.

TERMS

Block grants: ____________________

Categorical grants: ____________________

Cooperative Federalism: ____________________

Dual Federalism: ____________________

Federal system: ____________________

Implied powers: ____________________

Police powers: ____________________

Seventeenth Amendment: ____________________

Tenth Amendment: ____________________

Unitary system: ____________________

Welfare state: ____________________

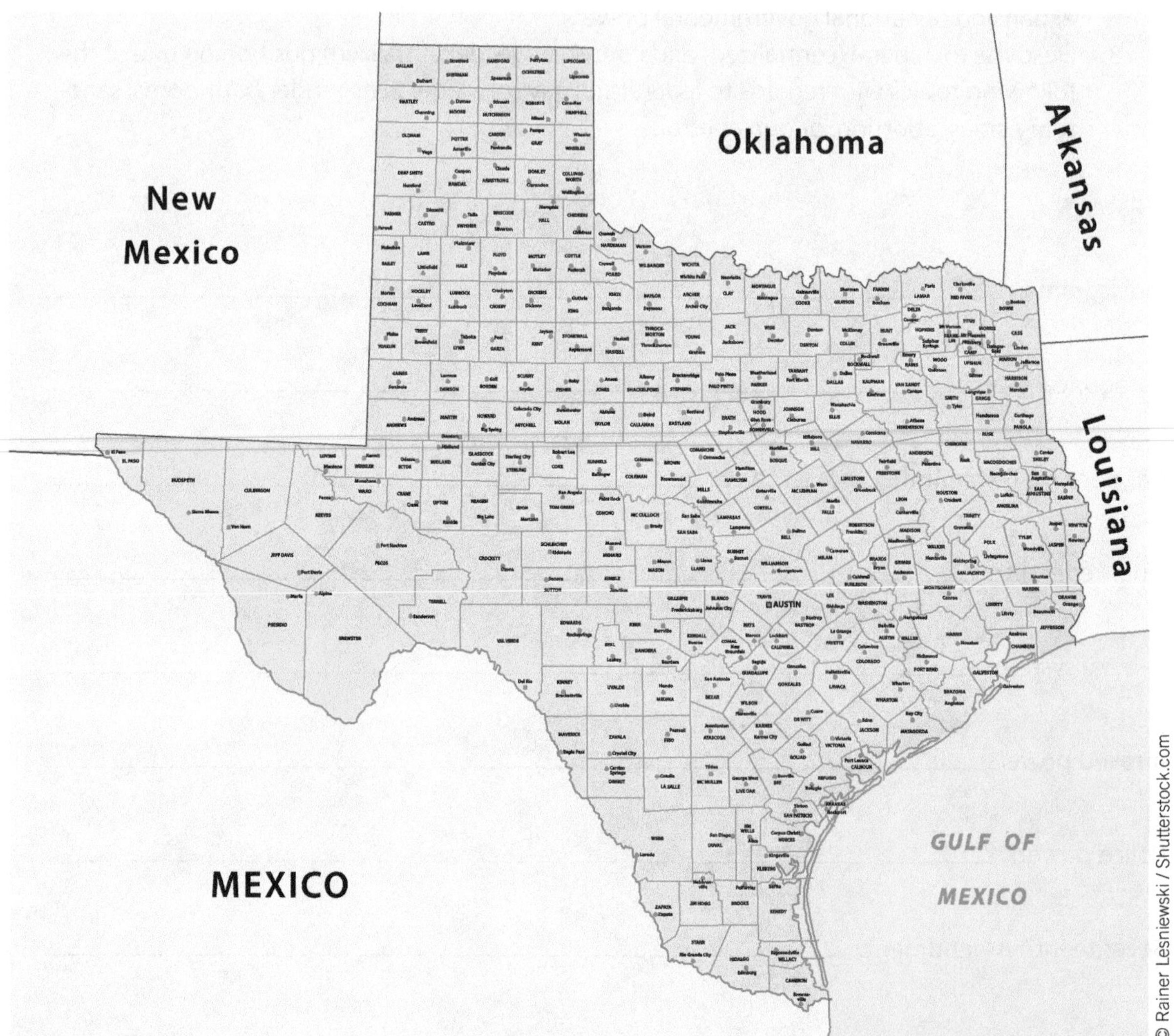

Texas County Map

CHAPTER 8

Local Government

TOPICS

- County Government
- City Government
- Three Types of City Government
- City Elections
- School Districts
- Special Districts

LEARNING OBJECTIVES

When you finish reading this chapter, you will be able to:

1. Describe the main functions and offices of county governments.
2. Explain the historical development of city government in Texas.
3. Discuss how city elections are conducted.
4. Describe the features of special districts, including independent school districts.

The US Constitution established a decentralized form of government, known as federalism, in which the national government shares power with fifty state governments. Furthermore, each state is divided up into several types of local governments. Today the United States consists of: 1 national government, 50 state governments, 3,031 county governments, 19,522 city governments, 16,364 townships, 12,884 school districts, and

37,203 special districts. This totals up to 89,004 separate governments in America!

In Texas, there are 254 county governments, 1,214 city governments, 1,079 school districts, and 2,600 special districts. More than the federal government, these local governments provide the services that affect us on a day-to-day basis. They provide clean drinking water, pick up the trash, take care of sewage, charter utility companies, establish schools for our kids, keep the police and fire departments, and maintain parks. This chapter will explain the different types of local governments and describe how they serve to enhance our lives.

There are tens of thousands of local governments in America.

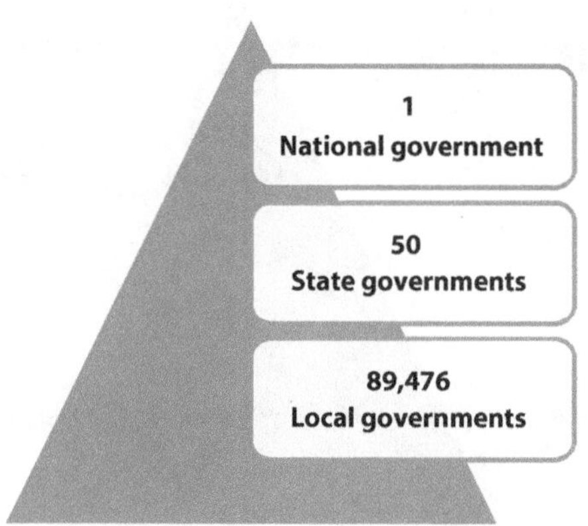

Number of governments in America
Courtesy Michael Young.

Creatures of the State: At the outset, we want to make a major distinction between state and local governments. Unlike state governments, local governments have no independent sovereign powers. Local governments are *creatures of the state*: They are legal entities created by state government by statute and derive all their powers from the state. Conversely, as we learned in the previous chapter, the states actually have independent power and authority from the national government.

And each state has wide latitude on what type of local government to authorize and how much power to grant local governments. *General purpose governments*, such as municipalities, are granted broad powers. *Limited-purpose governments*, such as school districts and counties, are granted narrow authority and have little control over revenue and manpower.

COUNTY GOVERNMENT

County governments are limited-purpose governments with narrowly defined powers. This is the oldest form of local government in America. Texas counties have their origin in the municipal unit of government under Spanish rule. The word "municipality" derives from the Latin "*municipium*," meaning "duty holders." It refers to communities in the Roman Empire that supplied Rome with troops in exchange for gaining Roman citizenship for its inhabitants and retaining a degree of local rule. Today, city governments are usually referred to as "municipalities," and county governments are usually referred to as counties.

Function of County Governments: In America, county governments may have different names (they are called "parishes" in Louisiana and "boroughs" in Alaska), but they have similar functions. Originally, they served as administrative subdivisions of the state government. Country governments would process things like marriage licenses, birth certificates, voter registration, auto registration, and driver's licenses for local state residents.

In Texas, most county governments are rural with small populations, thus they provide relatively few services—much less than city government in major urban centers. County governments in Texas typically provide police protection (Constables and Sheriffs), road and bridge construction, courts, records offices, tax collection, jails, election administration, and some welfare services. Some larger counties provide hospitals, libraries, and parks.

Commissioner's Court

The governing body for counties in Texas, it is composed of an elected county judge (at-large) and four elected commissioners (by district).

County judge

This county official serves as the chair of the commissioner's court, analogous to the mayor in a city government.

Structure of County Governments: *The governing body for counties in Texas is called the* **Commissioner's Court**, *composed of an elected county judge (at large) and four elected commissioners (by district).* It passes ordinances, approves budgets, and oversees minor officials. They usually serve four-year terms and run as partisans (the voters know if they are Democrats or Republicans).

The **county judge** *serves as the chair of the commission, analogous to the mayor in a city government.* The county judge may also have very limited judicial functions, but does not need to have an attorney's license. Unlike city governments that can pass city ordinances, county ordinances must

Texas has a great architectural heritage in its beautiful courthouses. This is the Tarrant County Courthouse, which was built in 1895.

be approved by the state legislature. The main source of revenue for the county government is the property tax.

County Government Offices: Just as in the state government of Texas, a prominent feature of county governments is decentralization and the plural executive. The chief executive, the *county judge*, is weak and has little appointment power. Each department head is elected by the people, not appointed by the county judge. There are seven major county offices: Sheriff, District Attorney, County Attorney, Tax Assessor/Collector, District Clerk, County Clerk, and Treasurer.

County Sheriff: The chief law enforcement officer of the county is the *sheriff*. They are elected by the people to a four-year term. The sheriff can appoint deputies. In big counties, the sheriff's primary duty is to operate the county jail. In small counties they may also serve as a tax assessor and collector. The citizens of a county also elect the *constable*, who serves as the court officer for the justice of the peace, serving subpoenas. A constable also provides law enforcement in their precinct.

County and District Attorneys: The leading prosecutor for all criminal cases in a county is the county attorney. They usually prosecute lesser criminal cases. The district attorney is the lead prosecutor at the district level. They usually prosecute more serious criminal cases. They both work in the county courthouse.

County Tax Assessor/Collector: The *tax collector* collects taxes (that makes sense!), primarily property taxes. Although "assessor" is often still in their title, they no longer appraise property values. Most counties also require the county tax collector to register voters and sell automobile licenses and permits. It might seem strange that the tax collector would be involved in voter registration, but this is a legacy of when Texas had a poll tax.

County and District Clerk: The chief record keeper of the county is the county clerk. They keep track of property records, birth certificates, marriage licenses, and sometimes voter registration. The district clerk keeps court records, including all judgments, acts, and court proceedings. They also schedule cases and collect child support payments.

The County Treasurer: The county treasurer receives, maintains, and disburses all county revenue. The county treasurer deposits money into the banks and keeps records of all the transactions. He or she may also make investments for the county. They have a fiduciary responsibility that all transactions are proper and that the accounts balance at the end of the month.

In many counties the sheriff runs the county jail. This is the jail and courthouse of Victoria County, Texas.

County Auditor: They oversee the collection and disbursement of county revenue. They are not elected but are selected by and report to the county judge. The auditor serves as a check on the treasurer, who obviously handles a lot of money.

Assessment of County Governments: County governments provide many important services to its residents, most importantly road and bridge maintenance and criminal justice. But because counties in Texas vary greatly in size, some of the smaller counties have difficulty paying for these services. In 2010, Harris County had 4 million residents, and Loving County had eighty-two residents! So, perhaps some of the smaller counties should get state financial assistance.

Another critique of county government is that there are too many elected officials. The idea is to hold government officials accountable to the people, but it also overburdens the voter. As we will see in Chapter 14, Texas has one of the lowest voter turnouts in the country. One explanation for low turnout is that Texas voters must vote to fill too many elected offices. This is a negative consequence of the plural executive at the state and county levels.

CITY GOVERNMENT

City governments have more power than county governments: they can pass ordinances and they are responsible for more services. The governments of large cities such as Houston, Dallas, and San Antonio exercise a large degree of power and independence from state government and serve to enhance the lives of millions of people.

The Creation of City Governments: The Texas Constitution establishes two types of city governments: *general law* and *home rule.*

General Law City: *Cities with fewer than 5,000 citizens that are governed by city charters created by state legislature are called* **general law cities.** Their powers are limited by the legislature and specified in the statute that established the city government. After the legislature grants the formation of the city, the city must choose from seven charters provided by statute. General law cities are the most common in Texas: there are about 938 general law cities.

Home Rule City: *Cities with over 5,000 citizens that were created by action of local citizens is called* **home rule cities.** In these cities, the citizens can pass their own laws, as long as they do not conflict with state law. Home rule cities are given great latitude in governing local affairs.

City Charter: Unlike general law cities that are assigned a charter by the state legislature, home rule cities make their own **charter**: *a document, like a constitution, that defines the governmental structure and rules by which the city operates.* The charter defines officer's responsibilities, establishes the court system, sets up the rules for elections, and provides the tax authority.

Function of City Governments: In Texas, city governments typically have the primary responsibility for police and fire protection, water, waste, parks and recreation, and libraries. And the city council can pass *ordinances*, pieces of legislation that have the force of law in a city.

Initiative, Referendum, and Recall: In special circumstances, the citizens in home rule cities can make their own laws. This can be done in a two-step process: first, if they get a certain number of registered voters to sign a petition, the city council must place the proposed ordinance, an *initiative*, on the ballot. Second, the initiative is placed on the ballot as a *referendum* and if it gets a majority of votes, it becomes law. This is a way for the people to make laws that the city government may be reluctant, for whatever reason, to support.

In home rule cities the people can kick out officials before the regularly scheduled election. This is called a *recall* election. If enough people sign a petition, the city will conduct a special recall election to replace the mayor or a city council member. The recall was designed to remove corrupt government officials from office.

General Law Cities

Cities with fewer than 5,000 citizens that are governed by city charters created by state legislature.

Home Rule Cities

Cities with over 5,000 citizens that were created by action of local citizens.

Charter

A document, like a constitution, that defines the governmental structure and rules by which the city operates.

Typically, cities manage their parks through their Parks and Recreation Departments. This is Austin's famous Zilker Park.
© Trong Nguyen / Shutterstock.com

THE THREE TYPES OF CITY GOVERNMENT

In America, most states, including Texas, have two forms of city government: *mayor-council* and *council-manager*. There is also a third type of city government, *the commission*. Although the commission was invented in Texas, it no longer exists in any city in Texas.

(1) Council-Manager: Arising during the Progressive Era (1900–1921), it has become one of the most popular forms of city government in America. The Progressives were concerned about corrupt, inefficient local governments that were controlled by city bosses and their political machines. Texas was a leader in developing the council-manager form of city government. Amarillo and Terrell were the first to adopt it in 1913. Except for Houston, all major cities in Texas, including Dallas and San Antonio, use it.

Council–Manager Form of Government

A type of city government that consists of an elected city council that makes policy and hires a professional city manager to administer the daily operations of the city.

The **council–manager form of government** *consists of an elected city council that makes policy and hires a professional city manager to administer the daily operations of the city.* The voters elect a nonpartisan city council, usually with seven members, and a mayor. By majority vote, the city council passes ordinances, ratifies the budget, and establishes the policies and direction of the city. The city council is considered part-time, and so traditionally they received little or no salary. In recent years, however, the salaries of mayors and city council members have been increasing, especially in big cities.

The significance of the council-manager form of government is that it did away with the city bosses who hired city workers and officials in exchange for political favors (known as the *spoil system*). The council-manager form of government reassigned many of the duties of the traditional mayor to a professional city manager, who is chosen for his or her competence, not political connections. The council-manager form of government placed the legislative power with the city council and mayor, and the executive power with the city manager.

Mayor: The mayor is the presiding officer of the council. He has a vote with the council, but no veto. The mayor is the spokesperson and symbolic head of the city and presides over many ceremonies, such as the opening of a new park or building. The council, including the mayor, selects only four positions: the city manager, the attorney, the clerk (or secretary), and the municipal judge.

City Manager: *The* **city manager** *prepares the budget, appoints and removes agency heads, and manages the city.* The city manager is appointed and serves at the pleasure of the council, which means he can be removed at any time. The city manager executes the policies of the city council. Once the city council hires a city manager, he has administrative control over the city. In small towns he might be called a "city administrator." Most city managers are trained professions with master's degrees in public administration. Their primary role is to administer city government, but

City manager

In a council-manager form of government, the city manager, sometimes called a city administrator, is the head of the city's administration and prepares the budget, appoints and removes agency heads, and manages the daily operations of the city.

The council-manager form of government has been largely successful at getting rid of the old fashion, corrupt city mayor.

they also provide advice and information to the city council. As skilled professionals, they usually receive good salaries.

Strengths and Weaknesses of Council-Manager Form: By most assessments, it is a successful form of local government that eliminated the city bosses and the spoil system. But there are some weaknesses. City council members are part-time, low paid, and serve short terms, and thus they do not always have high skills or professionalism. Also, since the city manager is not elected, he can ignore the will of the people. Lastly, there have been some cases where city managers hid information from the council.

(2) Mayor-Council Form: This is the traditional form of local government that developed from the English model. The city council exercises the legislative power of the city, and the mayor exercises the executive power. There are two types of the mayor-council forms of government: those with strong mayors, and those with weak mayors.

Weak Mayor: Most mayor-council forms of government in Texas have a weak mayor, in which the mayor shares power with the city council and other elected officials. The weak mayor has little power over the budget and cannot select or remove city officials. And a weak mayor has no veto power and may have term limits.

Strong Mayor: The strong mayor has more independent powers from the city council. The strong mayor has significant appointment, removal, budget, and spending powers. There are no term limits. And he has a veto over the council. Houston has a strong mayor form of mayor-council government. The strong mayor usually has a much larger salary than a weak mayor.

(3) The Commission Form of Government: After the 1901 hurricane, the Texas legislature and the Governor of Texas created the commission form of government to quickly rebuild Galveston. The idea was to create a local government on a business model that was more efficient than the traditional mayor-council form of government. The voters selected five commissioners in a city-wide election, each combining legislative and executive authority and each responsible for their specific department: Police and Fire, Streets and Public Property, Water and Sewer, Finance and Revenue, and Parks and Buildings. And each commissioner sat on the city commission.

Because Galveston was rebuilt so promptly and efficiently, people thought it was due to the commission system, and it was adopted in many cities around the country. But by WWII most cities abandoned it. Why?

People attributed the successful rebuilding of Galveston to the Commission Form of Government, but it had more to do with strong public will.
© Eric V Overton / Shutterstock.com

(1) Citizens did not always vote for competent administrators. (2) Because it combined legislative and executive functions in one body, it lacked proper checks and balances. Commissioners seldom scrutinize actions of their fellow commissioners. And, (3) It lacked leadership. The commissions had no visible leader, like a mayor, to make the final decisions.

CITY ELECTIONS

For most local governments in Texas, there are two main ways to elect leaders: *at-large elections* and *district elections*. District elections have been successful at creating more diversity on city councils. And although local government provides many important services for the citizens, people are less interested in local politics than national politics, thus turnout for local elections remain extremely low.

Non-partisan elections

In this type of city election, there are no party affiliations (Democrat or Republican) printed on the ballot next to the candidate's name.

Non-Partisan Elections: Technically, all city elections in Texas are **non-partisan elections**, *on the ballot there are no party affiliations printed next to the candidate's name.* Non-partisan elections were a major feature of the Progressive reforms that created the council-manager form of city government. The idea behind non-partisan elections is that people should vote for candidates based on their competency, not their political affiliation.

In reality, however, elections may not be as non-partisan as claimed. Although the ballot does not show an R (for Republican) or a D (for

Democrat) next to the candidate's name, many voters know the political ideology or party affiliation of the candidate. Liberal and conservative interest groups provide voter guides. And the candidate's campaign rhetoric often provides strong clues about the candidate's political leanings.

At-Large Election Systems: This was the traditional way to elect city officials. In an **at-large election**, *all voters in the city elect the members of the city council.* In other words, elections are city-wide. In some cities, the seven candidates who receive the most votes win a seat on the council. Most cities, however, have a city-wide election for each open seat on the city council, designating a number for each seat, such as Place 1, Place 2,and so on. The citizens submit one vote for each opening, and the candidate who gets the most votes for an opening wins a seat on the city council.

At-large election

In this type of city election, all voters in the city elect the members of the city council.

Single-Member Districts: Due to the Voting Rights Act of 1965, as amended in the 1970s, many cities, including those in Texas, switched to the single-member district system to provide for more minority representation on the council. In a majority rule system, minority residents of a city may never get a chance to elect a minority candidate. But in a **single-member district election**, *a city is divided into districts, and only the residents of a district can vote for a city council member to represent that district.* Because minority groups still tend to live in their own neighborhood, this system has been effective in diversifying city councils across Texas.

Single-member district election

In this type of city election, a city is divided into districts, and only the residents of a district can vote for a city council member to represents that district.

SCHOOL DISTRICTS

Besides county and city governments, another form of local government in Texas is the independent school district (ISD). They are called "independent" because they are independent of other local governments in their area, such as the county or city government. The Texas Constitution established a public school system in Texas under Article 7, which states: "A general diffusion of knowledge being essential to the preservation of the liberties and rights of the people, it shall be the duty of the legislature . . . [to establish] an efficient system of public free schools." There are over 1,000 school districts in Texas.

Independent School District

A unit of local government that provides K–12 education to its residents and that is independent from other local governments.

Structure of School Districts: *A unit of local government that provides K-12 education to its residents and that is independent from other local governments is called an* **Independent School District.** They are governed by a *board of trustees*, elected to staggered terms in non-partisan elections. There are normally seven members, who are usually selected in at-large elections. The trustees manage the district by selecting personnel,

Texas public high schools are run by Independent School Districts (ISD), which are independent of local governments.
© B. Franklin / Shutterstock.com

establishing rules and policies, adopting a budget, setting the tax rates, selecting textbooks, overseeing construction projects, and determining salaries and benefits. They also hold public meetings on a regular basis and honor outstanding students, staff, and faculty. School districts are primarily financed through a property tax.

The trustees hire a school *superintendent* to serve as the chief executive officer of the school district. The position of the superintendent is analogous to city manager. He or she administers the day-to-day operations of the school district and carries out the policies of the board of trustees. The superintendent normally serves a five-year term.

People get passionate about the education of their children, and thus school policies often garner much public debate. Issues like testing, funding equity, sports programs, transgender locker rooms, nutrition, and safety often get considerable media coverage and parental feedback.

SPECIAL DISTRICTS

The last type of local governments we will discuss are special districts, sometimes called special purpose districts. Actually, school districts are considered special districts. Special districts have been the fastest growing type of local government in Texas. Currently, there are over 2,600 special districts. **Special districts** *are a unit of local government that provides a particular service to residents, such as fire protection, transportation, sewage, or water.* They exist because the other types of local government fail to provide this specific function.

There are many different kinds of special districts. Some special districts serve one county (single-county districts), while others function in several counties (multi-county districts). River Authorities are special districts that span several counties. And special districts may provide one service, such as a hospital (special-purpose), while others may provide several services, such as water, sewage, and soil conservation (multi-purpose).

Special districts

A unit of local government that provides a particular service to residents, such as fire protection, transportation, sewage, or water.

Special districts are run by governing boards. In single-county districts, the residents usually vote for board members. In multi-county districts, the board members are selected by the leadership of the cities and counties they serve. This is the case with transportation special districts, such as the METRO in Houston and DART in Dallas, that provide a service to several cities and counties. Special districts may receive revenue from sales taxes, from property taxes, or by charging a fee for their service. Special districts are sometimes called "shadow governments" because few people even know that they exist.

NOTES

Texas Almanac. Edited by Elizabeth Cruce Alvarez. Denton: the Texas State Historical Association, 2016.

ESSAY QUESTIONS

1. Describe the most important officers in county government and the role of the county judge.
2. Outline the historical development of the three types of city government.
3. Why do single-member district elections create more diversity on city councils?

TERMS

At-large elections: ______________________________

Charter: ______________________________

City manager: ______________________________

Commissioner's Court: ______________________________

Council–Manager Form of Government: ______________________________

County judge: ______________________________

General law city: ______________________________

Home rule city: ______________________________

Independent School District: ______________________________

Non-partisan elections: ______________________________

Single-member district elections: ______________________________

Special districts: ______________________________

TEXAS FUN & FACTS SHEET 5

Texas Businesses

Retail/Food
Blue Bell Ice Cream
Brookshire Grocery
Church's Chicken
Chuck E. Cheese's
Dr Pepper/Snapple
Frito-Lay
Fuddruckers
GameStop
Gold's Gyms
HEB Markets
Imperial sugar
JC Penney
Jiffy Lube
Luby's
Michaels
Neiman Marcus
Pier 1 Imports
Pizza Hut
Scholtzsky's
7-11
Tony Roma's
TwinPeaks
Voit
Whataburger
Whole Foods Market
Zales

Transportation
American Airlines
Greyhound Lines
Peterbilt
Southwest Airlines

Petroleum
Apache Corp.
Baker Hughes
CITGO
ConocoPhillips
El Paso Corp
ExxonMobil
Halliburton
Schlumberger
Shell Oil
Valero

Technology
AT&T
Dell
Perot Systems
RadioShack

Other
D R Horton
Kimberly-Clark (Kleenex)
La Quinta Inn
Sysco
Waste Management
USAA

UNIT THREE

Three Branches of Texas Government

CHAPTER 9

Texas Legislative Power

TOPICS

- Structure of the Texas Legislature
- Qualifications of Membership
- Legislative Leadership

LEARNING OBJECTIVES

When you finish reading this chapter, you will be able to:

1. Cite the unique feature of the Texas legislature.
2. Explain the significance of a bicameral legislature.
3. Discuss the constitutional requirements to be a member of the Texas legislature.
4. List the powers and responsibilities of the Speaker and the Lieutenant Governor.

Along with the governor and the courts, the legislature is one of the three branches of the Texas government. It is considered the branch closest to the people. The primary **legislative power** *is to make law*. This is an awesome power: essentially, the power to make law is the power to order everybody in Texas to do what you want. In addition to the power to make law, the Texas legislature has many other formidable powers. The legislature has the "power of the purse" and controls taxing and spending. The

Legislative power

The primary power of the legislature is to make law.

legislature acts as a check on the governor, and it initiates the amendment process of the Texas Constitution. And more generally, the Texas legislature serves as a forum for the people of Texas to debate the issues that face the state.

This chapter begins Unit Three, which covers the three branches of government. Chapter 11 will focus on the powers and structure of the Texas legislature, while Chapter 12 will focus on how legislators get elected and pass bills.

Bicameral legislature

A legislature divided into two chambers, the Senate and the House.

Texas Senate

This chamber of the Texas legislature consists of thirty-one members who serve four-year terms.

STRUCTURE OF TEXAS LEGISLATURE

The Framers of the Texas Constitution greatly feared the abuse of government power. This is why they placed so many limits on the governor, but they also placed important limits on the Texas legislature.

Bicameral: If the Framers of the Texas Constitution wanted to create a powerful legislature to make laws quickly and efficiently, they would have created a legislature with one chamber, *unicameral.* Instead, they created a **bicameral legislature** *and divided the legislature into two chambers, the Senate and the House.* With two legislative chambers it is more difficult to make laws because they must pass both chambers by a majority vote. This gives the legislators more time to think about the issues, and, hopefully, only the best bills will make it through the more difficult process.

Terms: The Texas legislature consists of two chambers, the state Senate and state House of Representatives. The **Texas Senate** consists of *thirty-one members with four-year terms.* The Senate has staggered terms so that only half the membership is up for election every two years. In the election that follows reapportionment, the second year of each decade, all seats in the Senate are up for election. Lots are drawn to determine who stands for election in another two years or in another four years. They call the two-year term after reapportionment the "Houston seat" because when Texas joined the Union and sent its first two US Senators to Congress, Sam Houston drew the lot for the shorter term.

Terms are simpler in the House. The **Texas House of Representatives** *consists of 150 members with two-year terms.* So, every two years all the members of the House are up for reelection.

In the system of three branches of government, the primary power of the legislative branch is to make law.

Representation: As of the census year of 2010, each Texas Senator represents a senate district of 811,147 constituents. And each Representative serves a district of 167,637 constituents. There are 31 senate districts and 150 house districts.

Biannual Sessions: One of the striking features of the Texas legislature is its **biannual session**, *meaning the legislature meets every other year.* The legislative season starts on the second Tuesday in January in odd-numbered years and lasts for 140 days. At the end of the 140-day session, the Texas *legislature must adjourn and has no power to extend the session* (**sine die**). When the Texas Constitution was written, it was common for states to have biannual sessions. But as society modernized and legislatures struggled with increasingly complex issues, more and more states have turned to annual sessions. Today, only four states still have biannual sessions. Voters in Texas rejected a move to annual sessions in 1969 and again in 1972.

Texas House of Representatives

This chamber of the Texas legislature consists of 150 members who serve two-year terms.

Biannual Session

The legislature meets every other year

Sine die

The Texas legislature has no power to extend its session beyond 140 days.

Pros and Cons of Biannual Session: The biannual legislative session is in keeping with the traditionalistic/individualistic/classical liberalism/Populist political culture of Texas that we discussed in Chapter 4. Many Texans feel that the longer the Texas legislature is in session, the more damage the lawmakers can do! They consider most laws unnecessary. On the other hand, some people think that Texas should modernize and adopt an annual session like most other states. The following included some of the major arguments on both sides of the debate:

> **Advantages of biannual sessions:** The short legislative session forces legislators to concentrate on the most important issues facing the state. It makes it less likely that lawmakers will waste their precious time crafting frivolous laws. In general, more laws lead to bigger bureaucracies, additional regulations, and higher taxes. And when legislators are in the off-season, it gives them more time to meet with their constituents and reflect on the issues facing the state. Also, the short, biannual session is less expensive than long, annual sessions.
>
> **Support to switch to annual sessions:** In this modern, complex world, the legislature faces many problems they need to address. One hundred and forty days is not enough time to research and craft complex laws. Also, an annual session would enable the legislative branch to better check the governor. In the off-season, the governor is the primary voice of Texas. Furthermore, with longer legislative sessions, the Texas legislature could respond better to the ongoing needs of Texans.

The Texas Capitol Building in Austin, Texas.
© Chad Zuber / Shutterstock.com

Special Session: Although the legislature does not have the power to extend the session if they were unable to finish important business, the governor can . . . and often must. *The Texas Constitution allows the governor to call a* **special session**, *lasting only thirty days to complete unfinished business or deal with a special problem.* There is no limit on the number of special sessions the governor may call. And the governor decides the subject matter of each session, thus limiting the types of bills the legislature can initiate.

Special session

After the normal session ends, the governor can call a special session of the legislature, lasting thirty days, to complete unfinished business or deal with a special problem.

Compensation: Although Texas is a large, wealthy state, Texas legislators have one of the lowest salaries in the United States. Legislators receive an annual salary of only $7,200! When in session, they also get a per diem of $150. So, in years when the legislature meets, the 181 legislators get paid $28,200. By comparison, in 2013, California legislators made $90,526 and New York legislators made $79,500. The Texas Ethics Commission recommends the per diem rate. And they haven't recommended a salary increase since 1975.

Although Texas legislators have low salaries, they do get relatively generous retirement benefits, better than many other states. Legislators may retire at sixty years of age with eight years of service or at fifty with twelve years of service, with a compensation of about $25,000 a year. Also, Texas lawmakers are provided more generous staff accommodations than most other states. Most members keep a full-time office year-round in Austin and in their district. Texas state senators get a monthly office allowance of $38,000, and house members get $11,900.

The Citizen Legislator: *The low salary and the biannual legislative sessions fit with the concept of the* **citizen lawmaker**, *an amateur who is not a full-time, professional legislator.* The Framers of the Texas Constitution did not want to create a privileged class of professional lawmakers that live in a bubble and can no longer relate to the problems normal people face in their daily lives. Instead, in Texas lawmakers must go home and live under the laws they created. The idea is that the lawmaker's main life is outside of Austin and outside of government. He or she has a normal life with a normal job, and then every other year he or she serves in the legislature out of their patriotic duty.

The Texas legislature is based on the idea of the "citizen lawmaker," a person who lives a normal life and comes to Austin only every other year to serve briefly as a legislator.

QUALIFICATIONS OF MEMBERSHIP

The Texas Constitution provides a rather sparse list of qualifications to be a legislator, but in reality lawmakers need certain informal qualifications.

Formal Qualifications: To be a Texas state Senator, the Constitution stipulates that a person must be a US citizen, a registered voter, at least twenty-six years of age, and a resident of Texas for the last five years and a resident of the district for the last year. To be a Texas state Representative, a person must be a US citizen, at least twenty-one years of age, lived in the state for the last two years, and lived in the district the last year.

Informal Qualifications: Most adults meet the constitutional requirements for the job, but few can actually run for office. The first informal requirement to be a legislator is to have money or be able to attract money. Because the salary is so low, only wealthy people can afford to serve as a Texas legislator. Most Texas lawmakers are wealthy lawyers or businessmen. Also, they need connections and name recognition, perhaps by coming from a well-established family or by developing a business network or by holding some other political office. So, in order to launch a successful run for the state house, it helps to be wealthy and well-known.

Citizen lawmaker

An amateur who is not a full-time, professional legislator.

Although Texas is a majority-minority state, meaning minority groups comprise the majority of the state's population, the Texas legislature still consists mostly of white, middle-aged males. About 57 percent of the

Texas population is considered "people of color," although many Latinos identify as "white." Nonetheless, in a 2015 survey, only 35 percent of the Texas state legislators identified as persons of color. In the area of race and ethnicity, the two political parties could not be more different. For the Eighty-fifth Legislature, about 91 percent of Democrats are people of color, while only 4.3 percent of Republicans are. Meanwhile, women make up 20 percent of the legislature.

LEGISLATIVE LEADERSHIP

Article III, Section 9 of the Texas Constitution describe two powerful leadership positions of the Texas legislature: the Speaker of the House and the Lieutenant Governor. Without their approval, no bill can successfully make it through the legislature.

Speaker of the House

The presiding officer of the Texas House who controls the legislative agenda of the chamber.

Speaker of the House: The Speaker is one of the most powerful positions in Texas. **The Speaker of the House** *is the presiding officer of the Texas House and controls the legislative agenda of the chamber.* He has the power to direct legislation behind the scenes and to determine which bills come up for a vote. He appoints the chairs and most of the members of the important committees. The Speaker serves as presiding officer over all sessions, choosing who will speak, counting the votes, and interpreting house rules. And he chooses what bills will go to what committees. In essence, the Speaker has total control over the Texas House.

The Speaker is the leader of the Texas House of Representatives.

At the beginning of each legislative session, members of the House select a Speaker by majority vote. The person running for Speaker usually lines up support before the session starts. Most of the time there is no doubt who will win. Most speakers were long-time members of the house before they decided to seek leadership. Key lawmakers who supported his candidacy often become chairs of important committees and thus part of his working "team." In 2003, Tom Craddick became the first Republican Speaker since Reconstruction. The current speaker is Joe Straus, a Republican from San Antonio. He was elected in 2009.

Lieutenant Governor: *Elected to office by state-wide elections, the* **Lieutenant Governor** *is the presiding officer of the Texas state Senate.* He serves a four-year term. The Lieutenant Governor is not a senator, and he cannot vote except to break a tie. The powers of the Lieutenant Governor, however, are significant. He appoints the chairs and members to all senate committees, including the important conference committee. When in session, he serves as the presiding officer of the chamber and can recognize any senator for any floor action. He refers all bills to committees. And if there is a dispute, the Lieutenant Governor interprets all senate rules. In other words, no bill can pass the state Senate without his support.

Lieutenant Governor

The presiding officer of the Texas state Senate who is elected to office by statewide elections.

From 1876 to 1999, the Democrats maintained a majority in the senate, and all Lieutenant Governors were Democrats. Then in 1999, Rick Perry

The Lieutenant Governor is the leader of the Texas Senate.

became the first Republican Lieutenant Governor since Reconstruction. When George Bush won the presidency and left Texas in 2000, Perry became governor. David Dewhurst was elected Lieutenant Governor in 2002. In 2012, Dewhurst ran for the US Senate seat that was vacated by Kay Bailey Hutchison when she retired, but he lost to Ted Cruz in the Republican primary. Dewhurst continued to serve until 2014, when he was replaced by Dan Patrick, the current Lieutenant Governor.

The Speaker and Lieutenant Governor have powers beyond their leadership duties in the legislature. The Texas Constitution mandates that the Speaker and Lieutenant Governor have **extra legislative powers,** *they serve on boards outside of the legislature.* For example, they serve on the Legislative Redistricting Board (LRB). This board has the consequential job of drawing the district lines if the legislature fails to act. The Speaker and Lieutenant Governor also serve as chair and vice chair of the powerful Legislative Budget Board (LBB), which plays a key role in the budgetary process. The Speaker and Lieutenant Governor also appoint members to several important state boards.

Extra legislative powers

As part of their office, the Speaker and the Lieutenant Governor are automatically assigned to certain boards outside of the legislature.

The Texas Speaker and Lieutenant Governor are much more powerful than their counterparts in the US Congress: The Speaker of the House of Representatives and the Senate Majority Leader. Combining their legislative and extra legislative powers, the Texas Speaker and the Lieutenant Governor not only have more control over their chamber, but they are given more power over the budget and redistricting than any national office holder. Indeed, some have argued that the Lieutenant Governor is more powerful than the governor, who has limited appointment and budgetary power and little influence over the legislature.

NOTES

The Texas Handbook online: https://tshaonline.org/handbook

ESSAY QUESTIONS

1. Compare the pros and cons of biannual sessions.
2. Describe the "citizen legislator" and give your opinion if you think it is better than a professional legislator.
3. Delineate the main powers of the Speaker and Lieutenant Governor.

TERMS

Biannual session: ______________________________

Bicameral legislature: ______________________________

Citizen lawmaker: ______________________________

Extra legislative powers: ______________________________

Legislative power: ______________________________

Lieutenant Governor: ______________________________

Sine die ______________________________

Speaker of the House: ______________________________

Special session: ______________________________

Texas House of Representatives (term and number): ______________________________

Texas Senate (term and number): ______________________________

CHAPTER 10

Texas Legislative Process

TOPICS

- Getting Elected to the State Legislature
- Role of the Legislator
- Committees
- How a Bill Becomes a Law

LEARNING OBJECTIVES

When you finish reading this chapter, you will be able to:

1. Explain why it is easier for an incumbent lawmaker to win an election than a challenger.
2. Compare the three models of the lawmaker.
3. Describe the importance of legislative committees.
4. Delineate the steps of how a bill becomes a law.

While Chapter 9 focuses on the power and structure of the Texas legislature, this chapter concentrates on the legislative process—broadly speaking, what members of the Texas legislature do. We will begin by discussing how a lawmaker gets elected and conclude by outlining how Representatives and Senators actually make legislation.

GETTING ELECTED TO THE TEXAS STATE LEGISLATURE

It takes a lot of money to get elected to the Texas legislature, but once you get elected, it is easier for an incumbent to hold office.

Money: As stated in Chapter 9, the most important informal qualifications to become a member of the Texas legislature are name recognition and the ability to raise money. Running for office is expensive, especially if a challenger is running against *somebody who is currently holding office* (*an* **incumbent**). But whether you are an incumbent or challenger, it costs a lot of money to run for a seat in the legislature, usually several hundred thousand dollars.

Incumbent

Somebody who is currently holding office.

Interest groups

Groups of people that get together to form organizations in order to change public policy.

Where do lawmakers get money? Candidates raise money by asking for contributions from friends and family, from business associates, from like-minded citizens in their district or across the state, or from themselves—a rich candidate can finance his or her own campaign.

Candidates also get money from **interest groups**: *organizations that try to influence the government to adopt certain policies.* For example, an interest group that supports the environment, such as the Sierra Club, will donate money to environmentally friendly candidates, hoping that they will sponsor environmental laws. Legally, interest groups must form a Political

The capitol building grounds are adorned with several statues, including this one of a Texas Ranger.

Action Committee (PAC) to donate money directly to a campaign. PACs and interest groups will be discussed in more detail in later chapters, but for now know that a significant amount of the money that candidates raise to run for office comes from PACs, mostly from outside of their district.

Advantages of Incumbency: It is a lot easier for an incumbent to win an election than a challenger. As a powerful member of the state legislature, an incumbent gets media coverage and attends all sorts of public events. If people can identify the name and face of a candidate, they will be much more likely to vote for that person. This is because it is human nature to support a person one "knows," rather than a newcomer.

Besides name recognition, it is a lot easier for an incumbent to raise more money than a challenger. Individuals and interest groups are eager to give money to an incumbent because they want access to power. On the other hand, few people are willing to give money to a challenger who will likely lose.

Because the incumbent enjoys such an advantage, many legislative elections are *uncontested*, meaning that only one person runs for office. Most of the time, this is due to the fact that the incumbent scares off any challengers. For example, in 2010 there were 150 House races, but only eighty-nine elections had two candidates running. In the 2016 senate race, there were sixteen seats on the ballot (of thirty-one state Senators). In six of the races, there were no challengers. But if you count races in which a major party candidate faced a third party candidate that had no chance of winning, such as a Republican versus an unknown Libertarian, then eleven of the sixteen races were uncontested or nearly uncontested.

Turnover

A measure of new membership in a legislative session.

Term limits

Limitations on the number of years a government official can remain in a particular office.

As a result of the power of incumbency, a sitting legislator seldom loses an election. However, this does not mean that there is not a relatively high degree of turnover in the Texas legislature. **Turnover** *is a measure of new membership in a legislative session.* In 2013, the turnover rate in the House was 27 percent (with forty-one freshmen members) and 19 percent for the senate (with six freshman members). Incumbents most often leave office not because they lost an election, but voluntarily.

There are many reasons why an incumbent legislator may voluntarily leave office: the low pay, the heavy work burden, the expense of living in Austin during the legislative session, fatigue from fundraising, or to go on to higher office. Also, once lawmakers are eligible for retirement benefits, they often leave office and seek another job.

Term Limits: Some states consider high turnover a good thing and institutionalize it with **term limits**: *limitations on the number of years a* *government official can remain in office*. Currently, fifteen states have legislative term limits. In California, a legislator may serve a maximum of twelve years in the House or in the Senate, or split between both chambers.

There are pros and cons of term limits. Advocates of term limits argue that it brings in fresh members with more energy and new ideas. They also argue that it breaks up the legislative culture of careerism that tends to cause members to look out for themselves more than for their constituents. Those opposed to term limits argue that lawmaking is an extremely complicated business and that the state needs experienced, professional legislators to craft good laws. Texas has no term limits.

Delegate role

The idea that a lawmaker should represent the constituents in his or her district and vote in accordance to their views and wishes, even if the lawmaker holds contrary views.

Trustee model

The idea that a lawmaker represents Texas and uses his or her judgment and experience to do what is best for the long-term interests of the whole state.

ROLE OF THE LEGISLATOR

Once a lawmaker gets elected, he or she may have a different understanding of their role as a legislator than what their constituents do. Political scientists describe two major legislative roles: the *delegate role*, which focuses on the wishes of the constituents, and the *trustee role*, which focuses on the expertise of the lawmaker.

Delegate Role: Once elected to the legislature, who does a lawmaker represent? According to the **delegate role**, *a lawmaker represents the constituents in his or her district and votes in accordance to their views and wishes, even if the lawmakers holds contrary views*. Most of the voters think that this is the proper role of a lawmaker. Their job is to do what is best for the economic and political interest of the people in the district that the lawmaker represents in the legislature. That is precisely why the people elected her.

Trustee Role: Many lawmakers, however, think that they were elected to serve as a member of the Texas state legislature, which serves the whole state of Texas. According to the **trustee model**, *a lawmaker represents Texas and uses his or her judgment and experience to do what is best for the long-term interests of the whole state*. In this view, a lawmaker is a statesman who does not merely read the polls and do whatever the people back home want, but instead has the courage to sometimes go against popular opinion and do what she thinks is right for the whole state. The danger of this role is that if a politician ignores the people at home, he or she may find it hard to get reelected!

Sam Houston not only served as a governor, he was also a legislator that served in the US Senate. This is the 70-foot high statue of Houston in Huntsville, Texas.
© W. Scott McGill / Shutterstock.com

Mix of Both Roles: In reality, most lawmakers mix both roles. If a lawmaker represents a cattle district, for example, then he will likely vote for a bill that is beneficial to the cattle industry. And as a smart politician, a lawmaker will often support the hot-button topics that get a lot of media attention, such as gun rights. But most of the time the people back home have no idea what bills are working their way through the legislature. On these more mundane and technical issues, a lawmaker will use his judgment and do what he thinks is best for Texas.

Another reality of the state legislature is that every lawmaker is a member of a political party: they are either a Republican or Democrat. So, another role of the lawmaker is that of a **partisan**: *one who is devoted to a political party and wants that party to be successful.* If, for example, a lawmaker is a member of the Republican Party, he or she will often feel political pressure from party leaders to support a certain bill, regardless of whether the people back home support it, nor whether the lawmaker personally supports it. It is dangerous to go against the party leadership because it could make a legislator unpopular with his colleagues and he or she could be punished by losing a coveted committee seat or losing financial support for reelection.

Partisan

One who is devoted to a political party and wants that party to be successful.

COMMITTEES

After a legislator wins a seat in the Texas legislature, he or she will want to get a good committee assignment. The legislature is organized into dozens of committees, where bills are actually crafted. It makes sense that the legislature is divided up into specialized committees, such as the education, finance, or agriculture committees. This way, lawmakers can become experts in a few particular fields and hopefully better laws will be passed.

Because the committees have so much power in crafting legislation, the leaders of the majority party have a lot of control over their formation and membership. The Speaker of the House and the Lieutenant Governor choose the chair and, in many cases, the members of each committee. Also, whatever party has the majority of seats in the chamber will also have the majority of seats in all committees. This allows the majority party to control the legislative agenda. Lawmakers hate it when their party loses control of a chamber and suddenly they find themselves in the minority in their committee and thus lose all power to pass laws.

Legislative committees will often hold hearings to hear the testimony of experts.

Types of Committees: There are several types of committees. Most of the committees are called **standing committees**, *which are permanent committees that convene every session and make most of the legislation.* They are the real workhorses of the legislature. Normally, there are fourteen standing committees in the Senate, and forty-one in the House. You can look these up online at the Texas legislature's website (www.capitol.state.tx.com).

Committees deal with specific areas of lawmaking. For example, some senate committees include Transportation, Veteran Affairs, Criminal Justice, and Higher Education. And some House committees include Agriculture and Livestock, Technology, Ways and Means, and Urban Affairs. The chairman of each of these committees is very powerful. They preside over meetings and hearings and set the agenda. A chair has the power to kill bills that he may not like by several methods, such as sending it to a subcommittee where it may languish until the session is over. *Subcommittees* are smaller groups working under the standing committee. In reality, few bills can become law if they don't get the support of party leaders.

Standing committees

Permanent legislative committees that convene every session and make most of the legislation.

Beyond standing committees there are a few other types of committees. An *ad hoc committee* is a temporary committee formed for a special purpose, perhaps to conduct an investigation. A **conference committee** *is created to reconcile Senate and House bills.* This is very important. A bill must pass both chambers of the legislature in the exact same language in order to become a law. But sometimes a bill changes when it goes to the other chamber. So, they must form a conference committee and craft one compromise bill, which then must pass both chambers before it is sent to the governor's desk. Lastly, there is the **interim committee,** *which meets when the legislature is out of session to prepare bills, study issues, and conduct business in preparation for the next session.*

Conference committee

A legislative committee consisting of members of the Senate and House that reconcile bills from each chamber.

Interim committee

A legislative committee that meets when the legislature is out of session to prepare bills, study issues, and conduct business in preparation for the next session.

HOW A BILL BECOMES A LAW

The primary power of the Texas Legislature, along with preparing the budget, is to make law. It is said that laws are like sausages, it is better not to see how they are made. This saying reflects the fact that lawmaking is often a complex, messy process. In this section, we will, in a simplified manner, explain the major steps of how a bill becomes a law. And at each step, a bill can die. Indeed, the vast majority of bills die before they could become law.

(1) Introduce a Bill: The first step in the legislative process is for somebody to have an idea. Let's say that a concerned mother decides that it should be against the law to smoke in a car with children. Then she will

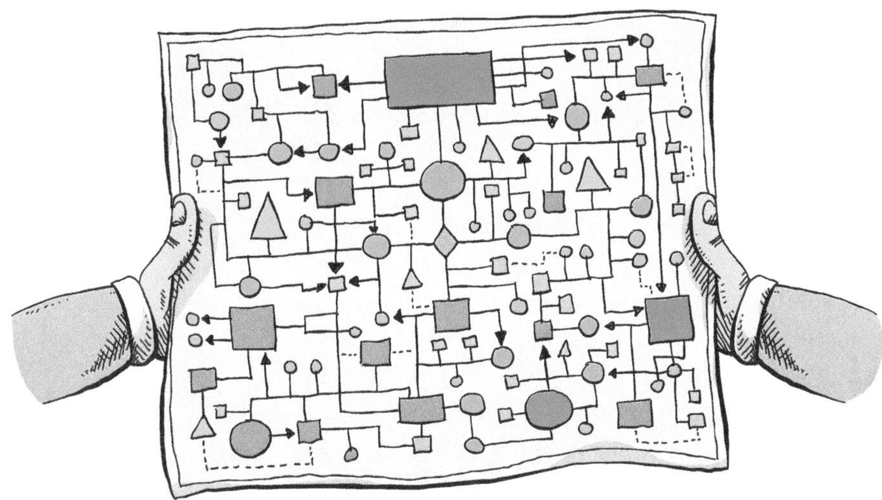

Getting a bill through the Texas legislature is a complicated task, filled with many arcane parliamentary rules. We have simplified the process into nine steps.
© blambca / Shutterstock.com

need a legislator to introduce the bill: a state Representative must introduce a bill in the House, and a state Senator must introduce a bill in the Senate. Once a bill is submitted, the clerk gives it a number. House bills are "HB 32," for example, and senate bills are "S 32." According to the Texas Constitution, each bill must be read aloud three times before it can be voted on. Before it is assigned to a committee, it is read for the first time.

(2) Committee Assignment: Next, the bill is assigned to a committee. Our no smoking in a car with children bill would likely be assigned to the Transportation Committee. In the House, the Speaker assigns bills to committees, and in the Senate this is done by the Lieutenant Governor. If it is a smaller bill, it may be assigned to a subcommittee.

(3) Mark-Up and Discharge: Once the bill is assigned to a committee, they get to work actually crafting the legislation. They do this by consulting with interest groups and experts and by holding hearings. For our proposed bill, the Transportation Committee might hold hearings and invite a lung doctor to discuss the dangers of second-hand smoke on children. During this time, legislators and their staffs will "mark-up" a bill, meaning they will change, add content, and amend the bill. "Mark-up" refers to the pencil marks that will cover a bill at this stage.

Once the bill is ready, committee members will vote for or against the bill. If a majority of members vote yes, then the bill is "reported favorably," meaning that it is approved by the committee and sent to the floor. Most bills actually die in committee unless the chamber leadership supports the bill.

(4) Calendar: If a House bill gains the support of the Speaker, it will be assigned to one of the eight house calendars, otherwise it will die. In the Senate, they only have one calendar. By senate rules, as soon as a bill is reported favorably it should be placed on the calendar. Before the sixtieth day of the legislative session, a bill can clear the Senate with a simple majority vote. But few bills passed before the sixtieth day. After the sixtieth day, a bill requires a two-thirds vote to be recognized and placed on the calendar. Therefore, most bills that are placed on the Senate calendar after the sixtieth day pass in some form because it has already won the backing of the Lieutenant Governor and a super majority of the senators.

(5) Floor Debate: When the time arrives for the bill to go to the floor, members of the legislature will debate the merits of the bill. At this time the bill is read for the second time. In the House, debate is limited because there are so many members. In the Senate, debate is unlimited. The Speaker and the Lieutenant Governor are the presiding officers of their perspective chambers, and they recognize members who wish to speak and enforce the rules and points of order. At this time, bills may be amended in order to gain support.

Since senators have the privilege of unlimited debate, a senator may launch a **filibuster**, *a long speech made as a delay tactic in order to prevent a vote on a bill.* In 2013, Democratic state Senator Wendy Davis performed a filibuster to block a vote on Texas Senate Bill 5, which would have banned abortion after twenty weeks of pregnancy. On the last day of a special session, Davis spoke for eleven hours and was successful at blocking a vote on the bill. However, since Republicans controlled the governorship and held a majority in both chambers of the legislature, Governor Rick Perry called another special session and the bill was passed 19-11 in the Senate and 96-49 in the House.

(6) Floor Vote: Before the floor vote, bills will continue to be amended. Often legislators attach **riders**, *provisions added to bills, sometimes to bring money to the lawmaker's district, which often have nothing to do with the subject matter of the bill.* Riders and earmarks are common in the US Congress, but Texas has a type of rider that is a bit sneaky. Closed riders are provisions added to appropriation bills that are not made public until the conference committee convenes, when there is little anybody can do to remove it!

Filibuster

A long speech made by a Senator as a delay tactic in order to prevent a vote on a bill.

Riders

Provisions added to bills, sometimes to bring money to the lawmaker's district, which often have nothing to do with the subject matter of the bill they are attached to.

In 2013, state Senator Wendy Davis filibustered an abortion bill for eleven hours.
© Albert H. Teich / Shutterstock.com

Then the bill, in its final form, is read for the third time. Once this is complete, lawmakers vote "yea" or "nay" for the bill. To become law, a bill must pass both chambers by a majority vote.

(7) Conference: If a bill passes the House, for example, and then passes the Senate in an altered form, then it must go to a conference committee. All bills must pass both chambers with the exact same language. To form a conference committee, the Speaker will choose five Representatives, and the Lieutenant Governor will choose five senators. Often, these lawmakers are members of the committees that originally marked-up the bill. To be reported out of the conference committee, the bill must win approval of six or more members of the committee.

(8) Final Passage: The compromise bill is then sent first to the chamber from which it originated, and then to the other chamber. To become law, the compromise bill must win a majority of votes of both chambers without amendments.

(9) Governor's Signature: The bill is then sent to the governor. If the governor does not like the bill, he can veto it. The legislature, however, can override a veto with a two-thirds vote in both chambers. If it is late in the 140-day legislative session, however, it is unlikely that his veto will be overridden due to lack of time. On appropriation bills, the governor can also use the *line-item veto* and strike out specific spending provisions. But if the governor likes the bill, he can sign it and it becomes law.

NOTES

Texas Legislature's website: www.capitol.state.tx.com

For information about turnover in the Texas legislature, refer to the Legislative Reference Library of Texas: www.lrl.state.tx.us

ESSAY QUESTIONS

1. Why do incumbent legislators so often win reelection?
2. What are the pros and cons of legislative term limits?
3. Compare the delegate, trustee, and partisan roles of the legislator.
4. List and explain the major steps of how a bill becomes a law.

TERMS

Conference committees: ____________________

Delegate role: ____________________

Filibuster: ____________________

Incumbent: ____________________

Interest groups: ____________________

Interim committee: ____________________

Partisan: ____________________

Riders: ____________________

Standing committees: ____________________

Trustee model: ____________________

Turnover: ____________________

Term limits: ____________________

TEXAS FUN & FACTS SHEET 6

Texas State Song

© Lorelyn Medina / Shutterstock.com

Texas, Our Texas is the official state song of Texas, being so designated by an act of the Texas legislature in 1929. It was written by William J. Marsh and Gladys Yoakum Wright.

Lyrics

Texas, Our Texas! All hail the mighty State!
Texas, Our Texas! So wonderful so great!
Boldest and grandest, withstanding ev'ry test
O Empire wide and glorious, you stand supremely blest.
(chorus)
Texas, O Texas! Your freeborn single star,
Sends out its radiance to nations near and far,
Emblem of Freedom! it sets our hearts aglow,
With thoughts of San Jacinto and glorious Alamo.
(chorus)
God bless you Texas! And keep you brave and strong,
That you may grow in power and worth, throughout the ages long.

CHAPTER 11

The Texas Governor

TOPICS

- Aspects of the Governorship
- Constitutional Powers of the Governor
- Legislative Powers
- Political Powers of the Governor

LEARNING OBJECTIVES

When you finish reading this chapter, you will be able to:

1. List the unique aspects of the governorship of Texas.
2. Outline the major powers of the Governor of Texas.
3. Explain how the governor can influence the legislature.
4. Describe how successful governors can maximize the informal powers of the office.

The Governor of Texas is the chief executive and leader of Texas, but the Texas Constitution places many limits on the office. The reason for this is that the delegates to the Texas constitutional convention of 1875 were influenced by two factors: the governorship of E. J. Davis and Jacksonian democracy.

After the Civil War, in the period known as Reconstruction, Texas was under the control of a powerful governor by the name of Edmund J. Davis. Davis was an ex-Union soldier and a Republican, while nearly all of Texas was populated by pro-Confederate Democrats. The

Reconstruction Constitution centralized power under the authority of the governor, lengthening his terms and giving him tremendous power over appointments and budgeting. In 1875, after the hated E. J. Davis and the despised Republicans were kicked out of office, the Democrats regained control of Texas and wrote a new constitution, which created a weak, decentralized governorship.

The other influence on the delegates that created a weak Texas governorship was the political values of Jacksonian democracy. Andrew Jackson was the seventh President of the United States, serving from 1829–1837, but the influence of the "Jacksonian Era" lasted to the Civil War and beyond. Jacksonian democracy is marked by suspicion of educated elites and celebration of the "common man." Jacksonians believed that all white men—rich or poor, educated or barely literate—had enough common sense to vote and hold office. In general, Jacksonians believed in westward expansion, white supremacy, free markets, limited government, elected not appointed judges, and the rotation of political offices. Andrew Jackson was opposed to long tenure of office that created a politically elite class of rulers.

The Framers of the Texas Constitution were highly influenced by Jacksonian democracy.

With these historical influences, the Framers of the Texas Constitution created a decentralized executive branch with many limitations on the governor. The Texas governor has weak appointment and removal powers, limited budget authority, and little direct control over the administration. But a talented politician with excellent persuasive skills can still assert influence over the Great State of Texas.

ASPECTS OF THE OFFICE OF GOVERNORSHIP

This section will describe several basic constitutional and historical aspects of the governorship of Texas.

Qualifications: The constitutional qualifications for Governor of Texas are quite simple: one must be thirty years of age, an American citizen, and a citizen of Texas five years prior to election.

Experience: The common career path to becoming governor is to serve in a chamber of the legislature, then run for statewide office, and then run for governor. Rick Perry (governor from 2000-2015) was typical in this regard. He was elected to the state legislature before serving as agricultural commissioner and then Lieutenant Governor. Greg Abbott also had a somewhat conventional career path to the governor's mansion. He served as Associate Justice of the Supreme Court of Texas and Attorney General before he assumed office as the forty-eighth governor in 2015.

George W. Bush was atypical. Before becoming Governor of Texas, Bush had never served in elected office. Instead, he was part owner of the Texas Rangers baseball team. Bush, however, was no stranger to politics. In 1978 he had run unsuccessfully for a seat in the US House of Representatives. And in 1988 and 1992 he had helped run his father's (George H. W. Bush) presidential campaigns.

Ann Richards, the second woman Governor of Texas, served in the Travis County Commissioner's Court (a county government body) before she was elected to state treasurer. From there she was elected governor and served one term, from 1991 to 1995.

Some governors served in national office before becoming Governor of Texas. Price Daniels served in the US Senate before he became Governor of Texas in 1957. John Connally was the US Secretary of Navy before he was elected governor in 1963. And Sam Houston was governor of Tennessee and President of the Republic of Texas before he became Governor of Texas in 1859. Houston is still the only man who ever served as governor of two states.

Tenure of office of the governor

The Texas governor serves a four-year term with no term limits.

Acting governor

The person, usually the Lieutenant Governor, who officially and legally functions as Governor of Texas when the elected governor is travelling out of the state.

Tenure: The Texas governor's **tenure of office** *is a four-year term with no term limits*. For most states, the governor's tenure of office is two four-year terms. In 1972, the term for the Texas governor changed from two years to four years. But because of the contentious nature of Texas politics, most governors have only served a couple terms.

Three popular governors, however, broke the trend of only serving a few years. Allen Shivers served eight years—four two-year terms (1949–57). Bill Clements also served eight years—two non-consecutive four-year terms (1979-83 and 1987–91). And Rick Perry was the longest serving Texas Governor with fifteen years in office (2000–2015). Perry served three consecutive four-year terms and (because he was the Lieutenant Governor) finished out George Bush's term when Bush left the governorship to become president in 2000.

Succession: If the governor dies, gets impeached, or can no longer continue in office, the Lieutenant Governor will become governor. In Texas, the order of succession is as follows: President Pro Tem of the Senate, Speaker of the House, and Attorney General. When the governor leaves the state, the Lieutenant Governor becomes **acting governor**: *the person*

The portraits of all the governors of Texas are displayed in the rotunda of the capitol building.
© Nagel Photography / Shutterstock.com

who officially and legally functions as Governor of Texas when the elected governor is travelling out of the state.

Lieutenant Governor Rick Perry served many months as acting governor when George W. Bush was running for president in 2000, as did Lieutenant Governor David Dewhurst when Perry was running for president in 2012. When serving as acting governor, the Lieutenant Governor gets the daily salary of the governor.

Impeachment: Like most states, Texas has a similar **impeachment process** as the US President. *For the Governor of Texas to be impeached, a majority of the members of the House must vote for the articles of impeachment, and two-thirds of the members of the Senate must vote for the governor to be removed from office.*

Impeachment process

For the Governor of Texas to be impeached, a majority of the members of the House must vote for the articles of impeachment, and two-thirds of the members of the Senate must vote for the governor to be removed from office.

Only two Texas governors have been impeached. James Ferguson was impeached in 1917. He was convicted on ten charges, including misapplication of public funds and receiving $150,000 from a secret source. And in 1976, Governor O. P. Carrillo was removed from office for abuse of power and misuse of public funds.

Compensation: Unlike Texas legislators (who only make $7,200 a year), the Governor of Texas makes a good annual salary at $150,000. By comparison, the governor of New York makes $179,000. The Texas Governor also gets a mansion, a car with a driver, an airplane, and reimbursement for travel and entertainment expenses. But compared to a CEO of a major American corporation, this is a very small salary.

It may seem strange, but there are several Texas government officials that make more money than the governor. The Commissioner of Education makes $215,000. The Texas State Auditor makes $198,000. The Commissioner of Insurance makes $175,000. The Chief Justice of the Texas Supreme Court makes $171,000, while Associate Justices make $168,000. And the Texas Land Commissioner makes $167,070.

Incidentally, the highest paid government employees in Texas work for universities, either as coaches or medical professors and doctors at public hospitals. In 2015, Charles Rena Strong, the head football coach at UT Austin, makes $5,085,228! Stephen W. Patterson, athletic director at UT Austin, makes $1,642,000. And August E. Garrido, the head baseball coach at UT Austin, makes $1,202,500. The highest paid doctor is Walter Lowe, professor of orthopedic surgery at UT Health Science Center in Houston. Dr Lowe makes $1,811,271. The president of Texas A & M, Michael Young (no relation to me) makes $1 million. The president of UT Austin, Gregory Fenves, actually turned down a $1 million salary and agreed to take $750,000.

Staff: Also unlike Texas legislators, the governor gets a large staff. About 200 staff members work in the governor's office. If you go to the office of the governor's website, you will see that the staff serves many functions: budget and policy, criminal justice, constituent communication, economic development and tourism, and media, just to name a few. One area of special importance of which the staff helps the governor is in appointments. Over a four-year term, the governor will make about 3,000 appointments to boards, commissions, and other offices. The staff plays an important role in looking for new talent and vetting potential appointees.

Elected in 1859, Sam Houston was the seventh Governor of Texas.

Post-Gubernatorial Office: For most Texas governors, the governorship marks the peak of their public career and they retired from office after they leave the governor's mansion. Some, however, have gone on to serve in national office. W. Lee O'Daniel, the thirty-fourth Governor of Texas, became a US Senator. Price Daniels, the thirty-eighth Governor of Texas, was chosen by Lyndon Johnson to serve as a member of his National Security Council. John Connally, the thirty-ninth Governor of Texas, served as Secretary of Treasury under Richard Nixon. And George W. Bush, the forty-sixth Governor of Texas, became President of the United States.

CONSTITUTIONAL POWERS OF THE GOVERNOR

The constitutional powers of the Governor of Texas are weak. The Governor of Texas functions in a decentralized executive branch and is restricted by limited appointment and budgetary powers.

Plural Executive: The governorship of Texas must be understood in the context of the *plural executive,* which means that the executive department is decentralized and department and agency heads are independently voted in by the people.

This is in stark contrast to the US Presidency, which is a single executive. When the people elect a president, he will appoint all the department and agency heads, such as Secretary of State, Secretary of Defense, and head of the Environmental Protection Agency (EPA). In other words, the people only elect one person in the national executive department, and the president appoints all the leaders in his administration. This allows the chief executive to implement his agenda. But this is not the way the executive department is set up in Texas.

Removal powers

The ability of the governor to fire or remove somebody from office.

Appointment Power: A key aspect of the plural executive is that the governor has weak appointment powers. As mentioned above, the major department and commission heads are voted into office by the voters, but the governor makes many appointments to smaller boards and commissions. All together, the governor appoints nearly 3,000 officials. Chapter 12 will describe in more detail the major administrative heads appointed by the governor.

The way the Texas administrative boards and commissions are set up also diminishes the governor's influence. Texas is run by dozens of boards and commissions. These boards and commissions usually have three, six, or nine members, which are appointed by the governor for six-year terms. But the terms are overlapping and staggered, normally with one-third of the membership appointed every two years. So, unless a governor serves at least two terms, he or she will not be able to appoint all the members of a board or commission. This scheme minimizes the governor's ability to control the executive department.

Removal Powers: Even though the Texas governor makes many lesser appointments, he or she has very weak **removal powers:** *the ability of the* *governor to fire or remove somebody from office.* This greatly diminishes the governor's authority. In contrast, the President of the United States has tremendous removal powers. All executive officers "serve at the pleasure of the president," meaning he can fire anybody without cause. A 1981 amendment to the Texas Constitution clarified the governor's removal powers. A governor can remove any person he appointed, provided that two-thirds of the Senate approves—something very difficult to achieve. Also, the amendment stipulated that a governor may not remove any appointment of the previous governor.

There was one unique way Governor Perry was able to remove somebody from office—but not without tremendous cost. In 2013, Rosemary Lehmberg, a Texas District Attorney, was arrested for drunk driving and was abusive to the police officers. After Perry viewed the video of Lehmberg's verbal abuses, which went viral, he requested that the district attorney's office fire Lehmberg for unprofessional conduct. When they refused, Perry threatened to veto the $7.5 million budget of the Public Integrity Unit of the district attorney's office.

The Travis County District Attorney's Office (known to have many Democrats) indicted Perry (a Republican) for this mere threat. After eighteen months, and millions of dollars, the Texas Criminal Appeals Court threw out the case, saying that there are no constitutional limits on Perry's line-item veto power or his freedom of speech. In the meanwhile, Lehmberg didn't run for reelection.

Legislative Budget Board (LBB)

A ten-member state agency that is headed by the Speaker and the Lieutenant Governor that writes the budget.

Budgetary Powers: Power is often defined by who controls the money. Without the ability to spend money on policy priorities, a governor cannot really implement an agenda. In most states, the governor enjoys a central role in formulating the budget. The Texas Governor's budgetary powers, however, are very weak.

Unlike the president, the governor does not submit a budget to the legislature. Instead, the budget is crafted by the **Legislative Budget Board (LBB)**: *a state agency that is headed by the Speaker and the Lieutenant Governor that writes the budget.* So, the legislative leadership has most of the power with regards to the state budget. Indeed, every two years the governor's office submits a budget to the legislature, but there are no constitutional mandates that the legislature must follow this budget. Instead, they usually follow the LBB's budget.

Others Constitutional Powers: Besides these major powers, the Texas Constitution also grants the Governor of Texas several other powers. For example, the governor has *law enforcement powers.* These powers are decentralized in Texas, but the governor is the head of the two state law enforcement agencies: the Texas Rangers and the Highway Patrol (through the Public Safety Commission, whose three members are selected by the governor).

And the governor enjoys *military powers* as the head of the state militia. He can call in the guard in times of natural disasters or riots or to suppress insurrection. In times of emergency, the Texas governor can call martial law. And he appoints the Adjunct General of Texas (described in Chapter 12).

Clemency powers

The Governor of Texas has the authority to grant pardons, executive clemency, and parole.

And lastly the governor has **clemency powers**. *The governor can grant pardons, executive clemency, and parole.* In the old movies, every person about to be executed would be waiting for a phone call from the governor to stay the execution. In Texas, however, the process is not so simple. By law, a defendant on death row can only make an appeal to the Texas Board of Pardons and Paroles. If the board recommends a commutation of the sentence, the governor can accept or reject the recommendation. If, however, the board does not recommend commutation, there is no way the governor can pardon the defendant. This is due to a 1936 law that was enacted by the legislature after James Ferguson was accused of selling pardons.

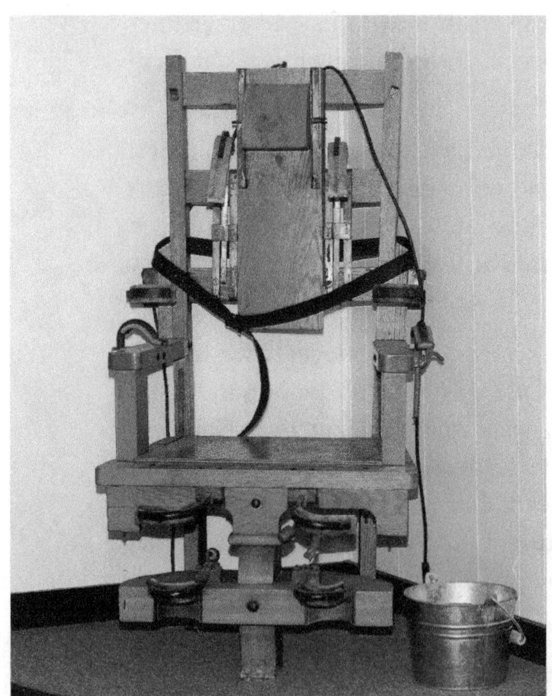

Contrary to popular belief, the governor cannot simply pick up the phone and pardon somebody. This is a photo of "Old Sparky" at the Huntsville Penitentiary.

LEGISLATIVE POWERS

As we learned above, the governor is weak because of the nature of a plural executive. One area where the Governor of Texas has more power is in his shared legislative powers. These give the governor real power over the Texas legislature. Since the rise of the powerful presidents, such as Teddy Roosevelt, Woodrow Wilson, and Franklin Roosevelt, state executives have also gained power. They are expected to introduce legislation and put pressure on the legislature to pass the governor's agenda. Today, people expect the governor to set the policies and long-term objectives of the state.

Qualified veto

The governor can veto any bill passed by legislature, but it can be overridden by a two-thirds vote of both chambers.

General Qualified Veto: As does the President of the United States, the Governor of Texas is given the **qualified veto**: *the governor can veto any bill passed by legislature, but it can be overridden by a two-thirds vote of both chambers.* If the legislature is in session, the governor has ten days to either sign the bill or it becomes law. If the legislature is out of session, he has twenty days to sign the bill or it becomes law. Because the legislative session is so short (only 140 days), it is very difficult for the Texas legislature to override a veto, especially if a veto occurred near the end of the session. From 1876 to 1968, only 25 of 936 vetoes were overridden. And since 1979, no bills have been overridden in the legislature.

The veto brings the governor into the legislative process. The line-item veto is the governor's most powerful tool.

Line-Item Veto: The one area in which the Texas governor has significant control over the budget is in the **line-item veto**: *the ability of a governor to veto specific provisions of an appropriations bill without vetoing the whole bill.* This gives the governor tremendous leverage over the legislature and nearly every government agency in Texas. For example, the governor may line-item veto funds to one state park or one agency within a department. The legislature can override a line-item veto with a two-thirds vote of each chamber. But because appropriation bills are normally passed in the last days of the session, a line-item veto is nearly impossible to override.

Veto-Threat: Actually, the mere threat of a veto (a general veto or a line-item veto) by the governor can influence a bill and bring the governor into the legislative process. For example, if the governor announces that he will veto an education bill unless they make certain changes, the legislature will often comply with governor. Again, this is due to the short legislative session, which is biannual. Legislators know that if the governor vetoes a bill, they will probably not have the time to override the veto and will have to wait two years to try to introduce the legislation again. Not wanting to take this risk, it is wiser to comply with the governor's requests.

Line-item veto

The ability of a governor to veto specific provisions of an appropriations bill without vetoing the whole bill.

Call Special Session: Besides the line item veto, calling a special session of the legislature is one of the most important powers of the Texas governor. *The governor can call a* **special session** *of 30 days after the regular session ended.* This often happens if the legislature was not able to complete an important piece of legislation before the regular session expired. *And the governor sets the agenda of the special session.* The ability to set the agenda is significant. For example, if the legislature didn't have time to override a bill during the regular session, they cannot do it during the special session unless it is included in the agenda.

Special Session

After the normal session ends, the governor can call a special session of the legislature, lasting thirty days, to complete unfinished business or deal with a special problem.

POLITICAL POWERS OF THE GOVERNOR

Compared with other large states, the Texas governor's constitutional or legal powers are very weak. But there have been many very powerful Texas governors over the years, such as James Ferguson, Bill Clements, and Rick Perry. The best governors weld power and influence by not only maximizing their constitutional powers, but by maximizing their *informal* or *political powers*. As the most prominent and visible public official in the Great State of Texas, a talented politician can assert real influence over the state.

Governor as Party Chief: The governor is the head of his party. He sets the priorities and goals of the party, helping to decide what issues to focus on. Also, the governor can reward supporters by appointing them to

Here Governor Greg Abbott is talking with a reporter. A successful governor needs to know how to communicate with the media.

boards, commissions, and party leadership positions. Through this power, the governor can influence things behind the scenes. Furthermore, the governor has the ability to raise enormous funds for members of his own party in the legislature, state-wide office, and in local government. In general, a popular governor can add to the growth and strength of his party.

Media: As the leader of one of the largest and wealthiest states in the Union, the governor receives a lot of local and national media coverage. The Governor of Texas can call attention to a particular policy issue by calling a news conferences or granting interviews to influential journalists or popular media outlets. The governor can also stage events to garner media attention. The governor's media and political advisors will try to orchestrate media events to gain popularity and craft a popular image. If a governor enjoys high approval ratings in the polls, then this ads to his power in all aspects of his governorship.

Chief of state

The governor is the symbolic leader of Texas and acts as the official representative of the state of Texas.

Ceremonial Role: The governor is chief of state, and as such, he can use the pomp and ceremony to his full advantage. As **chief of state**, *the governor is the symbolic leader of Texas and acts as the official representative of the state of Texas.* In public addresses, the governor articulates the values and unique history of Texas—he or she describes what it means to be a Texan. Riding in a parade, opening a new factory, awarding heroes, throwing the ceremonial first pitch at a Rangers game: these are all opportunity

Every other year, at the beginning of the legislative session, the governor gives the State of the State Address to a joint session of the Texas legislature.

© Nagel Photography / Shutterstock.com

to enhance the governor's image. If a governor performs well at these functions, he can add to his popularity.

The State of the State Address is another ceremonial event that offers the governor a great opportunity to enhance his image and set an agenda for the state. *At the beginning of each legislative session, the Governor of Texas gives a* **State of the State Address** *to both chambers, describing the condition of Texas and providing the governor's plan for the coming year*. This event is widely covered by the state media, and the governor can not only highlight his past accomplishments, but focus on his agenda and priorities for the future.

State of the State Address

At the beginning of each legislative session, the Governor of Texas speaks to both chambers of the legislature, describing the condition of Texas and providing the Governor's plan for the coming year.

Crisis Manager: In recent years, people expect the governors to take a leading role in dealing with natural disasters and internal uprisings, such as riots. Texas, which is situated on the Gulf of Mexico, is frequently hit by hurricanes. If a governor performs effectively during a natural disaster, and brings in federal money to help local people, he can gain popularity, as was the case with Governor Greg Abbott's strong performance during Hurricane Harvey.

Intergovernmental Coordinator: The governor's planning powers have grown in recent years. In order to get federal money, states must submit plans in advance. So the governor's office is highly engaged with Congress and other federal agencies to seek federal funds and to lobby against laws that may hurt Texas. Also, as the governor of the second largest state in the

Union, many Texas governors become chair of the National Governor's Association: an organization consisting of all the governors of the states that voice opinions on national policy, share best practices, and coordinate on inter-state initiatives. This can enhance the profile and influence of the Texas governor.

Persuasion: In general, successful governors take advantage of all the formal and informal powers by utilizing his or her political skills. The most important political skill is the power to persuade. Not only must politicians be able to persuade the public to vote for them, they must also be skilled at persuading members of the legislature, reporters, state officials, business leaders, and foreign dignitaries. When a governor's charm and communication skills are united with the prestige of the office, the governor of the Great State of Texas can be an undeniable force.

NOTES

For information on public employee salaries see this chart published by the Texas Tribune: https://salaries.texastribune.org/

For story on Rick Perry and Rosemary Lehmberg: Jim Malawitz, "Years after Rick Perry defunded the Public Integrity Unit, Texas may revive part of it." *The Texas Tribune*, 3/30/2017.

ESSAY QUESTIONS

1. Describe the key features of the governorship and explain how the Texas Constitution limits the governor's powers.
2. Explain how the governor can influence the legislature.
3. Describe how a successful governor can maximize his or her political powers to overcome the weak constitutional powers of the office.

TERMS

Acting governor: ______________________________

Clemency powers: ______________________________

Chief of state: ______________________________

Impeachment process: ______________________________

Legislative Budget Board (LBB): ______________________________

Line-item veto: ______________________________

Qualified veto: ______________________________

Removal powers: ______________________________

Special session: ______________________________

State of the State Address: ______________________________

Tenure of office of the governor: ______________________________

CHAPTER 12

Texas Executive Department

TOPICS

- Elected Statewide Offices
- Appointed Statewide Offices
- Boards and Commissions
- Characteristics of a Bureaucracy
- Dangers of a Large Bureaucracy
- Controlling the Government Bureaucracy

LEARNING OBJECTIVES

When you finish reading this chapter, you will be able to:

1. Explain the characteristic of the plural executive.
2. Cite the major elected and appointed statewide offices.
3. Describe the decentralized Texas system of boards and commissions.
4. List the ways Texas has tried to control the government bureaucracy.

In the three-branch system of government, the judicial branch interprets the law, the legislative branch makes the law, and the **executive branch** *implements and enforces the law written by the legislature.* Headed by the chief executive (the governor) and the department heads, the executive branch carries out public policy, oversees government agencies, and administers the day-to-day management of the government.

Executive branch

The primary power of the executive branch is to implement and enforce the law written by the legislature.

The most prominent feature of the Texas executive branch is the **plural executive**: *the executive department is decentralized and department and agency heads are independently voted in by the people.* This limits the ability of the governor to control the administration. Instead of having the chief executive select individuals to head administrative departments, as the President of the United States does, the people of Texas vote for the department heads.

Texas Plural Executive A multiplicity of elected office		
Governor LT Governor	Attorney General Comptroller	Boards & Commissions: Railroad Agriculture Land Education

Courtesy Michael Young.

Plural Executive

An executive branch in which many powerful state officials are elected by the people and are independent from the governor.

Besides the governor, the people of Texas vote for seven department leaders, including Lieutenant Governor, the Attorney General, and the Comptroller. These people are accountable to the people, not the governor. In addition to the seven major statewide offices, there are hundreds of independent agencies, boards, and commissions over which the governor has little direct influence. Thus the governor is not responsible for the planning and the implementation of all the functions of the Texas bureaucracy.

The Framers of the Texas Constitution decentralized the Texas government in order to make it more accountable to the people. However, in recent years it has become apparent that due to the multiplicity of so many government agencies and commissions, entities that most people are not aware of, they get less public scrutiny, not more. It remains a major challenge of government to make these agencies more efficient and responsive to the wishes of the people of the Great State of Texas.

In this chapter we will look at the Texas executive branch, which can be divided into three categories: statewide offices elected by the people, statewide offices appointed by the governor, and administrative boards and commissions. We will conclude by describing the state bureaucracy and recent attempts to make it more efficient.

ELECTED STATEWIDE OFFICES

Besides governor, there are seven major elected statewide offices in Texas. The people that run for these offices are independent from the governor and can even be of a different political party. In our democratic system of government, they are accountable to the people of Texas.

Lieutenant Governor: Elected to a four-year term, the Lieutenant Governor is the second-highest office in the Texas government. The Lieutenant Governor is first in line to assume the governorship of Texas if the Governor can no longer hold office and serves as *acting governor* if the governor is out of the state.

The real power of the Lieutenant Governor, however, is in his or her position as president of the Texas Senate. Additional power comes from automatically becoming a member (*ex officio*) of several very important boards, including the Legislative Budget Board, which draws up the biannual budget, and the Legislative Redistricting Board, which redistricts the state if the legislature fails to do so.

Attorney General: Elected to a four-year term, the **Attorney General** *is the chief lawyer for the state of Texas, constitutionally required to defend the laws and Constitution of Texas, to represent the state in litigation, and to provide legal advice to state officials.* Beyond writing legal opinions to the governor, other state agencies and the legislature, the attorney general's office has taken on several roles over the years: it approves public bond issues, enforces child support laws, files civil suits, and enforces consumer protection laws. With nearly 4,000 employees, the attorney general's office is one of the largest departments in the state. Several governors had previously served as Attorney General, including Governor Greg Abbot.

Comptroller of Public Accounts: This office was originally established by the provisional government of Texas in 1835, but many more responsibilities have been added over the years. The **Comptroller** *is the chief tax collector, accountant, revenue estimator, treasurer, and steward of the state's finances.* The Comptroller collects thirty-one different types of state taxes, as well as the sales taxes for all county and city governments. The property tax division conducts

Attorney General

The chief lawyer for Texas who is constitutionally required to defend the laws and Constitution of Texas, to represent the state in litigation, and to provide legal advice to state officials.

Comptroller

The chief tax collector, accountant, revenue estimator, treasurer, and steward of the state's finances.

Dan Patrick was elected Lieutenant Governor in 2015.
Fort Worth Star-Telegram/Contributor/Getty

an annual audit of property appraisal districts. And the Comptroller is responsible for investing state funds, which for a large state like Texas is several billions of dollars.

The Comptroller plays an important role in maintaining the balanced budget mandate for Texas. Before each legislative session, the Comptroller provides an estimate of tax revenue for the next two years. The legislature cannot spend more money than this. The comptroller's office also publishes important economic data and forecasting which is valuable to the private sector.

Commissioner of the General Land Office: Elected to a four-year term, the **Land Commissioner** *is responsible for the administration and oversight of the state-owned lands of Texas.* This office was established by the Republic of Texas immediately after the Texas Revolution of 1836. Unlike other states, when Texas joined the Union it retained its public lands. Not only this, but Texas is the only state to own its submerged lands 10.3 miles into the Gulf of Mexico. The land office leases this land to oil, gas, and mining companies, providing significant revenue to Texas. Much of this money helps pay for public schools through the *Permanent School Fund*, and helps veterans through the *Texas Veterans Land Board.*

Land Commissioner

This official is responsible for the administration and oversight of the state-owned lands of Texas, as well as the management of the Permanent School fund.

Texas Railroad Commission (RRC)

A state agency that regulates the Texas oil and gas industry

Commissioner of Agriculture: The Texas Department of Agriculture (TDA) was created in 1907. Agriculture is a major segment of the Texas economy, and so it is an important office. The TDA promotes Texas agriculture and livestock. Texas is the nation's leaders in the production of cattle, cotton, hay, sheep, wool, goats, mohair, and horses. The TDA has several other important responsibilities as well. It regulates all the fuel pumps in Texas, as well as all the weights and measuring devices, such as the scales in grocery stores. The TDA regulates pesticides and certifies organically grown products. And the TDA administers school lunch and breakfast programs for the Texas public schools.

Two of these functions pose a potential conflict. The TDA promotes Texas agricultural products and it also regulates pesticides. Texas farmers may not like the expensive regulations that make pesticides safe. So, the TDA must balance the interest of farmers AND the interest of consumers of farm products as well as the environment.

The Texas Railroad Commission: The **Texas Railroad Commission (RRC)** *is a state agency that regulates the Texas oil and gas industry.* It is one of the most powerful state agencies in the US. The RRC was created in 1891 under the administration of Governor James S. Hogg to regulate the railroad "monopolies." The commission was also given regulatory authority over other aspects of transportation.

George P. Bush, the son of Jeb Bush, was elected land commissioner in 2015

The commission consists of three members who are elected to six-year terms, staggered by having one member elected every two years. The chair of the commission is the member who is next up for election. In the 1920s, during the oil boom, it was given the additional task of regulating the oil and gas industry. Later, it was also given the power to regulate the trucking industry. Today, the RRC's major responsibility is regulating the oil and gas industry, which is the largest in the country. Like the ag commission, it has the conflicting role of promoting Texas oil and gas, but also protecting public and environmental safety. Considering that today the RRC plays a minor role in railroad regulation, some suggest that it change its name to the "Oil Commission."

The State Board of Education: The last of the seven major elected offices is the State Board of Education (SBOE). This board has changed several times over the years, but today it consists of fifteen members elected from each of the fifteen Texas school districts. The governor appoints one member to chair the board. The State Board of Education sets the curriculum standards for all the public schools in Texas. In addition, the SBOE adopts textbooks, establishes graduation requirements, oversees the Permanent School Fund, appoints board members to special school districts, and approves the establishment of new charter schools.

Incidentally, today there are 8,317 public schools in Texas serving 4.3 million students. There are 613 charter school campuses with 227,827 students. And there are 800 accredited private schools serving 250,000 students. In addition, an estimated 300,000 Texas children are being home schooled.

APPOINTED STATEWIDE OFFICES

These officers are selected by the Governor of Texas. The governor will try to select people that share his policy views, and so in this way the governor can indirectly influence these departments. It is common on the federal as well the state level that people who support the president's or governor's campaign often get appointed to government offices. This is true in Texas. Studies show that many people that significantly contributed their time and money to gubernatorial campaigns are often appointed to office.

Secretary of State (SOS): The **Secretary of State** *oversees state elections and keeps the state records*. This office was one of six state officials named in the Texas Constitution to form the executive department. The first Secretary of state was Stephen F. Austin. The governor makes the appointment of the SOS with majority approval of the state Senate.

The Secretary of State has three main areas of responsibility. (1) Elections: The SOS is the chief elections officer for the state, overseeing the uniform application of election laws in the state. (2) Records: The SOS is the keeper of records for Texas, publishing state, business, and commercial records. Many of these public records are published by the SOS in the *Texas Register*. And (3) International protocol: The SOS is the senior advisor to the governor for issues related to the Texas border and Mexican affairs, and serves as the chief international protocol officer for Texas.

Secretary of State

This official oversees Texas state elections and keeps state records.

The Health and Human Services Commissioner (HHSC): As Texas developed more health and human services agencies to serve the public, it became necessary to create an office to oversee and coordinate these many programs. So, in 1991 the legislature created the *Commissioner for Health and Human Services*, who is appointed by the governor for a two-year term with senate approval. The HHSC oversees and provides some administration to four major agencies: Department of Aging and Disability Services (DADS), Department of State Health Services (DSHS), Department of Assistive and Rehabilitative Services (DARS), and Department of Family and Protective Services (DFPS).

The HHSC also administers eight major programs, many of these you may have had contact with or have heard of: Medicaid, Children's Health Program (CHIP), Texas Woman's Health Program, Temporary Assistance for Needy Families, SNAP Food Benefits and Nutrition Programs, Family Violence Services, Refugee Services, and Disaster Assistance. If you or a

In natural disasters, such as in Hurricane Katrina, governors can call the national guard to protect property and provide food and water.
© Brian Nolan / Shutterstock.com

family member needs help in any of these areas, a good place to go is the HHSC website: www.hhsc.state.tx.us.

Adjunct General of the National Guard: This is another office created by the Texas Constitution. Although the governor is the commander-in-chief of the guard, the *adjunct general* of Texas is the state's senior military official appointed by the governor. The Texas Military Department is composed of three branches: the Texas National Guard, the Texas Air National Guard, and the Texas State Guard. Additionally, the adjunct general is also the commander of the Domestic Operations Task Force.

The President of the United States can activate the Texas guard by executive order, but normally they are under the command of the governor. This command, however, is limited to protecting the citizens during times of natural disasters and civil unrest. During natural disasters, such as hurricanes, the guard will evacuate areas, protect property, and send in food and water. Although the adjunct general is appointed by the governor, he can only be removed with approval of the state senate.

Director of Office of State-Federal Relations (OSFR): As the federal government became more involved in sending revenue to the states and making regulations that the states must comply with, in 1965 the Texas legislature created the Office of State-Federal Relations. The director of the OSFR is appointed by the governor with approval by the Senate. The OSFR essentially lobbies on behalf of the state of Texas to the US Congress and other federal agencies. In addition, the OSFR coordinates the activities of state agencies with a federal agenda, it works with members of Congress when they are making laws that might affect Texas, and it provides information to Texas agencies about federal initiatives.

Minor Agency Heads: The above officials are the most powerful leaders of state agencies appointed by the governor, but there are many other agency heads that the governor appoints. These agencies may not get a lot of public attention but are important in their sphere of influence. These include the Department of Housing and Community Affairs; Department of Commerce; State Office of Administrative Hearing; Insurance Commissioner; Public Utilities Commission Council; and the Fire Fighters Pension Commission Executive Director. The governor also appoints the director of the river authorities, such as the Upper Neches River Authority.

BOARDS AND COMMISSIONS

Besides the major state-wide departments and agencies, Texas is administered by over 200 state boards and commissions. Many of the members of these boards and commissions are appointed by the governor, but some are elected (such as the Board of Education and the Railroad Commission) and some are assigned **ex officio**: *automatically assigned to a board because they hold a particular office*. For example, once the Lieutenant Governor is elected, he or she is assigned, *ex officio*, to the Legislative Budget Board, the Legislative Council, the Legislative Audit Board, the Legislative Redistricting Board, and others.

Ex officio

Automatically assigned to a board because they hold a particular office.

This complex network of boards and commissions epitomizes the decentralized administrative system of Texas. These units do most of the administrative tasks of the state and work very independently. Some of the boards can be categorized—revealing a high degree of redundancy: eighteen agencies deliver health care and welfare, ten agencies have authority over aspects of the environment, thirty-eight boards issue professional licenses and give exams, and twelve college boards oversee Texas colleges and universities.

Because they have such an influence on Texas, in this section we will highlight two categories: the licensing and examining boards and the higher education boards.

Professional and Licensing and Examining Boards: Considering that Texas is such a conservative state, which celebrates free markets, it is somewhat surprising that Texas has so many licensing and examining boards. The thirty-eight licensing and examining boards regulate and limit access to many professions, including accountants, architects, barbers, chiropractors, funeral directors, exterminators, medical doctors, dentists, and cosmetologists—just to name a few.

The idea is that to become a professional somebody must pass the proper exams and get licensed in order to protect the public safety. In cases like medical doctors, this seems obvious. In occupations such as cosmetology, it seems less obvious. Does somebody really need a license if they want to braid hair in their garage? These rules limit the number of people who enter the profession, thus allowing them to charge higher fees.

Some question if so many professions need a license from the state of Texas, such as a hairstylist.

Boards of Higher Education: In Texas, there are twelve college governing boards that oversee the institutions of higher education in the state. They all fall under the supervision of the State Higher Education Coordinating Board. Each college, however, is relatively free to set its own standards, policies, and control its own budget. In Texas, education is decentralized. But in recent years the *State Higher Education Coordinating Board* is setting more policies that affect all the colleges in the state.

CHARACTERISTICS OF A BUREAUCRACY

Many of the characteristic of a bureaucracy were first described by Max Weber in his landmark book *Theory of Social and Economic Organization* in 1920. Weber said the primary feature of a modern bureaucracy is a *hierarchical structure*: Each level controls the level below and is controlled by the level above. A formal hierarchy is the basis of central planning and centralized decision making.

Besides *hierarchy*, Weber described four other features of the modern bureaucracy. (1) *Management by rules*: established rules and procedures allows decisions made at high levels to be executed consistently by all lower levels. (2) *Specialization*: A bureaucracy has a division of labor. Work is to be done by specialists, and people are organized into units based on the type of work they do. (3) *Impersonal*: The idea is to treat all employees and customers equally, and not be influenced by individual differences. And (4) *Merit-based hiring*: Employment in the bureaucracy should be based on merit, often proven by passing civil service exams. Also, bureaucrats are protected from arbitrary or politically motivated dismissal.

Contrary to the federal government, the Texas bureaucracy does not fit into the description of the modern bureaucracy. The Texas bureaucracy is not a centrally organized hierarchical structure. And to a large degree, employment is not based on merit and specialized knowledge but instead is based on popular elections and political appointments.

Managing large government bureaucracies is one of the challenges of modern government.

The Civil Service System: The national government began forming into a modern bureaucracy at the end of the nineteenth century. With the passage of the Pendleton Act of 1883, the national government started the *civil service system*: government employees will be hired based on their knowledge and merit as demonstrated by passing civil service exams. And government employees cannot be fired for political reasons. The civil service system replaced the old **spoil system** *in which government employees were hired after an election based on which political party or candidate they supported.*

Advantages to Decentralization: Texas never adopted the civil service system and to a large degree it remains a spoil system. And with over 200 independent departments, boards, and commissions, not to mention hundreds of local governments, Texas remains highly decentralized. But it must be remembered that even though the national administration is a centralized bureaucracy, the US government as a whole is also decentralized: there are fifty state governments and thousands of local governments.

Spoil system

Government employees are hired and fired after an election based on which political party or candidate they supported.

The Framers of the US and Texas Constitutions created a decentralized system because they knew it contained many advantages. (1) A decentralized system *democratizes decision making*: officials at the lower levels can make decisions to better serve the people without waiting for approval from the top of a lethargic, monolithic system. (2) A decentralized system *fosters innovation*: officials of local units are free to come up with their own ideas and experiments. And (3) decentralization is more *efficient*: officials at the local unit can take care of a problem far more quickly and efficiently than if they had to wait for a decision at the top of a bloated bureaucracy.

DANGERS OF A LARGE BUREAUCRACY

Although Texas is a conservative state, which believes in smaller government, Texas state government is still quite large. Payments to state personnel are the number one expenditure in the state budget. And the state of Texas is the number one employer in Texas. Government tends to grow because government departments are very good at protecting their existence once they are established.

But a large government is detrimental to the economy on many levels. First, large state governments tend to spend more and more money, creating enormous public debt. According to report by Truth in Accounting, Illinois has $213.8 billion in debt, New Jersey has $185.6 billion, and Connecticut has $72.2 billion. Second, large state governments tend to raise taxes. This takes money that consumers would have spent on goods and services, stimulated the economy and created jobs. And third, large state governments tend to create more and more regulations, which make it very difficult to run a business or start a new business, thus decreasing jobs.

Controlling the bureaucracy has become the great challenge and dilemma of modern government: modern governments create more and more government programs to better serve the people, but as the bureaucracy grows, it becomes less and less efficient at serving the people.

CONTROLLING THE GOVERNMENT BUREAUCRACY

Aware of the problems of a growing government, the Great State of Texas has implemented many programs to try to control the bureaucracy. Although many of these programs have had some success in increasing accountability and efficiency, they continue to face many challenges.

Voter Accountability: In Texas, greater accountability is achieved by making the eight major executive branch offices elected. If these officials are not running their departments properly, they will be kicked out of office by the people. Ideally, this will help eliminate incompetence, corruption, and going against the will of the people. The problem is that few voters even know who the top officials are, let alone how well they are running their departments.

Legislative Oversight: All boards and commissions are created by the legislature, and thus the legislature has the power to terminate any board or commission if it is not doing its job properly. To monitor these government agencies, various *legislative committees* have oversight authority.

Texas has developed several ways to try to fight the corruption and wasteful spending that often comes with large government bureaucracies.
© matrioshka / Shutterstock.com

But because of the biannual and short legislative sessions, these legislative committees have very little time to properly oversee the hundreds of agencies they have created.

One legislative tool that is effective is the *sunset clause.* When the legislature creates a program or agency, it can insert a sunset clause that stipulates that the program or agency will expire in ten years, or whatever amount of time, unless the legislature votes to renew it. This forces the legislature to review the program and determine if it is worthy of continuing.

Sunset Advisory Commission: Another program that has been efficient at cutting wasteful government is the **Sunset Advisory Commission**: a ten-member *agency that reviews the purpose and efficiency of each state agency every twelve years and makes recommendations to the legislature concerning whether an agency should be abolished or reformed.* Since its

Sunset Advisory Commission

A ten-member agency that reviews the purpose and efficiency of each state agency every twelve years and makes recommendations to the legislature concerning whether an agency should be abolished or reformed.

creation in 1977, it has closed down thirty-seven state agencies, including the Boll Weevil Commission and the Battleship of Texas Commission.

Privatization: Another attempt to reform and shrink the size of the bureaucracy is *privatization*: turning over services that were once performed by government to private contractors. Over the last few decades, Texas has privatized many services, such as collecting garbage, running prisons, and building and maintaining roads.

Performance Audits: In 1991 the legislature ordered the comptroller to review all state government agencies in an attempt to deal with a massive budget shortfall. As a result, the legislature cut $2.4 billion in spending. Since it was so successful, the comptroller's office continues to perform regular audits of all government programs and provides the legislature with recommended cuts. Although much of this responsibility has been turned over to the Legislative Budget Board, the comptroller's office publishes a detailed report of the expenditures of each agency.

Open Records and Meetings: Another way to create more government transparency and accountability is to open up records and meetings of government officials. The Open Records Act provides citizens access to government records. And Open Meetings Act mandates that all government meetings, including commission meetings, city council meetings, and even homeowner association meetings, follow certain procedures. They must post in advance the time and location of the meeting. The public must be allowed to observe the meeting. And after the meeting, the minutes must be published. The idea is that openness will reduce corruption and wrongdoing.

Whistleblower Protection: Lastly, the state of Texas passed *whistleblower* laws that protects government employees that expose corruption, wrong-doing, or incompetence. If a government employee exposes mismanagement and abuse, they cannot be fired.

NOTES

The Attorney General of Texas: https://texasattorneygeneral.gov/

Texas Comptroller of Public Accounts Office: http://comptroller.texas.gov/

The Texas Land Office: http://www.glo.texas.gov/the-glo/about/commissioner/

Texas Department of Agriculture: https://texasagriculture.gov/Home.aspx

Railroad Commission of Texas: http://www.rrc.texas.gov/about-us/

Education Bug: http://texas.educationbug.org/public-schools/

Texas Charter Schools Association: http://www.txcharterschools.org/

Texas Home School in Texas: http://www.thsc.org/

Texas Private School Association: http://www.texasprivateschools.org/

Texas Secretary of State: www.sos.state.tx.us

Texas Health and Human Services Commission: www.hhsc.state.tx.us

ESSAY QUESTIONS

1. Describe the characteristic of Texas's plural executive and the advantages of decentralization.
2. What are some of the problems that come with a large government bureaucracy?
3. Explain at least three ways Texas tries to control the government bureaucracy.

TERMS

Attorney General: ______________________________

Comptroller: ______________________________

Ex officio: ______________________________

Executive branch: ______________________________

Land Commissioner: ______________________________

Plural executive: ______________________________

Secretary of State: ______________________________

Spoil system: ______________________________

Sunset Advisory Commission: ______________________________

Texas Railroad Commission: ______________________________

TEXAS FUN & FACTS SHEET 7

The Main Rivers of Texas

Courtesy Texas Water Development Board.

The Six Longest Rivers in Texas

1. **Rio Grande**: 1,900 miles
2. **Red**: 1,290 miles
3. **Brazos**: 1,280 miles
4. **Pecos**: 926 miles
5. **Canadian**: 906 miles
6. **Colorado**: 865 miles

Texas Rivers with Biggest Flow

1. **Brazos**: 6,074,000 acre-feet
2. **Sabine**: 5,864,000 acre-feet
3. **Trinity**: 5,727,000 acre-feet
4. **Neches**: 4,323,000 acre-feet
5. **Red**: 3,484,000 acre-feet
6. **Colorado**: 1,904,000 acre-feet

CHAPTER 13

Texas Judicial System

TOPICS

- Constitutional Republic
- Aspects of the American Legal System
- Federal and State Court Hierarchy
- Judicial Qualifications and Removal
- Judicial Selection
- Judicial Democracy

LEARNING OBJECTIVES

When you finish reading this chapter, you will be able to:

1. Explain the significance of judicial review in a constitutional republic.
2. Describe the key features of the American legal system.
3. Outline the five levels of the Texas state court system.
4. Describe how judges can be removed from office.
5. Compare the Texas judicial selection system to other states.

In the three-branch system of government, the legislative branch makes the law, the executive branch executes the law, and the **judicial branch** *interprets the law*. What does this mean?

Judicial branch

The primary power of the judicial branch is to interpret the law.

When the legislature makes a law, it is written in general language so that it applies to everybody. But a situation may arise in which two parties have a disagreement over the law—the conflict may even be over the meaning of a phrase or single word in the law code. Once the case reaches a court, then the judge will interpret the part of the law under dispute and decide the case.

In our system of three branches of government, the primary function of the judicial branch is to interpret the law.
© JPL Designs / Shutterstock.com

Courts interpret two types of law: statutory law and constitutional law. *Statutory law* is written by the legislature and becomes a statute. For example, the Texas State Legislature wrote a statute that the speed limit on Texas highways is seventy-five miles per hour. *Constitutional law* refers to cases dealing with interpretations of the US Constitution. When the legislature writes a statute, it must be consistent with the Constitution. The US Supreme Court is the final court of appeal on constitutional matters.

CONSTITUTIONAL REPUBLIC

The role of the Supreme Court illustrates that America is a constitutional republic, not a democracy. In a democracy, the majority makes all the rules. But in a constitutional republic, the content of the Constitution and the Bill of Rights are withdrawn from the political process. For example, if the majority of the people voted to ban all firearms, the Court would vacate this law (if it heard a case on this matter) because it violates the Second Amendment. So, the role of the Supreme Court is to protect the Constitution from the political process and majority rule.

The power to interpret the Constitution and declare a congressional law, a state law, or an executive order null and void if it violates the Constitution is called **judicial review**. A constitution is higher law than statutory law. Article VI of the US Constitution states that the Constitution is "the supreme law of the land." It not only applies to the citizens but to all three branches of government as well as the states. If Congress or state legislatures were permitted to write laws in violation of the Constitution, then soon there would be no Constitution.

Judicial review

The power of the Supreme Court to interpret the Constitution and declare a congressional law, a state law, or an executive order null and void if it violates the Constitution.

For example, in *Texas v. Johnson* (1989) the Supreme Court declared a Texas law unconstitutional and thus null and void. At the 1984 Republican National Convention held in Dallas, Gregory Lee Johnson burned an American flag and was arrested under a Texas state law. The state of Texas argued that flag burning is not "speech" and thus is not protected by the free speech clause of the First Amendment. The Supreme Court, however, ruled against Texas and declared that burning the flag was a type of symbolic speech, and as such was protected under the First Amendment.

In our constitutional republic, the Supreme Court protects the Constitution.
© Erik Cox Photography / Shutterstock.com

ASPECTS OF THE AMERICAN LEGAL SYSTEM

Over the centuries, America has developed a legal system that is designed to carry out justice and at the same time protect the rights of the innocent. The following are some basic aspects of the American legal system.

Criminal and Civil Law: In the America legal system, cases are divided into two categories: criminal and civil. **Criminal law** *is a system of law concerned with punishment of those who commit crimes.* The state develops a penal code that outlaws certain behavior, such as murder, bank robbery, or speeding. If a person violates these rules, the law states that a certain punishment will be exacted. Criminal law cases are between an individual and the state (*State of Texas v. Jones*). The judge and jury decides who is guilty and what the punishment will be.

Civil Law *is a system of law concerned with private relations between two individuals.* These types of cases involve such things as property disputes, divorce, and breach-of-contract quarrels. These cases are usually between two individuals (*Jones v. Smith*), and the judge and jury decides who is responsible and rewards the person who has been injured with a monetary remedy.

Criminal law

A system of law concerned with punishment of those who commit crimes.

Civil law

A system of law concerned with private relations between two individuals.

In the American system of justice, the government must follow many due process procedures in order to protect individual rights.

Burden of Proof: In the American legal system a person is "innocent until proven guilty." In criminal cases, the burden of proof falls on the state to prove, "beyond a reasonable doubt," that the defendant is guilty.

Grand Jury: When government officials decide to bring a criminal case against a defendant, they must first submit all their evidence to a **grand jury**: *a body of citizens that decides if the state has enough evidence to proceed to a trial.* If a prosecutor does not have enough evidence, the grand jury will dismiss the case. In Texas, grand juries consist of twelve individuals, but in most other states they consist of sixteen to twenty-three members. Grand juries are an important institution designed to protect the individual against the arbitrary or malicious prosecution of the innocent by the government.

Grand jury

A body of citizens that decides if the state has enough evidence to proceed to a trial.

Petit Jury (pronounced petty): If a case goes to trial, the defendant can choose whether he or she wants the case to be decided by a judge or a jury. It is an important constitutional right that a citizen can choose to have a *jury of 12 peers*, a **petit jury**, to hear a criminal or civil case. Typically, jury pools are made from voter registration lists and drivers licenses. Serving on a jury is an important responsibility of a citizen in a democracy.

The American right to a jury of one's peers goes back to the Magna Carta. Like the grand jury, this is another important institution that protects innocent people from government abuse. If a judge, a government employee, decides all cases, then an innocent person has little ability to protect herself against malicious prosecution by the government.

Due Process: Broadly speaking, everything listed above falls under what is called *procedural due process*. This is a constitutional principle that the government must follow certain rules and procedures when denying a citizen life, liberty, or property (arresting or fining a person). Police cannot search a suspect's property unless they have reasonable suspicion and get a court ordered warrant. If evidence is unlawfully collected, it will be thrown out of court. When brought into custody, all suspects must be read their basic constitutional rights (Miranda Warning). And if somebody cannot afford a lawyer, one will be provided. Government officials must apply these legal procedures to all citizens in a fair and equal manner.

Petit jury

A jury of twleve peers that hears criminal or civil cases.

Trial courts

Courts that hear cases and juries determine the outcome of the trial.

FEDERAL AND STATE COURT HIERARCHY

The American court structure is a complicated system of federal, state, and local courts. The federal court system consists of three tiers: the Supreme Court at the top, the thirteen US Courts of Appeal in the middle, and the ninety-four US Districts Courts at the bottom. And each of the fifty states has their own court systems. Federal courts hear cases dealing with federal law, and state courts hear cases involving state law. And within the states there are many different kinds of city and county courts.

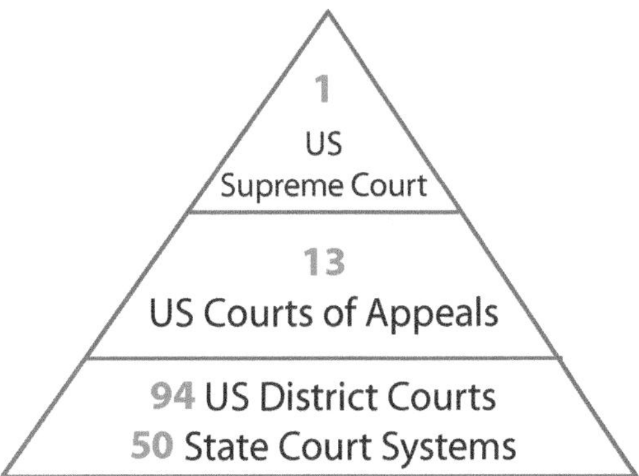

The US Supreme Court hears final appeals from federal, district, and state courts.
Courtesy Michael Young

Trial and Appellate Courts: In Texas, there are two types of state courts: trial and appellate. **Trial courts** *hear cases and the juries determine the outcome of the trial.* Cases are heard for the first time at a trial court. There is one judge and jury of citizens. They try to determine the facts in the case and then render a verdict: guilty or not guilty. **Appellate Courts** *are higher courts that hear appeals on questions of law from lower courts.* There are several judges and no juries. The judges decide points of law, not guilt or innocence. The decision of an appeals court can affect large numbers of people because the rulings are binding on lower courts.

Five Levels of the Texas Courts: The structure of the courts fits in with the decentralized system of Texas government. Most states have a three-level court system: one state supreme court, appellate courts, and trial courts. Texas is more complicated. It has five levels and no single supreme court. We will describe the five levels of the Texas court system by starting from the bottom and working our way up.

(1) Magistrate Courts (two types): The lowest level in the Texas court system deal with local misdemeanors and have some magistrate functions. *Justice of the peace courts* (JPs) are precinct courts within a county that hear minor criminal and civil cases, mostly traffic violations and criminal misdemeanors. They also hear small claim cases under $15,000. In addition, JPs issue marriage certificates. *Municipal Courts* are city courts that hear mostly violations of city ordinances, such as traffic violations. And they conduct preliminary hearings on serious crimes. Both JPs and municipal courts can issue search warrants and arrest warrants.

Appellate Courts

Higher courts consisting of a panel of judges that hear appeals on questions of law from lower courts.

(2) County Courts (three types): The Texas Constitution established 254 *constitutional country courts*, one for each Texas county. Since "judges" of county courts also have many administrative responsibilities as the presiding officer of the commissioner's court (as described in Chapter 8), the legislature has created 231 *statutory courts* in large, populated counties, such as Dallas or Harris county, to serve solely as statutory or "courts-at-law" courts to handle the case load. The legislature has also created eighteen *probate courts*, which deal with such matters as wills, estates, and guardianships. This totals 515 county level courts with 515 judges.

County courts mostly hear misdemeanor criminal cases, such as DUIs, bad checks, and drug violations. They also hear civil cases under $200,000. In addition, county courts hear appeals from JP and municipal courts.

(3) District Courts: The third level of the court structure of Texas consists of the *district courts*. There are 465 district courts, each with one judge. They hear felony criminal cases, such as murder, rape, armed robbery, and car theft. They also hear civil cases of significant monetary value. The

The Texas Supreme Court with Chief Justice Nathan Hetch center.
http://www.txcourts.gov/supreme

legislature creates these courts as the case loads increase. Large cities have several district courts to handle the many felony cases.

(4) Appellate Courts: Above the district courts are the appellate courts. In Texas, there are fourteen *courts of appeals*, with 80 judges. These courts hear all civil and criminal appeals from lower courts except for death penalty cases, which go directly to the Court of Criminal Appeals. The state of Texas is split up into fourteen jurisdictions for each of the appeals courts.

(5) State Supreme Courts (two types): All states, except Texas and Oklahoma, have one state supreme court, which serves as the court of last resort for all appeals. Not having a single supreme court fits into Texas's decentralized system of government. Instead, Texas has two courts of final appeal. The **Texas Supreme Court** *is the final appellate court in all civil and juvenile cases.* And the **Court of Criminal Appeals** *is the final appellate court in all criminal cases.* Each court has nine elected judges, which serve overlapping six-year terms.

Texas Supreme Court

The final appellate court in all civil and juvenile cases in Texas.

Court of Criminal Appeals

The final appellate court in all criminal cases in Texas.

JUDICIAL QUALIFICATIONS AND REMOVAL

Like most states, Texas judges can be removed from office by impeachment. But unlike most states, Texas judges, mainly because it's an elected office, have minimal qualifications.

Qualifications: In Texas, lower court judgeships tend to require little or no qualifications, while higher court judgeships require more qualifications.

There are no constitutional qualifications for justice of the peace, not even an attorney's license. The qualifications for municipal judges vary widely depending on the city charter that created that municipality. There are no qualifications for county judges, other than they must be "well informed of the law." Statutory county court judges, however, are usually required to have an attorney's license and four years of legal experience.

Higher court judges, including those that serve on the appeals court, the supreme court, and the court of criminal appeals, are required to be thirty-five years of age, possess an attorney's license, and have at least ten years experience as a lawyer or judge.

Judicial impeachment

Judges of the supreme court, court of appeals, and district courts can be removed by the governor with a two-thirds vote in each chamber of the legislature.

Removal: In Texas, judges can lose their seat on the bench by failing to win re-election or by **judicial impeachment:** *Judges of the supreme court, court of appeals, and district courts can be removed by the governor with a two-thirds vote in each chamber of the legislature.* The Texas Constitution says judges can be removed for "willful neglect of duty, incompetency, habitual drunkenness," and other reasonable causes.

And in Texas higher courts can remove or reprimand judges from lower courts. The state supreme court has the power to remove any judge from office. District courts may remove justices of the peace and county judges.

Also, the legislature has created a twelve-member commission, the *State Commission on Judicial Conduct*, to review judicial conduct. The State Commission on Judicial Conduct receives complaints about judges and holds hearings to determine if a judge has acted improperly. If they conclude a judge has acted improperly, they have the power to take several actions ranging from a private reprimand to recommendation to the supreme court for removal.

Senator John Cornyn was an Associate Justice of the Texas Supreme Court before he got elected to the US Senate.

JUDICIAL SELECTION

In recent years there has been much debate about what is the best process to choose judges. In this section we will discuss three major ways judges are selected in the United States. Judges for the federal government are selected by the president, confirmed by the senate, and serve for life. Texas judges run for election. Other states are trying various methods, such as appointing judges by the governor, appointing by the legislature, or by preselecting by a commission (the merit system).

Executive Selection	Fosters independent judiciary
Election of Judges	Makes judges more accountable to the people
Merit System	Tries to ensure more competent judges

The different judicial selection systems emphasize the importance of different values.
Courtesy Michael Young.

The different selection systems emphasize three different values: judicial independence, accountability, and competence. The federal method, in which judges serve for life, emphasizes judicial independence. The Texas system of elections focuses on accountability to the people. And the merit system highlights judicial competence.

National Judicial Selection: The Framers of the US Constitution created a non-political judicial branch. They did this through the judicial selection process. Federal judges, including those on the Supreme Court, are selected by the president, and with majority approval by the Senate, they serve on the bench for life. The Framers of the US Constitution thought that *life terms* for federal judges was the best system for securing the "impartial administration of the laws."

In *Federalist #78*, Alexander Hamilton said that life terms would create a judiciary independent from the other two branches of government and independent from the political whims of the people. The job of a Supreme Court is to protect the Constitution. But sometimes Congress passes unconstitutional laws and presidents make unconstitutional executive orders. Life tenure allows judges to protect the Constitution without fear of being removed from office by the President or by Congress or by losing an election. Also, Hamilton said that the job of a judge is intellectually demanding, requiring a life-time study of the law.

Texas Judicial Selection: The Framers of the Texas Constitution created an elective judiciary branch based on a different set of assumptions than those expressed by Hamilton. After suffering under the Reconstruction government, in which judges were selected by the much hated Governor E. J. Davis in order to impose his will on the state, the delegates at the Texas Constitutional Convention of 1875 made all judges elected by the people. They wanted to make sure that judges were accountable to the people and that they support the same political values as the citizens of Texas.

In Texas, most judges are elected in *partisan elections:* elections in which the voters know the party affiliation of the candidate—Democrat or Republican. Trial judges are elected to four-year terms, and appeals court judges are elected to six-year terms. Most municipal judges, however, are not elected but are appointed by the mayor or the city council.

Today the people of Texas still support an elective judiciary. The political values of Texans are conservative. The greatest fear of many Texans is that liberal judges will impose their values system on Texas by making biased rulings. This is made clear by watching the political ads of judges running for election in Texas. In nearly every ad, the person running for judge will boast that they will punish criminals, support gun rights, protect innocent life, defend private property, and strictly adhere to the letter of the law, not make law. These are the things that a majority of the Texas voters want from a judge.

Other Selection Methods: Although the Texas system keeps judges true to the political culture of the state, some people criticize certain aspects of judicial elections. They say that the people are not informed enough to properly evaluate the judicial competence of a person running for judge. And people often vote for irrational reasons, such as they recognize the candidate's name or they like his face or they thought his commercials were funny.

Merit system (or Missouri system)

The governor chooses a judge from a list compiled by a panel of legal experts. The judge serves a short term, after which the people vote on whether that judge should continue in office.

Another critique of judicial elections involves campaign finance. In order to run for office in a big state like Texas, it takes a lot of money. This means judicial candidates must accept money from all kinds of interest groups (environmentalists, teachers unions, labor unions, gun control groups, abortion groups), and this may bias their judgment in cases involving these issues. Furthermore, one of the groups that contributed funds to a judge might wind up in his or her court one day. Judges shouldn't be put in a situation that raises doubts about their impartiality.

To avoid the problems of popular elections and special interest groups, several states have tried different methods for selecting judges. These methods focus on judicial merit or competence. One popular method is called the **merit system (or Missouri system)**: *the governor chooses a judge from a list compiled by a panel of legal experts. The judge serves a short term, after which the people vote on whether that judge should continue in office.* This system tries to find judges that are competent in their field and it also provides accountability to the voters.

For appellate courts, twenty-four states use the merit system, but others states select judges by different methods: legislative election (two states), appointed by the governor (three states), nonpartisan elections (fourteen states), and partisan elections (seven states, including Texas). Actually, many Texas judges are initially appointed by the governor. If a seat becomes vacant due to death, impeachment, or resignation, or if the legislature created a new district, then the governor will appoint a judge to fill the seat until the next election.

In Texas, judges and sheriffs must run for office. This is based on the premise that law and order issues are not outside of politics.
Robert Daemmrich Photography Inc/Contributor/Getty

JUDICIAL DEMOCRACY

Winston Churchill once said that "Democracy is the worst form of government, except for all the others." Those that criticize Texas's judicial elections often point to problems of the lack of knowledge of the voter or problems related to interest groups. But this critique can be made about any democratic system, including the election of presidents and legislators.

In Texas, election of judges has prevented the problem that was foremost on the Framer's minds. They did not want to create an elite class of judges that thought they knew what was best for the people, even if the people disagreed. Elections are the only way to hold judges accountable to the will of the people.

The truth is that you cannot take politics out of the judiciary. Look at the issues that currently divide the country: abortion, affirmative action, gun control, immigration policy, the death penalty, gay marriage, environmental policy, and religion in the public sphere. On issues such as these, liberal judges will find a legal rational to decide cases based on their liberal beliefs, and conservative judges will find a legal rationale to decide cases based on their conservative beliefs. Only through elections will the people be able to select judges that share their political values.

NOTES

For information about the Texas court system: http://www.txcourts.gov/

For a description of the various judicial selection methods used by different states, go to National Center for State Court website: http://www.judicialselection.us/

Alexander Hamilton, John Jay, and James Madison. *The Federalists.* Indianapolis: Liberty Fund, 2001

ESSAY QUESTIONS

1. Describe at least three aspects of the American legal system that protect the citizen against the government.
2. Explain how a Texas judge can be removed or reprimanded.
3. Do you think the selection of judges should be part of the political process of elections? Why?

TERMS

Appellate courts: ______________________________

Civil law: ______________________________

Court of Criminal Appeals: ______________________________

Criminal law: ______________________________

Grand jury: ______________________________

Judicial branch: ______________________________

Judicial impeachment: ______________________________

Judicial review: ______________________________

Merit system: ______________________________

Petit jury: ______________________________

Texas Supreme Court: ______________________________

Trial courts: ______________________________

UNIT FOUR

The Texas Political Process

CHAPTER 14

Voting and Participation

TOPICS

- Election Districts
- Texas Legislative Districts
- Elections in Texas
- Texas Primaries
- General Elections
- Voter Turnout
- Political Participation

LEARNING OBJECTIVES

When you finish reading this chapter, you will be able to:

1. Describe the various election districts in Texas, including legislative districts.
2. Outline the important rules and regulations overseeing Texas elections.
3. Compare the features of the primaries and general election.
4. Explain the importance of voting and political participation in a well-functioning democracy.

In a democracy, voting is the primary responsibility of the citizens. Indeed, without fair and regular elections a country cannot call itself a democracy. As the Declaration of Independence says, no government is legitimate without the "consent of the governed."

Besides providing a way for the people to give their consent, elections do several things. Elections are the best way to select leaders to run the state. And by selecting leaders, the people are indirectly choosing the policies they think will best serve the economic and social interest of the Texas. Also, elections hold government officials accountable. If a governor, for example, is doing a bad job, the people will replace him or her with somebody new. And lastly, elections serve as a way for the people to express themselves and have a say in how their government is run.

But elections also place certain burdens on the citizens. In order for a democracy to work, the people must be informed about current events and know how government works. This is why the Texas legislature passed a law mandating that all college students take a course in Texas government. If the Great State of Texas is going to survive as a republic, then the people must be engaged, informed, and take up their civic duty.

ELECTION DISTRICTS

This chapter will explain how elections are conducted in Texas. First of all, the reader should know that each voter lives in several voting districts. Some elections are for statewide offices, others are for county offices, others are for city offices, and still others fit into special districts, such as for judges and legislators.

Without fair and regular elections, a country cannot claim to be a democracy.
© Aniwhite / Shutterstock.com

Statewide Elections: The citizens of Texas must elect officials for the seven major statewide offices. These include the Governor, Lieutenant Governor, Attorney General, Comptroller, Land Office Commissioners, Agriculture Commissioners, and Railroad Commissioners. Also, the citizens of Texas vote for the members of the Texas Supreme Court and the Court of Criminal Appeals.

County, City, and Legislative Districts: Also, every citizen lives within one of the 254 counties of Texas and can vote in county elections. And if you live within the city limits, you can vote in municipal elections as well. In addition, as will be described in more detail below, each resident lives in several legislative districts.

Other Types of Election Districts: There are still more districts that you may live in that require you to vote. Each resident lives in an Independent School District (ISD) and can vote for members of the school board and the superintendent. The state of Texas is also divided into fifteen school districts and citizens must vote for the members of the State Board of Education. Also, there are 465 district courts and fourteen courts of appeals. The residents in these judicial districts must vote for the judges serving in these courts. So, a typical Texan may be a voter in perhaps a dozen different election districts.

TEXAS LEGISLATIVE DISTRICTS

The election districts that usually receive the most attention are legislative districts. This includes the districts for the Texas Legislature and for the US Congress. Heated political conflicts always arise when these legislative district lines are redrawn, which occurs every ten years after the census is taken.

Districts of the Texas Legislature: In Texas, there are 31 senatorial districts and 150 house districts, each represented by one member of the Texas Legislature. This system allows for geographical representation. The candidate that wins the plurality of the vote of that district wins a seat in the legislature. Since 2010, a member of the state senate represented a district with 811,147 constituents, and a member of the state house represented a district of 167,637 constituents. The Supreme Court has ruled that all legislative districts should be of equal population size and thus comport with the concept of "one man one vote."

Congressional Districts: Texas is also divided up into US congressional districts. Since 2010, Texas has thirty-six members of the US House of Representatives, each serving a congressional district of 710,767 people. And of course each state gets two US Senators that represent the whole state. So, Texas has thirty-eight members in Congress, which is equal to the number of electors in the Electoral College that votes for the president.

Reapportioning: The US Constitution requires that every ten years a census will count the number of people in each state. If a state gains or

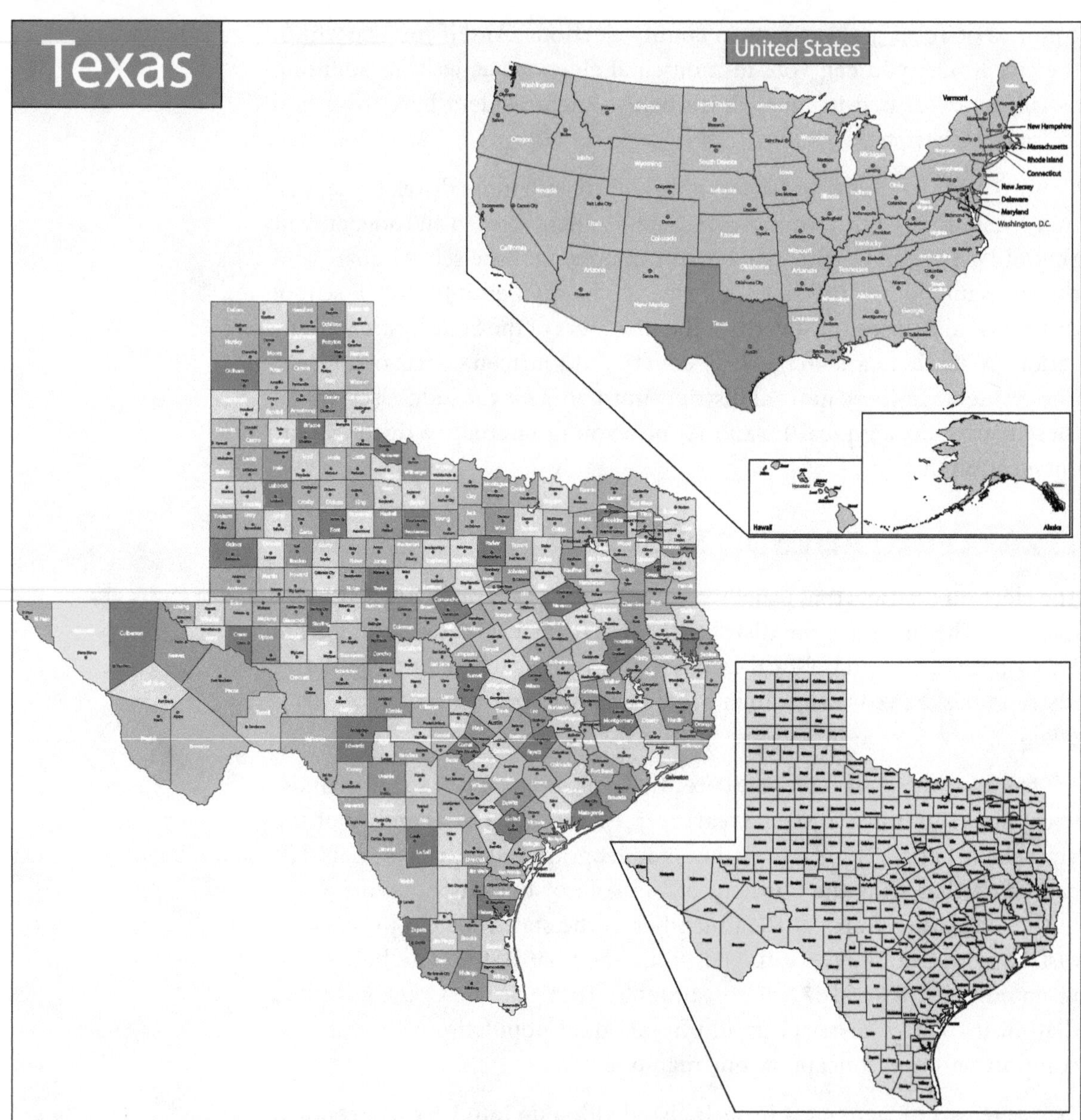

For the purposes of various elections, Texas is divided up into many different districts.

loses more than 710,767 people, then they will gain or lose a member of the US House of Representatives. The Texas Constitution also states that Texas will reapportion its districts after each federal census. *Reapportionment* refers to the process of allocating a number of representatives based on changes in the size of the population as reflected in the census.

Redistricting: If a state gains or loses representatives (reapportionment), then it must redraw the districts. This is called **redistricting**: *the process of redrawing the boundaries of legislative districts*. For example, in 2000 Texas had thirty representatives in Congress. But in 2012, due to Texas's rapid population growth, Texas was allotted thirty-six representatives in Congress. So, each time more representatives are allotted to Texas, it has to completely redraw the congressional district map for the whole state in order to fit in the new districts.

Whether it includes redrawing US House, Texas Senate, or Texas House districts, politics always enters the redistricting process. Political parties and special interest groups are very interested in how districts are drawn because it means one party or interest group can gain representation in the legislature, and thus gain power. In general, the majority party of a state ultimately controls the redistricting process.

Legislative Redistricting Board (LRB): In Texas, the legislature draws the district boundaries for members of the Texas legislature and Congress. If the legislature fails to act, the *Legislative Redistricting Board* (LRB) will draw district maps. The board consists of the Lieutenant Governor, the Speaker, the Attorney General, the Comptroller, and the Land Commissioner. In the past, when Texas was controlled by Democrats, they were in charge of redistricting. Now that a majority of the legislators and statewide office holders are Republican, they control the redistricting process. Each party tries to draw the districts maps in a way that gives them the maximum amount of political power.

Redistricting

The process of redrawing the boundaries of legislative districts.

Gerrymandered district

A legislative district drawn to give one party an advantage, especially if it has an unusual shape.

Gerrymandering: *A district drawn to give one party an advantage, especially if it has an unusual shape, is known as a* **gerrymandered district**. There are two major gerrymandering strategies: divide and isolate. If the Republicans control the state, for example, they will try to divide Democratic districts in a way that weakens their representation. Or they may try to put all the Democrats in a few, isolated districts.

Drawing districts in a way that gives advantage to a political party is called *political gerrymandering*. Drawing districts in a way that gives advantage to a racial group is called *racial gerrymandering*. For example, Hispanics may want to have a district drawn around an area of Texas with a high Hispanic population in order to gain Hispanic representation in the legislature. The Supreme Court, however, has ruled that racial gerrymandering cannot be a primary objective because laws should be colorblind. But in reality, since minorities overwhelmingly vote for Democrats, political gerrymandering is often essentially racial gerrymandering.

Safe Seats: The other goal of gerrymandering is to create as many safe seats as possible. A **safe seat** *is defined as one in which a candidate from either party wins 55 percent or more of the votes.* In 2012, 58 percent of the House seats were safe for Republicans, and 62 percent of the Senate seats were safe for Republicans. Most of the safe Democratic seats are in minority-majority districts, in which the majority of the population are ethnic minorities. Safe Democratic seats are in South Texas (with high Latino populations), the inner cities of Dallas and Houston (with high black populations), and in liberal Austin. Republicans are strongest in the Panhandle, German Hill Country, West Texas, East Texas, and in suburbs surrounding large cities.

Safe seat

A legislative district in which a candidate from either party wins 55 percent or more of the votes.

Political Polarization: As a result of political and racial gerrymandering, and the creation of safe seats, the Texas legislature and the US Congress have become more polarized. This means that legislators are either liberal Democrats or conservative Republicans, and fewer moderates from either party serve in the legislature. In the old days, when there were many conservative "blue dog Democrats" and many moderate "country club Republicans," political compromise was more common. But now with so many safe seats, lawmakers have no incentive to comprise and work across the political aisle. As a result, we have bitter fighting between the two parties, and the rhetoric seems to be getting nastier and nastier.

ELECTIONS IN TEXAS

Now that we have an understanding of all the election districts in Texas, let's discuss how all these elections are conducted. This section will outline all the rules and procedures regarding Texas elections, and the next two sections will discuss the primaries and general election. The rules for elections are specified in the Texas Election Code.

When: To be a legitimate democracy, elections must occur at regular intervals. In America, national elections always occur on the first Tuesday following the first Monday of November in even number years. The next presidential election will be held on November 3, 2020. Presidential elections are held every four years, and congressional elections are held every two years.

Joaquin Castro is the Democratic member of the US House of Representatives from the twentieth District of Texas.
Roy Rochlin/Stringer/Getty

The state of Texas also holds elections in November. All statewide offices, including the governor, are up for election every four years on non-presidential election years (also called midterm elections). The last gubernatorial election was held on November 4, 2014. And every two years, Texans vote for all 150 members of the Texas House of Representatives (two-year terms) and one-half of the members of the Texas state Senate (four-year terms). Elections for city council and mayor are also usually held in November.

Special Elections: But Texas also holds several elections on months other than November, these are called *special elections*. Many municipal and school board elections are held in May. Elections to decide Texas constitutional amendments are often held in January or August, when no other elections are held. Another type of special elections occurs to fill a vacant seat when a US Senator, a US Congressman, a Texas State Representative, or a Texas state Senator dies or resigns. This often happens, for example, if a US Senator is chosen by the president to fill a cabinet position. In these cases, the governor makes a temporary appointment until the special election in May.

Voter Qualifications: In order to vote in Texas, a voter must be eighteen years of age, a US citizen, a resident of Texas for thirty days, and a resident of the county for thirty days. And to be eligible to vote, a person must register to vote thirty days before an election. To make it easier to register, in 1993 Congress passed the *motor voter law*, which allows people to register to vote when applying for a driver's license or other government services. Two groups are forbidden from voting: felons who have not completed their sentence and those who a judge has ruled as mentally incompetent.

And there is another qualification to vote: one must provide a photo ID when voting. In order to help prevent voter fraud, in 2011 the Texas legislature (controlled by Republicans) passed a law requiring a photo ID when voting. Almost all countries around the world require a photo ID to vote. Several forms of ID are acceptable, including a driver's license, a passport, and an election identification certificate, which can be obtained free of charge. Democrats have vigorously opposed the law on the grounds that it will lower voter turnout for the poor, for the elderly, and for minorities—groups that typically vote for Democrats. Texas's voter photo ID law is currently being challenged in court and may go to the Supreme Court.

Ballot Form: Each county decides its own ballot form, which must be approved by the Texas Secretary of State. In the past, with paper ballots, there were several ballot forms. But since 2008, all 254 counties use electronic voting booths. Most computer ballots are in *Office Block Format*: each office title is at the top of a little box, and below that are the names of the candidates.

Straight party ticket

Voting for Democrats or Republicans for all offices listed on the ballot.

Electronic voting booths raise a few concerns. Computer voting makes it easy to vote a **straight party ticket:** *with one click, you can vote for all Democrats or all Republicans for each office*, but the voter can still select individual candidates from other parties. Some political scientists speculate that this is another factor that is contributing to political polarization. Others are fearful of electronic voting booths for other reasons. Each election, people and public officials voice concern that electronic voting booths may be open to hacking, viruses, and other computer related problems.

Financing Elections: Texas elections are paid for by the taxpayers and by the candidates via a *filing fee*: a payment to get a candidate's name on the ballot. Candidates must pay a filing fee for primaries and for the general election. Currently, the filing fee for statewide office is $3,700 and $1,250 for county offices.

Administration of Elections: Elections are regulated under the Texas Election Code and overseen by the Secretary of State. If there is a controversy or near tie, the secretary of state conducts a recount. In the primaries,

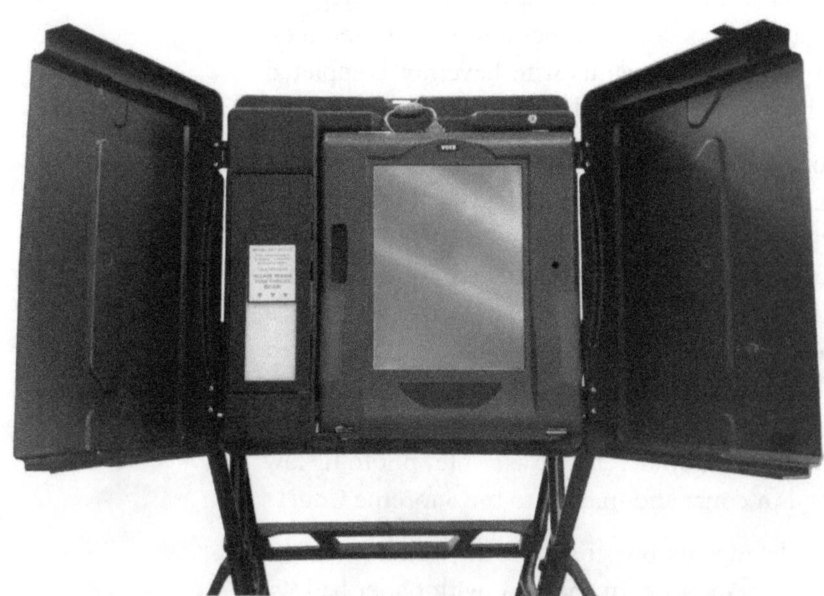

With electronic voting booths, it's easy to vote a straight party ticket. They also raise concerns about hacking.

the political parties play a more active role in administering the election. And for local election, city and county officials do much of the administrative work. But ultimately, the Secretary of State's office is responsible for the administration and oversight of Texas elections.

TEXAS PRIMARIES

In America, the candidates of the two major parties must run for election in a two-step process. First, is the *primary election*: an election used by the major parties to nominate candidates for the general election. The winner of the Democratic primary and the winner of the Republican primary will face each other in the *general election* in November.

Open and Closed Primaries: There are two types of primaries used in America. A **closed primary** *is an election by party members to nominate a candidate for the general election.* In the past, all primaries were closed. For example, only registered Republicans can vote to nominate a candidate to represent the Republican Party in the general election. This makes sense because a primary is when *party members* select their candidate to run in the general election. However, in recent years, as more people identify as independents, many states have turned to the **open primary**: *an election by people with any party affiliation to nominate a candidate for the general election.*

Technically, Texas is a *semi-open primary system*. When a citizen walks up to the voting location, he or she will be asked if they want a Republican or Democratic ballot. It doesn't matter if that person voted as a Democrat or Republican in the last election. They can now declare as a Republican, for example. Then the voter steps into the voting booth and votes as a member of the party for which they just chose. After the primary, the voter can re-register and vote for the other party in the general election.

Open primaries encourage *crossover voting*: when people leave their party to vote in the primary of the other party. When the motive to crossover is to *vote for the weaker candidate of the opposition party, this is called* **party raiding**. This has been a common feature of Texas politics for a long time. In 1996, many Democrats crossed over and voted for Pat Buchanan in order to weaken the Republican front-runner Bob Dole. And in 2008, many Republicans crossed over and voted for Hillary Clinton in order to weaken Barack Obama. Party raiding is controversial but there is little evidence that party raiding has actually changed the outcome of an election.

Runoff Primary Elections: *If no candidate wins a majority of the vote in the primary, then the top two candidates must compete in a* **runoff election**. In the past, the Texas Democratic primary was essentially the general

Closed primary

A primary election in which only party members can vote to nominate a candidate for the general election.

Open primary

An election by people with any party affiliation to nominate a candidate for the general election.

Party raiding

When a primary voter crosses over to another party in order to vote for the weaker candidate of the opposition party.

Runoff election

If no candidate wins a majority of the vote in the primary, then the top two candidates must compete in this election. The winner will run in the general election.

In the 2008 Texas primary, Hillary Clinton was the victim of party raiding as many Republicans voted for her in order to weaken Barack Obama.
© Harry Hu / Shutterstock.com

election because the Democratic candidate would easily beat the Republican. And since several Democratic candidates competed in the primary, the runoff was very common. Runoffs usually are held thirty days after the primary.

GENERAL ELECTION

The winners of the primaries go on to the general election. In the *general election*, people vote for the public official that will run the state. General elections are held in November on even number years. Elections for the statewide offices are held during the midterm election when the president is not up for election. This way the focus of the statewide election is on Texas issues, rather than national ones.

How do you get on the General Election Ballot? There are four ways to get your name on the general election ballot, depending on whether you are a major party candidate, third party candidate, independent candidate, or write-in candidate.

(1) Major Party Candidate: According the Texas Election Code, *major parties* are those that received over 20 percent of the vote for governor in the previous election. Only the Democratic and Republican parties qualify as major parties. There may be other names on the ballot, but in reality the general election is a contest between the individual who won the Republican primary and the individual who won the Democratic primary. So, winning the *primary* is how a candidate gets his or her name on the general election ballot.

(2) Third Party: Texas political history has been dominated by the Democrats and Republicans, but sometimes a minor or "third party" gains some support from the voters. The Texas Election Code defines a third party as a party that received 5 percent to 19 percent of the total vote for any statewide office in the previous election. In the past fifty years, only four parties have been granted official minor party status: Raza Unide Party in South Texas in the 1970s, the Socialist Workers Party in 1988, the Libertarian Party in the 1990s, and the Green Party in the 2000s. These last two still qualify. Third party candidates must nominate a candidate in a *party cause*: a meeting of members of a political party to nominate candidates.

(3) Independent Candidate: An *independent candidate* is somebody who is running for office without a party affiliation. To get your name on the general election ballot as an independent candidate, you must *submit a petition* with the secretary of state that has a certain number of signatures of registered voters. For statewide office, you must get a number of signatures equal to 1 percent of the votes cast for governor the previous election. And for the Texas legislature, you must get a number of signatures equal to 5 percent of votes cast for that office in the previous election. This requirement is designed to eliminate unserious candidates.

(4) Write-in Candidate: Somebody whose name is not printed on the ballot but the voter must write in the candidates' name is a *write-in candidate*. According to the Texas Election Code, a write-in candidate must file their intention to run with the secretary of state before the election. And they must pay a fee: for statewide office the fee is $4,000, for local officials it may be only a few hundred dollars.

Federal Voting Rights Act: The Voting Rights Act of 1965 has had a major impact on the elections of southern states, which had a racist legacy. This law forced many city councils and school boards to switch from at-large voting to district voting to elect more minorities. The law also requires Texas to print bilingual ballots in all counties that have over 20 percent Hispanics. In addition, the law requires pre-clearance by the US Justice Department of all changes in election procedures, including ballot form, time and place of an election, and method of electing legislators.

Absentee and Early Voting: In order to make it easier to vote, Texas has adopted two reforms that make it possible to vote without actually showing up at the polls on election day. *Absentee voting* is a process that allows

In the 2016 presidential election, over 3 million Texans voted in early voting.

a person to vote early, before the regular election. This practice was started to allow soldiers to vote when overseas. Since 1979, any Texan can vote absentee without restrictions. Also, the Texas legislature has created **early voting**: *people can vote between seventeen and four days before the election.* Polls are open between 7 AM and 7 PM. In recent years, early voting has become very popular in Texas.

VOTER TURNOUT

The percentage of eligible voters that actually cast a ballot is called **turnout**. Nationwide, about 55 percent of voters vote in presidential elections, about 40 percent of voters vote in gubernatorial elections, and sometimes as low as 5 percent of voters vote in local elections. With the introduction of absentee voting and early voting, it is surprising the turnout has remained low. And turnout in Texas is particularly low.

Early voting

People can vote between seventeen and four days before the election.

Turnout

The percentage of eligible voters that actually cast a ballot.

Turnout in Texas: Texas has lower turnout than the national average. In the 2012 presidential election, the national turnout was 58.2 percent, but Texas turnout was 49.7 percent, ranking Texas forty-seventh in the country. In the 2010 midterm elections, the national turnout was 41 percent, but Texas turnout was 32.2 percent, ranking Texas fiftieth. Why does Texas, a state known for its state pride, have such low voter turnout?

Socioeconomic Factors of Turnout: Certain types of people tend to vote more often than others. People who attained high levels of education, older people, higher income individuals, and people who are interested in politics have the highest turnout.

The socioeconomic make-up of Texas is contrary to the high turnout model. Texas has a significant high school dropout rate, Texas has a high poverty rate, and Texas has a young population. Much of this socioeconomic data is impacted by the fact that Texas is on the border of Mexico and receives a lot of immigrants. Latinos and recent immigrants tend not to vote because they came to America to work and raise a family and they have not yet focused on American politics.

Legacy of History of Discrimination: Some argue that the reason Texas and other southern states have low turnout is due to the continuing influence of past racial discrimination on voting. This argument is undermined by the fact that in recent election cycles black turnout has actually been higher than white turnout, but every Texan should know the history of discrimination in the South.

When the Democratic Party dominated the South, they instituted many practices designed to discourage Black Americans from voting. Until 1944 when the Supreme Court declared the *white primary* unconstitutional, only whites were allowed to vote in the Democratic primary. Democrats also instituted the *poll tax*, requiring that each citizen pay a yearly tax to remain eligible to vote. This was designed to discourage blacks, poor whites, and Hispanics from voting. Texas also required voters to register to vote every year at the local courthouse—something that was intimidating for many blacks and Hispanics. By 1972, when the poll tax and annual registration were finally abolished, minority turnout increased significantly.

Rational Explanations: Some political scientists have argued that low turnout is the result of rational human behavior. On election day, which occurs on a Tuesday (a work day), when an individual calculates the time and effort needed to vote, and knowing that their individual vote will not make a difference, it makes sense not to vote. On the other hand, there is another rational reason to vote. Clearly, if everybody failed to vote then our democracy would cease to function. So, people who vote do it out of a sense of civic and patriotic duty, knowing that their participation is needed to keep our democracy alive.

POLITICAL PARTICIPATION

When people vote or get involved in a political party, this is called **political participation**: *engaging in the political process*. In a democracy, voting is the most important way to participate in the political process, but there are other forms of political participation, such as telling a friend to vote for a candidate, going to a political rally, or placing a bumper sticker on your car.

A healthy democracy engages the public and encourages them to participate in the effort to bring about political and social change. In an unhealthy society, people feel disengaged, isolated, and alienated. They do not engage in political participate because they feel their actions do not matter, or if they do participation, it is in a radical or violent manner. Society benefits if there is a high degree of constructive political participation.

Political participation

Engaging in the political process.

Types of Political Participation: There are many ways that citizens can engage in political participation: voting; sending money to a candidate; attending a political speech, placing a sign on your front yard; attending a city, school, or neighborhood meeting; signing a petition; writing a letter to the editor; volunteering to work for a campaign; working with fellow citizens to solve a community problem; and joining an interest or civic group. According to a 2013 Pew Research Center survey, about 48 percent of the adults surveyed claimed that they did at least one of these activities over the last twelve months.

By participating in a community meeting or event, people get connected to society and develop important civic skills.

The Pew survey also revealed many interesting things about how people participate in the political process in the digital age. About 34 percent of people claimed to have contacted a government official via an online method. And about 39 percent of adults said they engaged in political participation on social networking sites. On such sites as Facebook or Twitter, these adults say that they have done one of the following: they "liked" or promoted political material, they encouraged other people to vote, they posted their political opinions, they posted links to political articles, or they followed an elected official or candidate. The Pew survey also found that in general people with higher education and income levels engage in more political participation, either on or off line.

Social capital

The sense of shared purpose and values that social connections promote.

Social Capital: In 2001, an influential book was published that highlighted the importance of political participation. In *Bowling Alone*, Robert Putnam said political participation and membership in social groups builds **social capital**: *the sense of shared purpose and values that social connections promote.*

It is not healthy for society if people are isolated and only concerned with themselves. It is healthier for an individual and for society if people join groups. This can be any group, such as a church, a book club, an environmentalist group, a kayak club, the Rotary, or a homeowners association. Participation in groups helps people develop "civic skills": the ability to communicate productively, work with others, and organize to accomplish a community good. A healthy democracy needs people to develop these skills.

NOTES

For information about the Republican Party in Texas: https://www.texasgop.org/

For information about the Texas Democratic Party: https://www.texasgop.org/

Mike Kingston, Sam Attlesey & Mary G. Crawford. *Political History of Texas.* Austin, Texas: Eakin Press, 1992.

Robert D. Putnam. *Bowing Alone.* New York: Touchstone Books, 2001.

ESSAY QUESTIONS

1. Compare the difference between open and closed primaries and explain why open primaries encourage party raiding. Do you think party raiding is good?
2. Explain why voter turnout in Texas is low. Cite textbook examples and then give your own opinion.
3. Describe several ways people can participate in the political process besides voting, and explain how political participation increases *social capital.*

TERMS

Closed primary: ____________________

Early voting: ____________________

Gerrymandered district: ____________________

Open primary: ____________________

Party raiding: ____________________

Political participation: ____________________

Redistricting: ____________________

Runoff election: ____________________

Safe seat: ____________________

Social capital: ____________________

Straight party ticket: ____________________

Turnout: ____________________

TEXAS FUN & FACTS SHEET 8

The Capitals of Texas

© Yevhen Tarnavskyi / Shutterstock.com

San Antonia (1771–1835): This was the capital during Spanish rule (1771–1821) and Mexican rule (1821–1836).

Washington-on-the-Brazos (March 1836): Texans met here for the Convention of 1836 to write a constitution and declare independence.

Harrisburg (1836): During the Texas war for independence, President David G. Burnet twice briefly occupied Harrisburg and used it as the capital.

Galveston (1836): Likewise, Galveston was also temporarily occupied by President Burnet during the war.

Velasco (to Sept 1836): During the last months of the war, Velasco served as the seat of government for Texas.

Columbia (October 1836–December 1836): This became the first capital of the Republic of Texas.

Houston (April 1837–1839): President Sam Houston ordered the capital to be moved to his namesake. During this time, a commission was established to find a permanent capital for Texas. They decided on La Grange in Fayette County, but President Houston vetoed this suggestion.

Waterloo (Austin): (1839–1845): Waterloo, later renamed Austin, was approved as the new capital on January 19, 1839. President Mirabeau B. Lamar and his cabinet arrived in October of 1839.

Austin (1845–to present day): Fearing that Mexico may attack Austin in 1842, President Sam Houston temporally moved the capital to Houston and then to Washington-on-the-Brazos. The Constitution of 1845 required that the capital remain in Austin to 1850, at which time there will be a vote. Austin won with 7,674 votes. Then in 1872 there was another vote to select a capital. Again, Austin won (63,297 votes), beating out Houston (35,188) and Waco (12,776).

Source: Texas Almanac

CHAPTER 15

Political Parties

TOPICS

- Characteristics of a One-Party Rule
- History of Texas Party Politics
- Texas Republicans and Democrats Today
- Party Power and Function
- Party Organization
- Parties Help Run the Government

LEARNING OBJECTIVES

When you finish reading this chapter, you will be able to:

1. Compare the characteristics of one-party and two-party rule.
2. Outline the history of party politics in Texas.
3. Contrast the current party platforms of the Democratic and Republican parties.
4. Describe the role of the political parties in organizing elections.
5. Describe how the political parties run and organize the three branches of government.

Political Parties are *organizations consisting of many coalitions that elect officials to government in order to carry out their agenda.* In the last 150 years, two parties have dominated the American political landscape: the Republican Party and the Democrat Party. Groups that tend to support the Republican Party include small business organizations, religious groups, veterans, pro-life supporters, gun rights advocates, and people

One aspect of the two-party system is that each party tries to hold the other accountable by exposing wrong-doing.

© Christos Georghiou / Shutterstock.com

with conservative beliefs. Groups that tend to support the Democratic Party are unions, ethnic organizations, lower socioeconomic groups, immigrants, pro-choice supporters, gun control advocates, and people with liberal beliefs.

Besides ideology, there are geographical differences between the two parties. Most of the people in small towns, in the South (including Texas), and in the Midwest vote Republican. Most of the people in big cities, especially along the West Coast, around the Great Lakes, and in the Northeast, vote Democratic.

Political parties

Organizations consisting of many coalitions that elect officials to government in order to carry out their agenda.

Another function of political parties is that they serve as an intermediary or a link between the people and the government. During a political campaign, not only is the candidate articulating her political beliefs, but the people are expressing their support or lack of support for a particular candidate. In this way the people are indicating what issues they support and how they want their government run.

This was illustrated by the Texas governor's race in 2014. State Senator Wendy Davis, a Democrat, came to national fame when she filibustered a strict abortion bill. And a main element of her stump speech was her pro-choice position. But Attorney General Abbot won the election by a landslide, 60 percent to 39 percent. Abbot, a Republican, ran on law and order, border security, and gun rights. He pledged to continue Governor Rick Perry's pro-growth economic agenda of less regulations, tax relief, and cuts in government spending. And he vowed to improve education and repair the roads. By voting for Abbott in such large numbers, the people of Texas expressed their support of his agenda.

CHARACTERISTIC OF ONE-PARTY RULE

While America has always had a two-party system, a unique feature of Texas politics is its history of one-party rule. In the past Texas was controlled by the Democrats, and today it is dominated by the Republicans. Several characteristics distinguish a one-party system from a two-party system. First, since all the political candidates are members of one party, they tend to agree on the issues, thus personality becomes the focus of the voters. This helps account for why Texas is known for politicians with big personalities.

Second, in one-party rule, since there is no serious opposition to unite the party, the dominate party becomes divided between two or three wings. After World War II, the Democrat Party was divided between the New Deal, liberal Democrats and traditional conservative, Democrats. Today, the Republican Party is divided three ways: traditional, establishment Republicans; religious, social conservative Republicans; and Tea Party, populist Republicans.

Third, in a one-party state the *primary* is the real contest. Today, everybody knows a Republican will win the general election, so the real battle is between the several Republicans competing in the primary. This also makes the *runoff* more probable. And whoever wins the runoff will likely win office.

A unique feature of Texas's political history is one-party rule, in which one party dominates.

And fourth, a one-party system presents a problem of accountability. One of the important functions of the two-party system is that one party will hold the other party to account. For example, if a Democratic governor commits an unethical act, then the Republicans in the legislature may publicize it and conduct an investigation. But in a one-party system, the opposition party may be too weak to hold the dominate party responsible for corruption, ineptitude, voter fraud, or cronyisms. Throughout the history of Texas, all four characteristics of the one-party politics have been on display.

HISTORY OF TEXAS PARTY POLITICS

As mentioned above, Texas has almost always been a one-party state. The Democratic Party dominated from the founding of the Republic of Texas to the Civil War (1836–1865). Then for a brief period, during Reconstruction, the Republican Party ruled Texas (1866–1874). The Democrats returned to dominance and enjoyed a century-long stretch of power from 1877 to 1977. This was followed by a transition period when the Republican Party was in the ascendancy and a two-party system existed in Texas. But since 1994, Texas returned to one-party status, this time governed by the Republicans.

Republic of Texas to the Civil War (1836–1865): From 1836 to 1846, when Texas was an independent nation, political parties did not substantively exist in the Republic of Texas. Politics, however, was very combative and personal. During this decade, Texas politics was dominated by two Democrats and their supporters. Sam Houston, the hero of the Battle of San Jacinto and the first and third president of Texas, promoted Texas statehood and peaceful relations with the Native Indians. Mirabeau B. Lamar, the second president of Texas, championed Texas nationhood and supported aggressive action towards the Indians.

Sam Houston tried to avoid the fight between the Democrats and Republicans before the Civil War by helping to form a third party, the Union Party.

In 1845, the US Congress approved the annexation of Texas and it became the twenty-eighth state of the Union. During this period, the Democratic Party, established by Andrew Jackson, dominated Texas. Most of the settlers in Texas were from southern states and brought their slaves with them. In general, the pre-Civil War Democratic Party was for state rights, the expansion of slavery, reduction of tariffs, and against the central bank. Although a national party, it was strongest in the South. For the most part, all Texas politicians of this era followed the policies of the national Democratic Party, with the exception of Sam Houston.

As a US Senator representing Texas from 1846 to 1859, Houston was often at odds with the Democratic Party. He was opposed to the expansion of slavery and took a more nationalistic view than most Democrats. In 1859, Houston ran for Governor of Texas as an independent and began building the

Union Party, a national party opposed to secession. After Houston was elected, the citizens of Texas voted for secession by more than a three to one margin. Houston refused to pledge allegiance to the Confederate flag and was removed from office. During the Civil War, Texans remained faithful Democrats.

Reconstruction (1866–1874): In the War Between the States, the Confederacy, controlled by southern Democrats, was defeated by the Union Army, led by Abraham Lincoln and the northern Republicans. After the war, the South was subjugated by northern Republicans in Congress. With the passage of the Thirteenth Amendment, slavery was abolished. Then northern Republicans implemented Reconstruction, dividing the South into five military zones and appointing Republican governors to the former Confederate states.

Before the war, Edmund J. Davis was a supporter of Sam Houston and the Union Party, but once the conflict started he fought for the Union Army, achieving the rank of brigadier general. In 1869, Davis, a Republican, was elected Governor of Texas when few white Democrats voted (members of the Confederacy were banned from voting that year). Davis centralized the government, gave the vote to blacks, tried to protect the safety of the freed slaves, and rebuilt the economy. Southern Democrats deeply resented Davis and the Republican Party. They called southerners who voted for Republicans "scalawags." A deep hatred of Reconstruction united southern Democrats against Republicans for generations.

Greenback Party

In the 1870s, this party represented the small farmer and promoted paper currency in an attempt to inflate farm prices.

Return of One-Party Democrat Rule (1875–1977): In 1875, Democrats returned to power and wrote a new constitution, ratified in 1876. This is the foundation of the current Texas Constitution. From 1875 to 1961, no Republican won statewide office in Texas. Although the Democratic Party dominated Texas during this era, a couple minor or "third parties" challenged Democratic rule. In opposition to the Democrats who represented large farmers, ranchers, and merchants, the first of these parties fought for poor farmers. In 1878, the **Greenback Party** won twelve seats in the Texas legislature. *This party represented the small farmer and promoted paper currency in an attempt to inflate farm prices.*

A decade later, the Greenbacks were replaced by another farmer's party, the Populist Party. Combining the Farmer's Alliance with other groups representing industrial labor, the *Populist Party* united the "common man" against the industrial and intellectual elite. In 1896, the Populist Party merged with the Democrat Party in support of the charismatic William Jennings Bryan. Although Texas threw its fifteen electoral votes to Bryan, he lost the presidential election to Republican William McKinley.

In the mid-1920s, a majority of the members of the Texas legislature were members of the Ku Klux Klan. This is an ad for the Klansman Cigars, made in Dallas, Texas.

Anti-Saloon League

A semi-third party/interest group that was successful at turning most counties in Texas dry and supporting Prohibition in 1919.

On the national level, both the Republican and Democratic parties were influenced by the *Progressive Movement* (1900–1920). Progressives were not as anti-elite as the Populists and the movement was centered in the cities, not the farms. Progressives sponsored government initiatives crafted by elites to reform education, regulate business, and fight political corruption. They supported woman's suffrage, prohibition, the primary, direct election of senators, a graduated income tax, and other egalitarian measures. Although Texas voted for Democrat Woodrow Wilson, the most progressive/liberal president in history, actual progressive reforms were less popular in Texas. The Texas Democratic Party, in partnership with large land owners and merchants, successfully stopped the most radical progressive reforms in the state.

Although the Democrats continued to dominate Texas, two other movements during the Progressive Era influenced Texas Democrats. The Texas **Anti-Saloon League**, *a semi-third party/interest group, was successful at turning most counties in Texas dry (prohibited alcohol).* In 1919, Texas ratified the Eighteenth Amendment (Prohibition), which prohibited the production, sale, and transportation of alcoholic beverages. Another organization that supported prohibition was the *Ku Klux Klan*, a secret organization that supported white supremacy. In 1922, the Texas KKK was successful at electing a US Senator (Democrat Earle Bradford Mayfield) and a majority of the members of the Texas legislature. Due in part to the efforts of Governor Miriam Ferguson, the Klan died out by 1928.

During this time the Texas Democratic Party disenfranchised two large segments of the voting population: blacks and poor whites, many of whom were *sharecroppers* (farmers that didn't own their land and paid rent with a percentage of their crops). In 1904, Texas implemented the **poll tax**, *an annual fee to register to vote.* Initially the poll tax was $1.50, but this was a lot of money for poor farmers back then. The poll tax was outlawed in 1964 with the passage of the Twenty-fouth Amendment. And in 1924 the Democrats enacted the **white primary** *that denied Black Americans the right to vote in the Democratic primary.* The argument was that a political party is a private organization and has the right to choose its membership. But in 1944, the Supreme Court declared the white primary unconstitutional because political parties are not truly private organizations but government entities.

Poll tax

An annual fee to register to vote.

White primary

The Texas Democratic Party denied Black Americans the right to vote in their primary.

In 1928, Texans voted for Republican Herbert Hoover for president over the New York Democrat, Al Smith, who was an anti-prohibition Catholic. From 1928 on, the national Democratic Party would become increasingly divided: southern Democrats remained conservative, while northern big city democrats turned liberal. During this era, Texans remained loyal to Democrats in local and statewide elections, but voted more and more often for Republicans for president. Texas voted for Dwight Eisenhower in 1952 and 1956 and for Richard Nixon in 1972. In other words, they engaged in **ticket splitting**: *when voters decide to vote for candidates from one party for some offices and candidates from another party for other offices.*

Ticket splitting

When voters decide to vote for candidates from one party for some offices and candidates from another party for other offices.

Party Realignment in Texas (1978–1993): *When the majority of the electorate switches over and supports another political party this is called* **party realignment**. On the national level, this occurred in 1932 when a majority of Americans left the Republican Party and supported Franklin Roosevelt and the Democrats. In Texas, the process developed more slowly as conservative Democrats gradually decided they would switch over to the conservative party, the Republicans.

Party realignment

When the majority of the electorate switches over and supports another political party.

Texans grew up with a strong identification as Democrats and a natural dislike for Republicans. So, even though they were conservative and agreed with the national Republicans on many issues, they were going to keep their Democratic affiliation. These people were known as **Yellow Dog Democrats**: *southern Democrats who remained loyal to the Democrat Party.* They said they would "vote for a yellow dog before they would vote for a Republican."

Yellow Dog Democrats

Southern Democrats who remained loyal to the Democrat Party by never voting for Republicans.

During this era, Texas Democrats split into two groups. Some Yellow Dog Democrats followed the national Democratic Party as it shifted leftward. They supported the big government, liberal programs initiated by Democratic presidents, such as the New Deal (Franklin Roosevelt), the Fair Deal (Harry Truman), and the Great Society (Lyndon Johnson). Yellow Dog Democrats always voted a straight party ticket.

But other, more conservative Democrats, sometimes crossed party lines. They became known as **Boll Weevil Democrats**: *conservative southern Democrats who sometimes voted for Republicans.* Today they are known as *Blue Dog Democrats.* These Democrats kept their Democratic affiliation, saying "I was born a Democrat and I am going to die a Democrat." But they voted increasingly for conservative Republicans in statewide and national elections.

A "Boll Weevil Democrat" was a conservative southern Democrat who sometimes voted for Republicans but stubbornly kept his Democratic affiliation.
© Koshevnyk / Shutterstock.com

The transition to the Republican Party started with the election of Allen Shriver, the conservative Democrat who served as the Governor of Texas from 1949 to 1957. He supported Republican Eisenhower for president and often fought with the national Democratic Party on many issues. Then in 1961, Texas elected its first Republican US Senator, John Tower. But the point at which Texas became a two-party state was when Bill Clements won the governorship in 1978. He was the first Republican Governor of Texas since E. J. Davis.

In 1980, 55 percent of Texans voted for Republican Ronald Reagan, the most conservative president since Calvin Coolidge, and only 41 percent voted for Democrat Jimmy Carter. Reagan's victory was certainly aided by his Texas running mate, George H. W Bush, who previously served as a congressman representing the Houston area. From this point on, Texans started voting for more Republicans. Phil Gramm, an economic advisor to Reagan, became the second Republican in Texas history to serve in the US Senate. Then Bill Clements came back and won the governorship in 1987. And in 1988, George H. W. Bush won the presidency. In that year, Republicans won four statewide offices and many important judgeships.

Boll Weevil Democrats

Conservative southern Democrats who sometimes voted for Republicans.

One-Party Republican Control of Texas (1994–Today): By the end of the 1980s, Texas Republicans were winning more local, statewide, and national elections, but the Democrats still held the majority of offices, including majorities in both chambers of the legislature. And in 1991, Democrat Ann Richards won the governorship, becoming the second woman governor in Texas history. But in 1994 she was defeated by George W. Bush, the son of the former president.

In the year 1994, the Republicans became the dominate party of Texas. Besides winning the governorship, Republicans won the majority of statewide offices. Four years later, in 1998, the Republicans established complete dominance of the state by winning the governorship, all statewide offices, and a majority in both chambers of the state legislature. And two years later, George W. Bush became President of the United States. Across the nation today, Texas is associated in the public mind with conservative Republicans.

TEXAS REPUBLICANS AND DEMOCRATS TODAY

As with national politics, today the Texas Democratic Party is becoming more liberal, and the Texas Republican Party is becoming more conservative. Texas, like the country, is *politically polarized* with few moderates in the middle. This polarization is clearly illustrated by the political platforms published by the Democratic and Republican parties of Texas. A **political platform** *is a document stating the set of principles of a political party*. It is made public during the party conventions.

Political platform

A document stating the set of principles of a political party.

On June 20, 2016, Texas Democrats held a convention in San Antonio and approved a new party platform, outlining the party's stand on a host of issues. The document says Texas Democrats "denounce efforts to build an unnecessary border wall," urge decriminalization of marijuana, and support a minimal wage of $15. The platform articulates opposition to

Today, the Democrats and Republicans seem to disagree on every issue. Republicans support a border wall, and the Democrats oppose it.

private school vouchers and calls for a repeal of the new open carry gun law. On elections, the Texas Democrats oppose voter ID and support same day registration. The platform also calls for the right of transgender individuals to use the bathroom of their choice and for Medicaid to cover the cost of sex-change operations. The Democratic platform also supports the right of a woman to choose to have an abortion.

On May 15, 2016, the Republican Party approved its platform which takes the opposite position on nearly every issue. The Republicans "oppose all laws that infringe on the right to arms," and they support the right to choose public, private, charter, or home schools. The platform urges the building of "high border wall" and opposes amnesty and in-state tuition for illegal aliens. The Republican platform calls for tax cuts and the elimination of the minimum wage. They support traditional marriage and oppose criminal prosecution of private businesses that do not wish to participate in a gay marriage ceremony. The platform also states that the "right to life . . . cannot be infringed" and it urges for criminal prosecution for persons who injure or kill an unborn life. Also, it says that people should only use the public bathrooms, showers, and locker rooms that correspond to their biological sex.

By comparing the two platforms, it is easy to see that the Democrats and Republicans disagree on nearly all the basic issues facing the state and nation today.

Australian ballot

People vote in private and the government prints the ballot which contained the names of all candidates from both parties.

Primary

The voters choose the candidates from each party that they wish to run in the general election.

PARTY POWER AND FUNCTION

In the past, political parties were much more powerful than today. Then around the turn of the century, several progressive reforms weakened their influence. Up to the 1890s, people voted in public by signing a ballot printed by the political parties. These ballots only contained the names of the candidates of one party, be it Democrat or Republican. With the adoption of the **Australian Ballot**, *in which people vote in private and marked a ballot printed by the government that contained the names of all candidates from both parties*, this kind of public intimidation on election day was eliminated.

A few decades later the Progressives were successful at accomplishing another major reform that weakened the parties: the direct primary. Before the primary, party leaders would select the candidate to run in the general presidential campaign. But since the implementation of the **primary**, *the voters of each state choose the candidates they wish to run in the general election.* This has significantly weakened the power of the party leadership.

Party Functions: In the past political parties served several functions in conducting political campaigns. Parties recruited candidates to run for office. They helped run and finance campaigns, including organizing campaign events such as rallies and parades. They printed campaign literature and posters and arranged for surrogates to speak for the candidate. And the parties encouraged people to vote by organizing get-out-the-vote campaigns.

In general, the main function of political parties is to organize the contest between two candidates with two different political agendas, thus simplifying things for the voter. When a voter sees an R next to a candidate's name, they know the candidate is a Republican and is more conservative than a Democrat. Think how difficult it would be to vote if each candidate ran as an individual with no party affiliation. Another way to think of elections is that it is when the voters decide what member of the two teams (Republicans or Democrats) win the contest.

Today, the political parties are weaker than they were in the past. Candidates decide to run on their own; they are not selected by party leaders. And a candidate hires her own campaign manager and raises money for her own campaign. And many independent groups raise money and run ads for the candidate. But the two political parties still offer some financial, media, and organizational assistance as well as provide voting and polling data to the candidates.

And today the people are less loyal to parties. In the past, a Texan, for example, would have strong emotional ties to the Democratic Party. But today more and more people view themselves as independent with no strong party affiliation. According to the Texas Politics Project, in 1952 about 20 percent of Texas voters identified as independent. And in 2008, 29 percent identified as independent. Another indication of weaker party loyalty is that many Republican candidates often rhetorically run against their own party. When Ted Cruz ran for the US Senate in 2012, he probably spent more time criticizing the "Republican establishment" than he did his Democratic opponent.

PARTY ORGANIZATION

Although the parties are weaker than they were in the past, party organization still plays an important role in how candidates run for office. Parties are organized on the national, state, and local levels.

National Party Organization: On the national level, the parties are weak and decentralized. With the exception of the presidential race, most campaigns are held at the local and state level where the national parties have

As the state with the second most Electoral College votes, Texas plays a large part in the national party conventions.
© Frontpage / Shutterstock.com

limited power. Today the chair of the national Republican Party is Ronna Romney McDonald, the daughter of former presidential candidate Mitt Romney. And the chair of the national Democratic Party is Tom Perez, the former Secretary of Labor in the Obama administration. The main event for the political parties is the national party conventions held every four years during the presidential elections. Usually meeting at the end of August, the national conventions agree on a party platform and officially confirm the presidential nominee, which was already determined in the primaries.

In 2016, two Texans ran for president: former Governor Rick Perry and current Senator Ted Cruz. Both lost the primaries to Donald Trump. Besides running the national conventions, the national parties play a minor role in presidential campaigns. Presidential candidates run their own campaigns with limited assistance from the parties.

State party chair

The head of the state executive committee and the leader of the party for the state.

State Party Organization: In Texas, each party has a *state executive committee*, a permanent party organization consisting of sixty-four members. At the top of the state party hierarchy is the **state party chair**: *the head of the state executive committee and the leader of the party for the state*. There is a state chair and a vice chair, and one must be a man and the other a woman. They are selected by the members at the state party convention for a two-year term.

A major responsibility of the state chair is to preside over the state convention, held every two years in June. The state convention selects state party officials, elects the sixty-four members of the state executive committee, and adopts a party platform. In presidential years, the state convention also conducts two very important tasks. First, it elects the party's presidential nominee. In 2016, the Republican state convention selected Ted Cruz. And second, it selects the state's thirty-eight electors, members of the Electoral College that votes for the presidential candidates in November.

County Party Organization: Each of Texas's 254 counties has a Republican and Democratic *county executive committee*. It consists of all the precinct chairs (see below) and is presided over by the *county chair,* elected to a two-year term by the voters in the county. The county chair and the county executive committee will help decide voting places for the primary,

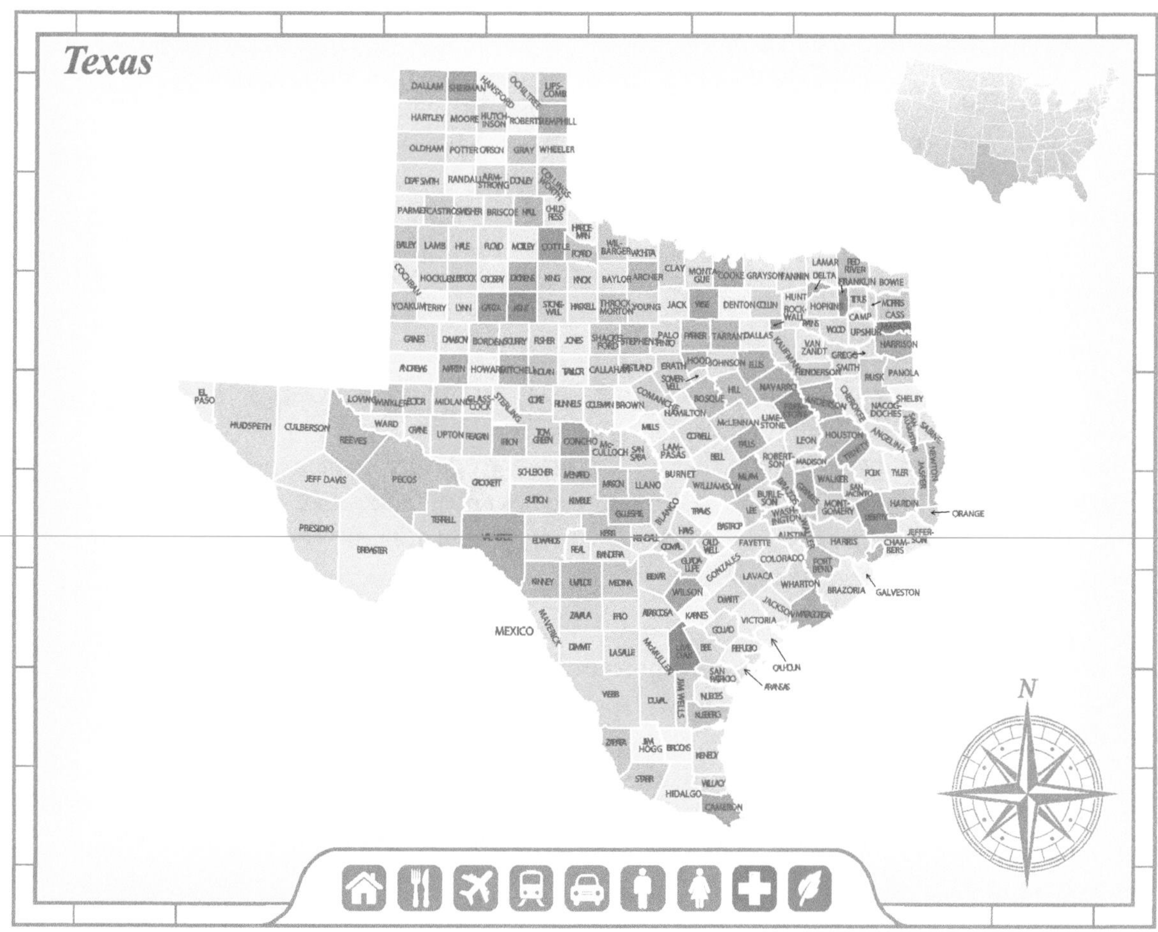

Every county in Texas has a Democratic and Republican county chair.

appoint election judges, collect fees, accept candidates to be placed on the ballot, and rent voting machines. And the county chair presides over the county convention, which votes on resolutions to be considered at the state convention and selects delegates to the state convention.

Precinct Party Organization: There are over 8,000 voting precincts in Texas. They are created by the county commissioner of each county. The precinct chair is elected to a two-year term by the voters of the precinct. Often the position is uncontested or vacant because nobody runs. In general, the **precinct chair** *is the lowest level party official who organizes and supports the party at the precinct level.* The precinct chair tries to increase party registration, organizes party events, and may serve as election judge on Election Day.

The precinct chair also serves as a member of the county executive committee and presides over the *precinct convention*, which is held on the same day as the party primary in March. Anyone who voted earlier in the day can attend the precinct convention. The convention starts as soon as the polls close at 7:00 PM. After the precinct chair certifies that the attendees have voted in the primary and that the officers are in place, the convention chooses delegates for the county convention. This is the most important task, but some precincts also conduct a straw poll to show their support for a presidential candidate, and they may also make recommendations for items to be included in the state party platform.

Precinct chair

The lowest level party official who organizes and supports the party at the precinct level.

PARTIES HELP RUN THE GOVERNMENT

At the beginning of this chapter, we defined political parties as organizations consisting of many coalitions that elect officials to government in order to *carry out their agenda.* The reason why parties are able to implement their agenda is because parties play such a significant role in how government is run and organized.

Parties in the Texas Legislature: Whatever party has a majority in each chamber of the legislature has enormous power. For example, if the Republicans have a majority in the Texas House, then they will choose the Speaker and the other leadership positions. Party leaders have many tools to force members to vote the party line. And the Speaker will select all the chairs and members of the legislative committees. This means that Republicans will be able to implement their agenda, effectively shutting out the Democrats from any legislative power.

Parties in the Executive Branch: Because of the plural executive and the weak appointment powers of the governor, the political parties have less independent power in the Texas executive department. But in Texas's traditional one-party system, whatever party dominates the state will control the executive departments. Texas governors make thousands of appointments to state committees, agencies, and boards. Thus, if one party controls the governorship for a few terms, they will control the bureaucracy and administration of the state.

Party in the Judicial Branch: In most states judicial elections are nonpartisan. But because Texas judges run in partisan elections, the political parties are able to implement their judicial agenda. For example, Republicans tend to be strict on law and order, approve the death penalty, oppose lax immigration laws, favor limiting late term abortions, and support gun rights. In these ways judges are able to implement the Republican agenda.

NOTES

Randolph B. Campbell. *Gone to Texas: A History of the Lone Star State.* Oxford: Oxford University Press, 2003.

Platform of the Republican Party of Texas: https://www.texasgop.org/wp-content/uploads/2016/01/PERM-PLATFORM.pdf

Texas Democratic Party Platform: http://www.cherokeecountytexasdemocrats.org/Platforms/Texas_Democrat_Platform_2016.pdf

ESSAY QUESTIONS

1. Describe the main features of a one-party state such as Texas.
2. Compare the 2016 platforms of the Republican and Democratic parties.
3. Explain how political parties are weaker today than they were in the past.

TERMS

Anti-Saloon League: ____________________

Australian Ballot: ____________________

Boll Weevil Democrats: ____________________

Greenback Party: ____________________

Party realignment: ____________________

Political parties: ________________________________

Political platform: ________________________________

Poll tax: ________________________________

Precinct chair: ________________________________

Primary: ________________________________

State party chair: ________________________________

Ticket splitting: ________________________________

White primary: ________________________________

Yellow Dog Democrats: ________________________________

TEXAS FUN & FACTS SHEET 9

Deep in the Heart of Texas

Deep in the Heart of Texas is one of the most popular songs about Texas. It was written by June Hershey and Don Swander. In 1942, it was recorded by two famous singers, Perry Como and Bing Crosby, and spent a combined twelve weeks on the *Hit Parade*.

Other artists who have recorded the song include Roy Rogers, Ray Charles, and George Strait, who has the song played at every concert before he comes on stage.

The University of Texas Longhorn Band performs the song during each football pregame. The Houston Astros play the song during the seventh inning stretch. And the Rangers play the song in the middle of the fifth inning.

LYRICS

The stars at night—are big and bright
Deep in the heart of Texas.

The prairie sky—is wide and high
Deep in the heart of Texas.

The sage in bloom—is like perfume
Deep in the heart of Texas.

Reminds me of—the one I love
Deep in the heart of Texas.

The cowboys cry—ki-yip-pie-yi
Deep in the heart of Texas.

The rabbits rush—around the brush
Deep in the heart of Texas.

The coyotes wail—along the trail
Deep in the heart of Texas.

The doggies bawl—and bawl and bawl
Deep in the heart of Texas.

© Kathy Hutchins / Shutterstock.com

Democrats **How USA voted 2016** Republicans

The winning Electoral Votes

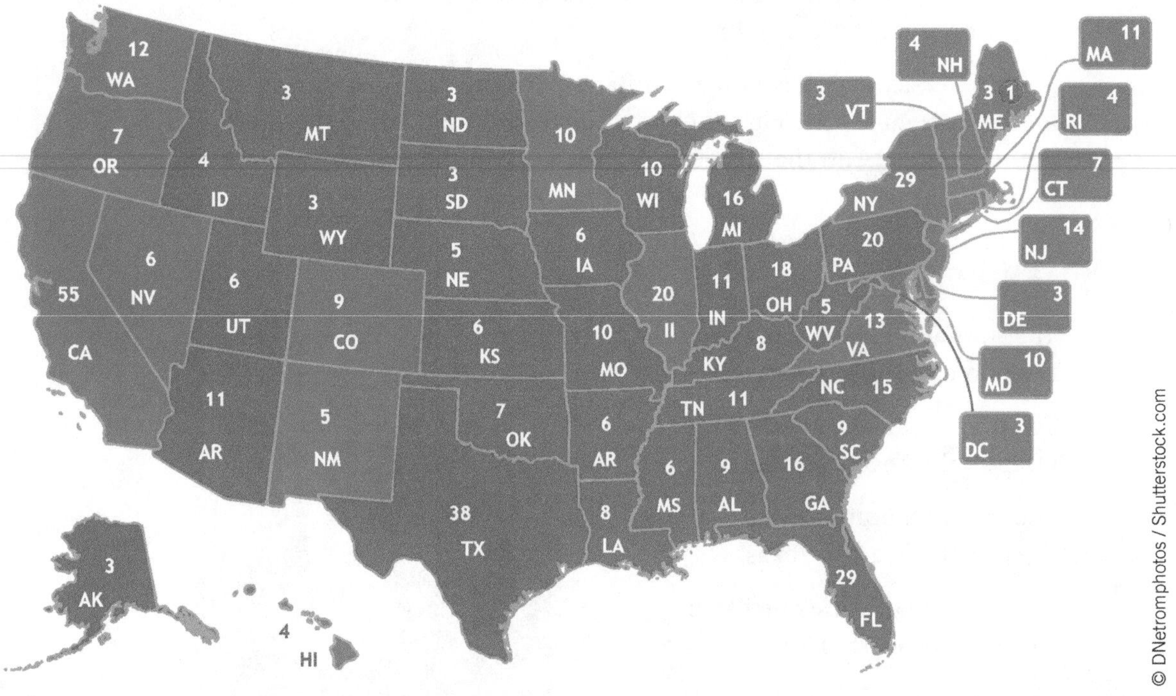

Electoral Map, 2016

CHAPTER 16

Political Campaigns

TOPICS

- Campaigning in Texas
- Who Wins Elections?
- Financing Campaigns
- Interest Groups and Electioneering
- Texas Campaign Finance Laws

LEARNING OBJECTIVES

When you finish reading this chapter, you will be able to:

1. Explain how the main feature of a political campaign, including the media campaign.
2. Describe what candidates are likely to win elections.
3. List ways candidates raise and spend money.
4. Describe the different types of interest groups and how they influence elections.
5. Summarize the federal and state campaign finance laws.

The word "campaign" comes from an Old French term, meaning military maneuvers in the open field. Over time the term has been extended to politics. A **campaign** *is political activity before an election, marked by organized action to influence voters and win an election.* To some extent a political campaign is like a military battle. Each side has its leaders, which decide the tactics. And each side has its masses of volunteers and recruits that spread out to win victory. At the end of the long, arduous, expensive,

The word "campaign" originally referred to military campaigns, of which there are many similarities.
© Nagel Photography / Shutterstock.com

and at times painful contest, there will be one victor and one loser. As the saying goes "campaigns aren't beanbag," and so anybody who decides to run for political office must be prepared for the physical, mental, and emotional strain of competition.

CAMPAIGNING IN TEXAS

In Texas, primary campaigns start in January and end on the second Tuesday in March. General election campaigns usually start on Labor Day and end on the first Tuesday after the first Monday of November. During this time candidates engage in many activities to win the battle and persuade citizens to vote for them. They pay for advertisements, go door-to-door, give speeches, kiss babies, consult pollsters, speak to interest groups, talk with reporters, make phone calls, and participate in debates. And to pay for all these activities, they go to fundraisers and talk with potential donors.

Campaign

Political activity before an election, marked by organized action to influence voters and win an election.

Political Consultants: Just as an army needs generals to plan and execute the military strategy, candidates hire political consultants to run their campaigns. In a major statewide campaign, such as a Texas gubernatorial race, a candidate will hire a team of political consultants. The three most important are the campaign manager, communications director,

Karl Rove was George Bush's campaign manager.
© MCT/Contributor/Getty

and the financial chair. The *communications director* talks with the press, supervises speech writers, makes the talking points, and oversees advertisement production. And the *financial chair* keeps track of donations, audits accounts, and fills out forms in compliance with federal and state campaign finance laws.

Of course, *the person who oversees the campaign staff and heads the campaign* is the **campaign manager**. The typical duties of the campaign manager include advising the candidate, determining where and when to allocate financial and human resources, making the day-to-day decisions, orchestrating the get-out-the-vote effort, and, perhaps most importantly, developing the strategy.

Campaign manager

The person who oversees the campaign staff and heads the campaign.

A good campaign manager will develop an *overarching theme* or narrative of the campaign. For example, in Rick Perry's 2010 campaign, his theme, although not explicitly stated, was "vote for me as I fight the liberal agenda of Obama and the overweening federal government." The voters must have a sense of why the candidate is running for office and what his political agenda is. If a candidate is just running to attain higher office, the voters will not feel particularly inspired to vote for that person.

In the old days, candidates had very small staffs and did most of the work themselves. A typical campaign would consist of driving around Texas, visiting as many towns as they could and delivering a **stump speech**: *a standard speech used by candidates running for office that is used over and over again with minor alterations depending on who they are speaking to.* This term derived from the nineteenth century custom of politicians standing on a tree stump to speak to people in rural areas. Today it is more difficult for politicians to rely on one stump speech because the media will broadcast the speech statewide and thus people will expect new material and new ideas as the campaign progresses.

Media: A major part of any modern political campaign is the media strategy. **Media,** *which is plural for medium, refers to all the forms of mass communication, such as television, radio, newspapers, internet, billboards, and mailings.* One of the primary tasks of any campaign is to use the media to make sure that potential voters know the candidate's name. This is called *name recognition.* People will not vote for you unless they know your name.

One of the best examples of the importance of name recognition comes from Bill Clements's victorious gubernatorial campaign in 1978. At the time, Clements was a successful business man who owned the world's largest offshore drilling company, but he had never held public office in Texas. He knew that the first thing he had to do was to get people to know his name. So, he paid hundreds of thousands of dollars for billboard and newspaper ads that feature CLEMENTS in large letters. It worked and he won. This is because only after voters know a politician's name will they pay attention to his candidacy.

Political Advertisements: Today, political advertisements are much more sophisticated and try to accomplish more than just raising name recognition. Political consultants will hire pollsters and conduct focus groups to test words, themes, and positions on the issues. All this data goes into the production of television and Internet ads. Typically, Texas political ads fall into three broad categories: The *feel good cowboy ads, positive ads,* and *negative ads.*

We have all seen the *feel good cowboy* commercial. It is especially common for candidates running for judge or sheriff, but is used by nearly all politicians running for office in Texas. Rick Perry effectively used it over his entire career. The feel good cowboy commercial depicts the candidate in cowboy boots and jeans walking through a ranch, usually in the orange glow of sunrise. While grooming a horse or drinking a cup of coffee or even holding a rifle, the candidate looks into the camera and talks about how he was raised on the values of hard work, community, and religion. If

Stump speech

A standard speech used by candidates running for office that is used over and over again with minor alterations depending on who they are speaking to.

Media

(plural for medium) refers to all the forms of mass communication, such as television, radio, newspapers, Internet, billboards, and mailings.

During Rick Perry's political career, Perry perfected the "feel good cowboy" commercial.
© ASSOCIATED PRESS

he brings up issues, they are broadly about law and order, gun rights, religious freedom, and small government, emphasizing the traditional values of self-reliance and individualism.

The feel good cowboy ad actually falls under the broader category of **positive ads**: *commercials that depict the candidate in a positive light, highlighting the candidate's ideas and accomplishments while making no reference to the opponent.* Positive ads will often display loving photos of the candidate's family or show him or her talking with regular people at a diner or gas station. These commercials hope to make the voter identify with the candidate and illicit positive feelings about the candidate as a person.

Positive ads

Campaign commercials that depict the candidate in a positive light, highlighting the candidate's ideas and accomplishments while making no reference to the opponent.

This is in contrast to the **negative ads**: *commercials that attack the opponent's character, record, or bring up some sort of scandal or misstep.* When launching a new campaign, candidates will often say: "I am going to run on my ideas and my record and not get in the dirt with my opponent." But invariably by the end of their campaign they run negative ads. This is because during any campaign the opposition will criticize the record or words of a candidate, and in turn the candidate will feel the need to retaliate and return fire. But there is another reason negative ads are so effective. It is human nature to remember the bad things we hear about somebody and forgot the good things.

Negative ads

Campaign commercials that attack the opponent's character, record, or bring up some sort of scandal or misstep.

WHO WINS ELECTIONS?

So, how do you win a political campaign? One way to look at it is that there are certain things a candidate can control and other things beyond the control of the candidate. The baseball player Lefty Gomez once said, "I'd rather be lucky than good," and this often applies to politics.

For example, at the end of the 2012 presidential campaign a major storm, "Hurricane Sandy," hit the northeast. This gave Barack Obama, as president, the opportunity to tour the devastated areas with the press and offer sympathy and federal funds to people whose homes and businesses had been destroyed. On the other side, Mitt Romney decided to suspend his campaign for a few days because it would look bad to continue campaigning while people were suffering. In the end, a significant number of people told pollsters that they decided to vote for Obama because he looked so presidential after the storm. This illustrates the fact that a candidate can never know what sort of thing will pop up and change the dynamics of an election.

Run a Good Campaign: Barring some unforeseen incident, the way to win an election is to execute a good campaign. A good campaign is marked by a high level of energy and few mistakes. Two things in particular are important. First, mobilize groups that traditionally support your party. For Democrats, these groups would include unions, minority organizations, pro-choice groups, government workers, and liberal interest groups. For Republicans, these would include small business organizations, religious groups, gun rights advocates, and conservative interest groups. Candidates will spend a lot of time speaking to these groups in order to energize the base, raise money, and seek their assistance in the get-out-the-vote effort.

The second aspect of a good campaign is for the candidate to pick the right issues to emphasize. In Texas, it is nearly impossible to win statewide elections unless a candidates supports lower taxes, gun rights, law and order, border security, smaller government, balanced budgets, right to life, and education reform. In the 2014 gubernatorial race, Wendy Davis was able to win the Democratic primary by focusing on women's rights and abortion. But these issues do not play so well in the general election, thus she tried to pivot to more conservative issues like gun rights. The voters, however, were not convinced that these were the issues she was passionate about and her opponent, Greg Abbott, won the election.

Party Identity: Even if a candidate runs a fantastic campaign, he or she can lose an election. This is because most people vote based on party identity and ignore everything else. The bottom line is that nearly all

Usually, the most likable candidate wins. Polls showed that President Obama had high candidate appeal, especially as a family man and father.
© Everett Collection / Shutterstock.com

Democrats are going to vote for the Democratic candidate even if he is Frankenstein. And nearly all of the Republicans are going to vote for the Republican candidate even if he is Dracula. Typically, 90–95 percent of people vote for the candidate of the party they identify with. So, if you are running as a Democrat today in Texas, you are going to have a more difficult time winning elections because there are less registered Democrats than Republicans.

Incumbency: Besides party identity, the other important factor that influences voters is incumbency (the incumbent is the person in office). It is a truism that the candidate that currently holds office almost always defeats the challenger. There are many reasons for this. The incumbent has better name recognition. The incumbent attracts more press coverage. And it is much easier for an incumbent to raise money. In Congress, the incumbent representative wins about 95 percent of the time.

Candidate appeal

A positive feeling a voter has about a candidate's personality, physical appearance, family, intellect, humor, and way of speaking.

Likability: Lastly, the final factor that determines who wins elections is likability. The most likable candidate usually wins elections. Another term for likability is **candidate appeal**: *A positive feeling a voter has about a candidate's personality, physical appearance, family, intellect, humor, and way of speaking*. The reason why candidate appeal so often determines election is that this is how the independent voter often casts his ballot. Democrats will vote for the Democratic candidate, and Republicans will vote for the

Republican candidate, but independents have no party loyalty. They often vote by a gut feeling on who they like best, not on the issues. So, likability is the last determinative factor in who wins elections.

FINANCING CAMPAIGNS

With 268,581 square miles, Texas is the second largest state in America, thus it is very expensive to run for statewide office in Texas. Anybody pondering running for office in Texas must first consider how he or she will raise enough money to finance a viable campaign. To run for governor, it takes tens of millions of dollars. According to the National Institute on Money in State Politics, in 2014 Gregg Abbott spent $47,464,000 and Wendy Davis spent $8,762,000 on their campaigns. And in 2010, Rick Perry spent $49,000,000 and Bill White spent $26,291,000.

Other statewide offices are also quite costly. In 2014, Dan Patrick spent $18,278,000 on his campaign for Lieutenant Governor. Ken Paxton spent $8,337,000 to become Attorney General. Glenn Hegar spent $5,000,000 on his campaign for comptroller. And George P. Bush spent $5,292,000 to become land commissioner.

Considering the size of Texas, it makes sense that running for statewide office is expensive, but today it is even quite costly to run for a relatively small legislative district. In 2014, Konni Burton spent $2,997,000 for her race for the state senate seat representing for district 10. Don Huffines spent $2,439,000 on his state senate race. And Wayne Faircloth spend $1,232,000 to become a state representative. Incidentally, these people spent millions of dollars to get a job that pays only $7,200 a year!

Where does the money come from? So, where do candidates get all this money? Politicians try to raise money via their websites from small donors. Although this looks the most democratic, it seldom brings in enough money to finance a strong campaign. Consequently, candidates must solicit large contributions from big donors such as wealthy individuals, corporations, banks, law firms, unions, and other interest groups. And some candidates borrow money. In 2002, David Dewhurst borrowed $12 million for his successful bid to run for Lieutenant Governor. Another option for some candidates, if they are rich, is to self-finance.

It takes a lot of money to run for office in Texas.

In 2002, Democratic candidate Tony Sanchez, who owned an oil and natural gas exploration company, spent $27 million of his own money to run against Governor Rick Perry. Although he spent more money than Perry, Sanchez lost. This illustrates two points. Wealthy people have an advantage in that they can spend their own money to run for office. But it also shows that the candidate that spends the most money is not always the winner.

Another way to raise money for a campaign is to get money from interest groups. Legally, interest groups must make their contributions to political campaigns through **Political Action Committees (PAC):** *An organization formed by an interest group to raise and contribute money to a campaign of a candidate that the organization thinks will advance its cause.* Much of the money candidates get comes from PACs.

A list of the top PACs in Texas can be found on the website of the National Institute on Money in State Politics. The following are some of the top Texas PACs: *Texans for Lawsuit Reform*, a pro-business PAC, contributed over $5 million to mostly Republican candidates in 2014, including $193,000 to Greg Abbott. The *Texas Association of Realtors*, which has given over $18 million to Republican and Democratic candidates over the last 20 years. *Empower Texans*, a conservative interest group, has contributed over $4 million to 130 Republicans over the last ten years. And *Border Health*, a PAC the represents the health care industry, has given nearly $8 million over the last thirteen years to mostly Democrats.

Political Action Committee (PAC)

An organization formed by an interest group to raise and contribute money to a candidate's campaign.

Why Do People and Groups Give Money to Candidates? Many have ideological reasons. Liberal people and groups will support liberal candidates, and conservative individuals and groups will support conservative candidates. In Texas, most PAC money comes from businesses. They tend to give money to both parties, especially incumbents with power. They are buying access. They want to be able to contact a lawmaker or government official to discuss issues that affect their business. Other individuals and groups will give money because they know the candidate. That is why successful candidates are often lawyers and businessmen who have developed a network of wealthy contacts.

Where Does the Money Go? Like a shopaholic on a spending spree, politicians can blow a lot of money on a campaign. Candidates spend money on newspaper ads, billboards, radio spots, bumper stickers, yard signs, phone banks, staff, consultants, and travel expenses. Paying for offices and travel expenses across a huge state like Texas is expensive. TV ads are expensive and prices go up before elections. A prime time ad during a popular show can cost $25,000 for thirty seconds. And media

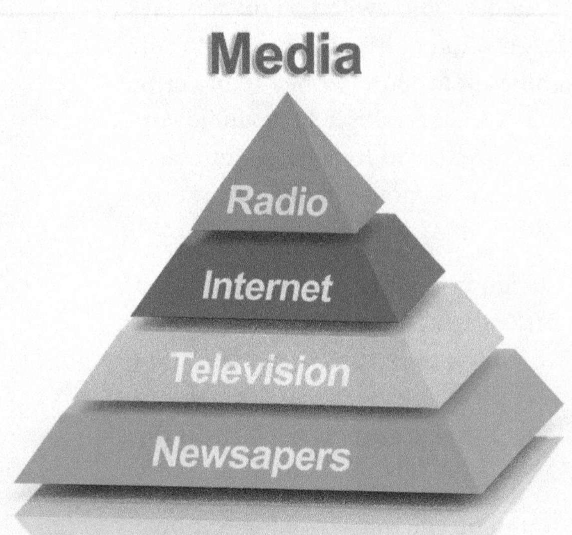

Political campaigns pay enormous amounts of money for media advertisements. Television commercials can cost tens of thousands of dollars for each airing.
© Stuart Miles / Shutterstock.com

and consulting firms charge a lot of money. A drive-time radio ad can cost $2,000 for sixty seconds. Billboards can cost up to $15,000 for a month in a major city. This gives you an idea how candidates can spend millions of dollars in a few months.

INTEREST GROUPS AND ELECTIONEERING

As the above discussion of PACs illustrates, interest groups play a major role in political campaigns. In Chapter 17, we will explain how interest groups influence public policy. In this section we will explain how interest groups work actively for a candidate or a political party, which is called *electioneering.*

Interest Groups

Groups of people that get together to form organizations in order to change public policy.

What Are Interest Groups? *Groups of people that get together to change public policy* are called **interest groups.** The US Constitution safeguards the right of interest groups to exist and to participate in the political process. The First Amendment protects freedom of speech, the right to assemble into groups, and the right to "petition the government for a redress of grievances." One way interest groups try to redress government grievances is to get people elected that will change the laws in a way that supports the concerns and goals of interest groups.

Interest Group Theory: There are two prominent theories about the nature of interest groups, one positive and one negative. James Madison, in the *Federalist Papers*, wrote about the positive nature of interest groups. He said that in any free society it is only natural that people will form groups to advance their beliefs. Madison argued that as long as there are a multitude of interest groups, with no one group dominating, society will benefit from this political participation. Madison pointed out that due to America's tremendous size, divided government, federal system, and diversity of economic and ideological interests, it is impossible for one group to dominate the political process of the United States.

James Madison formulated pluralistic theory in the *Federalist Papers*. In a pluralistic society power is distributed among many groups.

Madison's concept is often called **pluralistic theory**: *When many interest groups representing a wide variety of economic and ideological interests compete with each other in the political process, power is not concentrated in one group.* This is in contrast to monolithic society that may exist in a small geographical area. For example, in Texas before the Civil War, cotton was king and the cotton interests dominated Texas politics. If one interest group controls a state, society would likely stagnate or politics becomes corrupt. In Texas today, however, there are a wide-ranging, multiplicity of economic and ideological interest groups competing with each other. This type of pluralism is healthy for society.

In contrast to pluralistic theory, some people hold a negative view of interest groups. They argue the rich and powerful elements of society have undue influence on American politics. This is called **elite theory**, *which holds that a small group of wealthy and highly educated elites corrupt the political process for their own benefit at the expense of the general public.* This is actually a popular notion, but it is difficult to prove. There are so many rich people and powerful groups that it is impossible to point to one group and say they dominate American politics. For example, environmental groups have been successful at stopping oil companies from drilling in Alaska. And banks have been unable to stop the government from enacting strict financial regulations. But in general, it is certainly true that rich people have more political influence than poor people.

Pluralistic theory

When many interest groups representing a wide variety of economic and ideological interests compete with each other in the political process, power is not concentrated in one group.

Elite theory

The idea that a small group of wealthy and highly educated elites corrupt the political process for their own benefit at the expense of the general public.

Types of Interest Groups: Interest groups can be divided into three types: economic, social, and ideological. Economic interest groups would include corporations or industries, such as Microsoft, Apple, the movie industry, or the green industry. And trade associations represent another type of economic interest groups. The National Association of Realtors, the American Medical Associations (AMA), the American Bar

Association (ABA), and the Chamber of Commerce are very active in politics. Business and trade associations often give to both Republican and Democrats because they want *access* to whomever is in power. Perhaps the most politically active economic interest groups are unions. Labor unions, such as the AFL-CIO, and public sector unions, such as teacher unions and government worker unions, give tremendous money to Democratic candidates.

The other major type of interest group are social, representing a particular demographic segment of the population. Some of the top social interest groups include: groups representing older people, such as the American Association of Retired Persons (AARP), women's groups, such as the National Organization for Women (NOW), groups representing African Americans, such as the National Association for the Advancement of Colored People (NAACP), and Hispanic groups, such as La Raza. One of the top LGBT groups is the International Lesbian, Gay, Bisexual, Trans and Intersex Association. All these groups tend to give to the Democratic Party.

Ideological groups are motivated by an idea or a set of principles that apply to all social groups, regardless of race, class, or gender. Ideological groups include environmental groups, such as the Conservation Fund or the Sierra Club, Christian Groups, such as Focus on the Family, pro-choice groups, such as EMILY's List, gun rights groups, such as the National Rifle Association (NRA), and many others. Other groups are broadly liberal or conservative. Some of the most powerful liberal interest groups that give to Democrats are MoveOn.ORG, ActBlue, the American Civil Liberties Union, and People for the American Way. The top conservative groups that support Republicans are Americans for Prosperity, Freedom Works, the American Conservative Union, the American Family Association, and Citizens United.

Some of the most politically active interest groups are environmental organizations.

How Interest Groups Influence Elections: Interest groups participate in electioneering in a variety of ways. They give money, through their PACs, to candidates and political parties. They recruit candidates that share their values and train them to run for office. Some groups are known to endorse candidates and provide voter guides. Some interest groups provide staff, volunteers, phone banks, and office space. Other interest groups specialize in mobilizing voters and get like-minded people to the polls on Election Day. Lastly, many groups focus on paying for media commercials that support their candidates.

TEXAS CAMPAIGN FINANCE LAWS

People have long been concerned about the possible deleterious effects of money in politics. For over a hundred years, federal and state legislatures have made laws to regulate financial contribution to campaigns. Most of these laws, however, have been unsuccessful. The general pattern is as follows: legislatures pass a law to limit big money in politics, and interest groups and businesses find ways around them, resulting in a continuous escalation of money in politics.

This pattern has led some people to say, we might as well give up on the idea of banning money in politics. Instead, let's allow all groups to compete with each other and make the candidates disclose what contributions they accept. This is pretty much where Texas is today. Candidates in Texas can accept money as long as they list all the contributors on their website. The following is a basic summary of federal and state campaign finance laws.

Federal Campaign Finance Laws: The Federal Elections Commission (FEC) regulates and enforces federal election laws. In 2002, the Bipartisan Campaign Reform Act (BCRA), informally called the McCain-Feingold Act, established strict limits on campaign contributions. Now individuals can contribute $2,500 per candidate per election, and PACs can contribute $5,000. The Supreme Court, however, declared one aspect of BCRA unconstitutional. Originally, BCRA banned unions and corporations from running political ads sixty days before a general election. In *Citizens United v. FEC (2010)*, the Supreme Court ruled that the FEC cannot violate the freedom of speech of unions and corporations by prohibiting them from running political commercials.

Super PACs

These groups can raise unlimited funds to support a candidate as long as they report their contributions to the FEC and make commercials without coordinating with a campaign.

As a result of BCRA and *Citizens United*, today there are three entities that play a major part in federal elections. **Super PACs**: *these groups can raise unlimited funds to support a candidate as long as they report their contributions to the FEC and only engage in "independent expenditures," making commercials without coordinating with a campaign.* 501 (c) 4 Groups: These are non-profit groups that can participate in elections but only by engaging in generic civic functions. In 2012, the Obama administration faced a scandal when it was revealed that the IRS wouldn't recognize 501 groups that had "Tea Party" or other conservative titles. And bundlers are individuals that raise individual contributions of $2,500 to comply with FEC rules, but they bundle thousands of these contributions together and give a large sum to a candidate. For example, in 2012 Jeffrey Katzenberg, CEO of DreamWorks, bundled $1.8 million and gave it to the Obama campaign.

Texas Campaign Finance Laws: Texas campaign finance laws can be boiled down to six major points: (1) All candidates and PACs must file reports to the Texas State Ethics Commission. (2) All contributions of over $100 must be reported with the name of the contributor. (3) Each candidate must have an official treasurer, who is legally responsible to follow all campaign finance laws. (4) An expenditure report must be filed. (5) Direct contributions from corporations, unions, and banks are prohibited (but they can contribute through their PACs). And foreign contributions are prohibited. So, in Texas everything must be disclosed, but there are really no limits on individual or group contributions.

NOTES

Alexander Hamilton, John Jay, and James Madison. *The Federalists*. Indianapolis: Liberty Fund, 2001.

The National Institute on Money in Politics: https://www.followthemoney.org/

The Center for Responsive Politics: http://www.opensecrets.org/influence/

Texas Secretary of State, Election Information: https://www.sos.state.tx.us/elections/funds/primary-finance/index.shtml

ESSAY QUESTIONS

1. Describe how campaigns try to use media to influence voters and the three typical Texas political commercials.
2. Discuss the four factors that explain who wins an election.
3. List the three different types of interest groups and explain the ways interest groups try to influence elections.

TERMS

Campaign manager: ______________________________

Campaign: ______________________________

Candidate appeal: ______________________________

Elite Theory: ______________________________

Interest groups: ______________________________

Media: ______________________________

Negative ads: ______________________________

Pluralistic Theory: ______________________________

Political Action Committee (PAC): ______________________________

Positive ads: ______________________________

Stump speech: ______________________________

Super PACs: ______________________________

TEXAS FUN & FACTS SHEET 10

The Fishing Industry

© Harry Green / Shutterstock.com

- **Texas has 369 miles of coast line.**
- **In 2015, Texas brought in over 80 million pounds of seafood.**
- **The top fishing ports in Texas by pounds of fish:**

  Brownsville—Port Isabel (25 million pounds)
  Galveston (16 million), Palacios (15 million)
  Port Arthur (14 million)

- **The top species of fish caught in Texas with monetary value:**

  Brown Shrimp ($150 million)
  White Shrimp ($72 million)
  Eastern Oyster ($19 million)
  Red Snapper ($8 million)
  Marine Shrimp ($4 million)
  Blue Crab ($3 million)
  Black Drum ($2 million)
  Grouper ($1 million)

CHAPTER 17

Taxing and Spending

TOPICS

- Political Ideology and Economics
- State Taxes and Revenues
- Local Taxes
- Tax Issues
- Texas Spending
- Budgetary Process

LEARNING OBJECTIVES

When you finish reading this chapter, you will be able to:

1. Compare liberal and conservative economic viewpoints.
2. Discuss the main sources of revenue for Texas.
3. Explain important tax issues and concepts.
4. Discuss the main annual expenses of Texas.

Governments provide goods and services for the common good. Building roads and bridges, maintaining schools, providing for police and fire departments, and establishing libraries and parks are all things that state and local governments do to provide safety and happiness to the public. Governments pay for these services by collecting revenue from taxes, fees, penalties, and other sources. A big part of government involves making decisions about where to spend money and how to raise revenue.

Fights over the state budget are intense because it is when political rhetoric turns into tax and spending reality.

© dizain / Shutterstock.com

The government's policies about taxing and spending, as reflected in the budget, are called **fiscal policy**. Because the Texas legislature meets every other year in biannual sessions, it makes a two-year budget. The biannual budget is called the *biennium*. And every time the legislature begins to craft a new biennium it sparks a fight between Republicans and Democrats. This is because budgets reflect political values and priorities, and liberals and conservatives have different views on economics and fiscal policy.

This chapter will describe how Texas raises revenue and spends money, and it will explain some of the contentious issues involved in fiscal policy.

Fiscal policy

The government's policies about taxing and spending, as reflected in the budget.

POLITICAL IDEOLOGY AND ECONOMICS

Although economics deals with a lot of numbers and graphs, it is not a hard science like chemistry. Chemists do not argue about whether water consists of two hydrogen atoms or seven. But liberal economists will hold a completely different set of beliefs about economic principles than conservative economists. Most Texas government textbooks present the liberal economic point of view as if it was objective fact, but this textbook is different. We try to fairly present both sides so that the student can understand the economic and fiscal debates of our time.

Conservative economists hold that the profit motive is a good thing. It motivates people to work hard and innovate. Nobody would invent a cell phone or make you a hamburger unless they expected to make a profit. And conservative economists praise free market capitalism. No other system in world history has lifted more people out of poverty, sparked more scientific innovation, and provided for more individual freedom than capitalism. If you want to see examples of how socialism creates poverty, inequality, and despair, then look at the recent history of the Soviet Union, Maoist China, and Venezuela.

And conservative economists believe lower taxes benefits the whole economy. If individual tax rates are lower, then a person has more money to buy goods and services, which spreads money around to other businesses. And businesses that pay fewer taxes will make more profit and be able to hire more people. Nobody gets a job from a poor person or a failing business. And conservative economists think government should not spend more money than it collects in revenue. Huge government debt is irresponsible. Also, conservative economists think that too much welfare spending is harmful to the individual and to society. If a person gets dependent on government handouts, they lose the dignity of taking care of themselves and their own family. People gain a sense of self-worth if they struggle to achieve success on their own.

Liberal economists have a completely different view on these topics. Liberals disparage free market capitalism. As displayed by the popularity of Democratic presidential candidate Bernie Sanders (a socialist), more and more liberals are praising socialism. Instead of the profit motive, they want to achieve economic equality. They feel that money should be taken away from wealthy individuals and businesses and redistributed to the poor. This creates more fairness, harmony, and reduces class resentment.

Liberal economists argue for higher taxes and more government spending in order to create more material equality and to provide more services for the poor. Liberals believe in the welfare state that provides government programs from cradle to grave. They argue that government should provide childcare, preschool, college, school meals, housing, transportation, food stamps, medical care, and pensions. Liberal economists advocate deficit spending and have justified massive national debts as morally just because it is necessary to provide more government services for the poor. They feel that a robust welfare state creates more safety, equality, and social stability.

Since Texas is a conservative state, it is logical that Texas politicians would advocate conservative economic policies. This was made apparent by

Much of political debate revolves around economic issues. Conservative politicians like Ted Cruz support free markets, tax cuts, and economic growth.
© Crush Rush / Shutterstock.com

Governor Gregg Abbott's 2015 State of the State Address, in which he outlined a conservative economic agenda. Abbott said that Texas "leads the nation in job creation" because Texas has an agenda of smaller government, "individual liberty, and economic opportunity." If governments create a hostile environment for businesses by increasing taxes and regulations, then companies will move to other states and countries, taking their jobs with them.

And Abbott said that beyond lowering taxes, reducing regulations, cutting spending, and balancing the budget, there are other things the state of Texas should do. He pledged that his government will maintain law and order, secure the border, improve education, build more roads, and improve health care for all its citizens. These things are also ways the state government can stimulate economic growth.

Of course, Democrats were highly critical of Abbott's economic agenda as articulated in his State of the State Address. They have a different set of economic policies that they think are better. In our political system, the voters decide what candidate to elect based in large part on the economic policies they espouse. This is why it is important that the electorate is informed about economics and financial matters. Ultimately, the citizens will decide the economic agenda of the state and the country.

STATE TAXES AND REVENUES

Texas is one of only seven states that has no state income tax. And Texas is one of only four states with no corporate tax. But through a combination of other taxes and nontax revenue, Texas brings in enough money to run the state. According to the "Fiscal Size-Up for the 2016-2017 Biennium" (published by the Legislative Budget Board), it is estimated that Texas will bring in about $214 billion in 2016.

Consumer taxes

Taxes consumers pay when they purchase goods and services.

Excise taxes

Taxes on a particular good, such as gasoline, tobacco, and liquor.

Margin tax

A 1 percent tax on corporations and large partnerships.

Top Taxes Collected in 2016 with Percentages of Total Revenue

- Sales Tax (28 percent)
- Motor Vehicle Sales and Rental Tax (4.6 percent)
- Motor Fuels Tax (3.3 percent)
- Margin Tax (3.3 percent)
- Oil and Natural Gas Production Tax (2.7 percent)
- Cigarette, Tobacco and Alcohol Taxes (2.4 percent)
- Insurance Occupation Taxes (2.1 percent)
- Hotel Occupancy Tax (0.5 percent)
- Utility Taxes (0.5 percent)

Taxes: Altogether, revenue collected from taxes accounts for about 49 percent of the revenue for the 2016 budget. The single largest source of revenue for the state of Texas comes from **consumer taxes**: *these are taxes consumers pay when they purchase goods and services.* Consumer taxes mostly consist of *sales taxes*: a tax collected by the retailer at the point of sale, such as when one buys groceries or a refrigerator. Consumer taxes also include **excise taxes**: *a tax on a particular good, such as gasoline, tobacco, and liquor.* Sometimes these are called "sin taxes" because they are taxes on things that people choose to do that are harmful to the individual or society.

The largest category of revenue for Texas is consumer taxes, these are taxes on the purchase of such things as groceries, gas, and tobacco.
© bajinda / Shutterstock.com

Although Texas does not have an official "corporate tax," businesses in Texas pay a small tax in the form of a **margin tax** (what used to be called the franchise tax). *The margin tax is a 1 percent tax on corporations and large partnerships.* Small businesses do not have to pay the margin tax. Besides the margin tax, specific industries are targeted for taxes. Oil and natural gas companies pay "severance" taxes. The idea behind this tax is that these companies should pay a tax for extracting a natural resource that theoretically belongs to all the citizens of the state. And hotel, insurance, utility, and rental car companies are also targeted for special taxes. Sometimes it is not clear why some industries are expected to pay an extra tax, while others are not.

Federal Receipts: Besides taxes, the second largest source of revenue for the state of Texas is money from the federal government that was collected by federal income taxes. In the 2016–2017 biannual, it is estimated that the state of Texas will receive $73 billion in federal receipts, which accounts for 34 percent of state revenues. Most of this money goes to health and human services and to transportation.

The federal government provides these funds by two methods. **Categorical grants** *are monetary grants to states in which Congress appropriates funds for specific purposes, usually with certain conditions and regulations attached.* Categorical grants are used for things such as welfare or health care. But most of the federal funds come in the form of **block grants**, *which are Federal funds for a general purpose that give states significant leeway on how to spend the money, usually with less conditions and regulations.*

Categorical Grants

Federal monetary grants to the states for specific purposes, which comes with federal rules and regulations.

Block Grants

Federal money that is transferred to the states with no strings attached to be used for general purpose.

Non-Tax Revenue: There are other ways governments raise revenues besides what are officially called taxes. *Nontax revenue* is government revenue derived from fees that were paid for a variety of government goods and services and other investments. Often politicians raise fees and service charges rather than "taxes" because it is politically dangerous to raise taxes.

For the 2016–2017 biennium, it is estimated that nontax revenue will make up 15 percent of revenue. Nontax revenue includes (1) licenses, fees, fines, licenses, and penalties, (2) interest and income, (3) land income, (4) and lottery. In 2015, Texas lottery ticket sales totaled $4.5 billion, but only $1.2 billion went to the Foundation School Fund.

Various State Funds: One aspect of the Texas budget that makes it especially complicated to understand is that money comes from a variety of funds set up to pay for different state functions. Indeed, there are over 400 funds held in the Texas state treasury.

The following includes a brief description of four important Texas funds. The *Permanent School Fund (PSF)* was established in 1854 to provide funds for K-12 education. The *State Highway Fund* allocates financial resources for the construction, maintenance, and policing of the state highways. The money comes from taxes on gasoline, motor vehicle registration, and motor oil. The *Rainy Day Fund* was established by a constitutional amendment in 1988 to provide funds for the state during recessions or other periods of economic distress. At the end of 2015, it had $8.5 billion. And the *Permanent University Fund (PUF)* was established in 1876 to provide money to University of Texas and Texas A & M University systems. The PUF collects revenue from 2.1 million acres of land in West Texas.

LOCAL TAXES

The above sections describe taxes and revenue collected by the Texas state government, but local governments have their own taxes. Cities, counties, special districts, and school districts are financed primarily through two types of taxes: sales taxes and property taxes. These account for about half of their revenue, with the remaining revenue coming from the state and federal government. Like other states with no income tax, Texas has higher sales and property taxes than most states.

Sales Taxes: By Texas law, local sales taxes cannot exceed 2 percent. When this is added to the state sales tax of 6.25 percent, the highest sales tax permitted in Texas is 8.25 percent. But according to the Tax Foundation, the average sales tax across Texas is 8.17 percent, making it the twelfth highest sales tax rate in the nation.

Property Taxes: In Texas, property taxes provide most of the funding for public schools, but it also provides revenue for city and county governments. The effective real estate tax in Texas is 1.93 percent, the fifth

The effective real estate tax in Texas is 1.94 percent, the fifth highest in the nation.

highest in the nation. The median value of a Texas home is $131,400 with the average tax bill of $2,537.

TAX ISSUES

Issues related to taxes play a large part in the political debate between liberals and conservatives. In general, liberals like Barack Obama, Hillary Clinton, and Bernie Sanders advocate more taxes as a way to achieve income equality and to pay for government services. And conservatives like Donald Trump, Ted Cruz, and Gregg Abbott advocate lowering taxes to enhance economic freedom and to stimulate job growth. In this section we will discuss various tax issues, knowing that liberals and conservatives often interpret these issues according to their different political values.

Tax Fairness: How much should people be taxed? What is a fair amount of money people should give to the government for all the services it provides? In Vietnam (a communist country), the highest federal income tax rate is 35 percent. In Switzerland it is 33 percent, and in Russia it's only 13 percent. America actually has one of the highest tax rates in the world at 39.6 percent. When you add state income tax, sales taxes, and property taxes, a wealthy person in a state like California (with a 13 percent state income tax) can pay over 50 percent of their income in taxes.

A recent poll by the Pew Research Center shows that 61 percent of the American people feel that wealthy people do not pay "their fair share." But according to a report by the Tax Foundation that reviewed 2012 IRS data, the top 5 percent of earners pay 59 percent of all federal income taxes, and the top 10 ten pay 70 percent of all federal taxes. In stark contrast, the bottom 50 percent of earners pay only 2.8 percent of federal income taxes.

Tax Incentives: By using tax laws as carrots and sticks, taxes can be used to change human behavior. Governments tax things that are considered bad, like cigarettes and alcohol ("sin taxes"). While governments give tax breaks for behavior it considers good, like giving to charity, owning a house, or having children. And some taxes are used to stop people from depleting scarce resources. For example, fishing and hunting license fees are designed to protect fish and wildlife populations. And high water fees can be used to encourage people to conserve water in times of drought.

Governments also reward and punish businesses. The coal industry pays high taxes and licensing fees. But other businesses, such as the green industry and farmers, get generous tax breaks. Companies pay a lot of money to lobbyists to make sure that the government does not add taxes to their particular industry. And businesses pay a lot of money to tax attorneys to study the complex tax codes to find loopholes. In this way, large companies enjoy a big advantage over small businesses which cannot afford expensive lobbyists and tax attorneys to review all the regulations.

A complex tax code that rewards and punishes different types of economic activity can lead to **crony capitalism**: *a system in which business success is enhanced by connections to government officials, knowledge of legal loopholes and tax breaks, and by government favoritism.* Some economists argue that it is better to have a small flat tax on all businesses and get rid of the loopholes. The market, they argue, should determine businesses' success, not government.

Competitive Federalism: In our system of federalism, each state has the power to make its own fiscal policy and tax laws. Many states base their economic policy, in part, with an eye to encouraging businesses and people to relocate to their state. This is called **competitive federalism**: *when states compete with other states to attract businesses and people.*

Governor Rick Perry was an aggressive practitioner of competitive federalism. In order to create more jobs, Perry launched a campaign to attract businesses to Texas. He publicized that Texas has no state income tax, very low business taxes, and less regulations than other states. He also made it known that in 2003 Texas passed sweeping *tort reform* that made it more difficult to file frivolous malpractice and business lawsuits. Furthermore, Perry used the *Texas Enterprise Fund (TEF).* Created in 2003, the TEF provides funds to businesses as a "closing deal" reward for companies to help pay for the expense of relocating to Texas. All this helped bring about the "Texas economic miracle," which created 2.1 million jobs during Perry's tenure from 2000 to 2014.

Benefit-Based Taxes: Some people think that the people that use a particular government service should pay more for it, rather than the whole society. **Benefit-based taxes** *are taxes on a government service by the people who use that service.* For example, gas taxes pay for maintenance and construction of roads. People who drive a lot will pay more gas taxes. Other examples of benefit-based taxes are fees for such things as public golf courses, public pools, camping parks, garbage collection, college, hunting fees, and water usage. In recent years, benefit-based taxes have become more popular in Texas and other states.

Some benefit-based taxes are more controversial than others. For example, should libraries charge higher fees on the people that use libraries or should the general taxpayer pay for free public libraries? Most people

Crony capitalism

A system in which business success is enhanced by connections to government officials, knowledge of legal loopholes and tax breaks, and by government favoritism.

Competitive Federalism

The ideas that states compete with each other to attract businesses and people to their states by offering incentives.

Benefit-based taxes

Taxes on a government service by the people who use that service.

Benefit-based taxes are taxes on a government service that are paid for by the people that use that service, such as public golf course fees.
© romakoma / Shutterstock.com

feel that services that provide an important social benefit, like education, should be paid for by the general public. But when the usage of a thing is clearly recreational, like hunting or golfing, the user should pay a fee.

Progressive and Regressive Taxes: Political scientists have created two terms that describe how the burden of taxes affects the rich and poor. *Taxes in which wealthy people pay a higher percentage of their income* are called **progressive taxes**. The federal income tax is very progressive. For example, if you make $30,000 a year you pay a 15 percent federal income tax, and if you make $400,000 you pay a 39.6 percent federal income tax. Many people feel that since rich people have a large *disposable income* (money left over after they pay for necessities like food and housing), they should pay more taxes.

Progressive taxes

Taxes in which wealthy people pay a higher percentage of their income.

Regressive taxes

Taxes in which poor people pay a higher percentage of their income in taxes.

Regressive taxes *are taxes in which poor people pay a higher percentage of their income in taxes.* Since Texas does not have an income tax but instead relies heavily on consumer taxes, Texas has a regressive tax structure. Poor families in Texas pay a higher percentage of their income on sales taxes, alcohol taxes, tobacco taxes, gas taxes, and lottery tickets. One argument for creating a state income tax in Texas is that it would reduce the tax burden on the poor and shift it to the wealthy.

Tax Shifting: Tax policy is often more complicated than it may at first appear. For example, many people say that we should tax big businesses because they have all the money. But in reality, they often do not actually pay the tax due to **tax shifting**: *passing the tax on to other people.* Businesses seldom pay for a tax out of their own profits, but instead pass on the tax to consumers in the form of higher prices or to the workers in the form of lower wages. So in reality, taxes on businesses are often a tax on average people who buy things or work.

Since much of Texas's revenue comes from the taxes on the oil and gas industry, revenues fluctuate widely as the price of oil goes up and down.
© W. Scott McGill / Shutterstock.com

Income-Elastic Taxes: *When tax revenue fluctuates widely due to economic conditions, this is known* as **income-elastic taxes**. Texas is more sensitive than most states to economic conditions because Texas is very dependent on the tax revenue from the oil and natural gas industry, which is highly volatile. For example, in May of 2008, a barrel of oil cost $139. But by January 2016, a barrel of oil cost only $28! When the price of oil and natural gas drops the fossil fuel companies let go a lot of workers. This not only hurts the Texas oil and gas industry, it hurts the Texas budget. To help reduce revenue fluctuations triggered by recessions and the volatile fossil fuel industry, the Texas legislature created the Economic Stabilization Fund ("the rainy day fund") to provide money during economic downturns.

TEXAS SPENDING

According to the website "Texas Transparency" created by the comptroller's office (which certifies the budget), it is estimated that Texas will spend $209 billion in 2016.

Texas spending by agency for 2016 with expenditures:

1. Health and Human Services Commission ($226 million)
2. Texas Education Agency ($215 million)
3. Teacher Retirement System ($89 million)
4. Texas Department of Transportation ($84 million)
5. Comptroller State Fiscal ($61 million)
6. Comptroller Treasury Fiscal ($54 million)
7. Department of Aging and Disability Services ($49 million)
8. Employee Retirement System of Texas ($49 million)
9. Department of Criminal Justice ($28 million)
10. Department of Health Services ($24 million)

Tax shifting

When businesses pass the tax on to other people.

Income-elastic taxes

When tax revenue fluctuates widely due to economic conditions.

Like most states, Texas spends most of its budget on four items: education, health and welfare, transportation, and public safety.

Education: Education accounts for the largest expenditure for the state of Texas. There are 1,037 school districts in Texas with approximately 5 million students and 325,000 teachers. The Texas school system is financed from three sources: local, state, and federal governments. Local school districts fund their operations with local property taxes, paying for about 60 percent of the total school budget. Most of the state money comes from the Permanent School Fund and one-fourth from the motor fuel tax. And the rest of the money comes from the federal government, which mostly pays for school nutrition programs and special needs students.

Health and Human Services: The second largest category of state expenditure is health and human services. This accounts for about 36 percent of the budget. Much of the money for these programs also comes from the federal government, such as Medicaid and Medicare programs. These are redistributive services that move money from the taxpayer to low income individuals and families. To be eligible for most of these programs, the applicant must show that their income level is below the poverty line.

Public Safety: This category includes police departments and prison operations. The budget for the Texas Department of Criminal Justice is $3 billion. There are ninety-four prisons and twenty state jails in Texas, housing about 155,000 inmates.

Transportation: The state highways are built and maintained by the Department of Transportation, headed by a five-member commission appointed by the governor. Texas has over 80,000 miles of highways. The state finances about 53 percent of the transportation budget, with the rest of the funds coming from the federal government. Most of the state money comes from a gas tax, motor oil tax, and car registration fees.

BUDGETARY PROCESS

At no other time is politics more real than when the budget is being made. This is when lawmakers face tremendous pressure from interest groups, lobbyists, government agencies, constituents, and political consultants about where to spend the state's limited financial resources. Should we build more roads? Should teachers get a raise? Should colleges get more funding? Should we construct more prisons? Should we hire more police officers? Should we spend more to protect the environment? During the budgetary process, lawmakers must make these tough decisions as they decide what programs to fund and what programs to cut.

It is very expensive to maintain the 80,000 miles of Texas highways.

Major Entities in the Budgetary Process: One of the continual themes of this book is that the Texas government is decentralized and this is true once again for the Texas budgetary process. Unlike the federal government, which has developed a process by which the executive and legislative branch share in the task of making an annual budget, Texas has three independent entities that play a role in the Texas budgetary process: the Governor, the Legislature, and the Comptroller.

Legislative Budget Board (LBB)

A ten-member state agency that is headed by the Speaker and the Lieutenant Governor that writes the budget.

The governor's office prepares its own preliminary draft of the budget. This task is overseen by the *Governor's Office of Budget, Planning, and Policy* (GOBPP). For about a year before the budget is submitted, the GOBPP reviews agency budget requests, holds hearings, and strategically plans for the upcoming biennium. Finally, the governor's budget is submitted at the beginning of the legislative session.

Although the governor submits a budget to the Texas legislature, the legislature is free to ignore it, which it often does, especially if one or both chambers of the legislature are controlled by the opposition party. The Texas Legislature prepares its own budget through the **Legislative Budget Board (LBB)**, a ten-member legislative agency headed by the Speaker

Glenn Hegar is the Comptroller of Texas
© ASSOCIATED PRESS

and the Lieutenant Governor. They choose a budget director who evaluates the budget requests from each state agency. When the LBB budget is submitted, it constitutes the working draft from which the budget bill is crafted by the legislature.

The third major player involved in the budgetary process is the comptroller's office. At the beginning of the legislative session, the Comptroller submits a statement containing the estimate of the revenue expected over the biennium. This represents the spending ceiling above which the legislature cannot spend. For example, if the Comptroller says that the state will bring in $200 billion in revenue next year, then the legislature cannot spend more than that figure. This is in accordance to the Texas Constitution that mandates a balanced budget. And at the end of the session when the legislature finalizes the budget, the Comptroller must certify that the budget is balanced.

Steps in Budgetary Process: There are several steps in the budgetary process:

1. The GOBPP and the LBB prepare a budget proposal. This is based on an evaluation of the requests made from each state agency on how much money they need.

2. The comptroller's office submits the Biennial Revenue Estimate, which provides an economic forecast facing Texas and gives an account of all the money in the treasury. Most importantly, it provides an estimate of the revenue coming into the coffers of the state in the next two years. This sets the spending limit for the next session of the legislature.
3. The GOBPP's and the LBB's budget proposals are submitted to the legislature: In the Senate, it goes to the Senate Finance Committee. And in the House, it goes to the House Appropriations Committee.
4. Then budget bills go through the same process as any legislature, as described in Chapter 9 on the legislative process.
5. Each legislative chamber produces a budget bill and votes on it. Then the two bills are sent to the Conference Committee where they are reconciled. After much debate and compromise, the Conference Committee produces one bill.
6. Then the Comptroller must certify that the budget bill is balanced. If it is not balanced, it is sent to the House to be rewritten.
7. The certified budget bill must pass BOTH chambers with a majority vote.
8. The budget bill is then sent to the governor, where he can either sign it, veto it, or exercise his line item veto authority. At the beginning of the process, the legislature likely ignored his budget proposal. Now is the governor's chance to influence the state budget by striking out spending provisions that he doesn't approve of. These vetoes can be overridden by two-thirds of both chambers of the legislature, but the budget bill is usually the last bill to be passed and there is seldom any time to conduct an override.
9. The budget bill takes effect at the beginning of the next fiscal year, on September 1.

The 140-day legislative session is intense, and working on the budget is the final, exhausting task. After the Texas State Legislature passes the budget, they go home for a year.

NOTES

To view the 2016-17 Biennium Texas State Budget: http://www.lbb.state.tx.us/Documents/Publications/Fiscal_SizeUp/Fiscal_SizeUp.pdf

To view aspects of Texas's taxing and spending: http://www.texastransparency.org/

Greg Abbott's 2015 State of the State Address: gov.texas.gov/news/press-release/20543

Scott Drenkard and Nicole Kaeding, "State and Local Sales Tax Rates in 2016," *Tax Foundation*, March 9, 2016

Eric McWhinnie, "The 10 Worst for Property Taxes, The CheatSheet, May 30, 2016.

Jim McAlister, "Welcome to Houston, Texas—Still America's Economic Miracle," *Forbes*, Feb 27, 2015.

Pew Research Center, "Federal Tax System Seen in Need of Repair: Top Complaints: Wealthy, Corporations, 'Don't Pay Fair Share.' March 19, 2015.

ESSAY QUESTIONS

1. Compare the general economic ideologies of liberals and conservatives.
2. Compare progressive and regressive taxes. By citing at least three Texas tax policies, explain why the Texas tax system is progressive or regressive.
3. Explain where most of the Texas budget money goes.

TERMS

Benefit-based taxes: ______________________

Block grants: ______________________

Categorical grants: ______________________

Competitive federalism: ______________________

Consumer taxes: ______________________

Crony capitalism: ______________________

Excise taxes: ______________________

Fiscal policy: ____________________

Income-elastic taxes: ____________________

Legislative Budget Board (LBB): ____________________

Margin tax: ____________________

Progressive taxes: ____________________

Regressive taxes: ____________________

Tax shifting: ____________________

CHAPTER 18

Public Policy Process in Texas

TOPICS

- Who Makes Public Policy?
- The Public Policy-Making Cycle
- Problems with the Public Policy Process
- Red States versus Blue States
- Interest Groups and Public Policy

LEARNING OBJECTIVES

When you finish reading this chapter, you will be able to:

1. Describe the steps in the public policy process.
2. List the common flaws in making public policy.
3. Compare the public policies of liberal and conservative states.
4. Explain the strategies interest groups use to influence public policy.

What is Public Policy? *All the laws, regulations, funding, and priorities of government is* **public policy**. Actually, everything the government decides to do or not do is public policy. In the modern world, what the government has decided to do is much more than what the government has decided not to do. Government action is immense and far-reaching, touching nearly every aspect of our lives. Can you think of something you did today that government was not involved in? If you drove a car, turned on a light bulb, bought food, went to school, or texted a friend, those actions are regulated by some government body, and thus are part of public policy.

WHO MAKES PUBLIC POLICY?

All three branches play a part in making public policy: the legislative, judicial, and executive, including the bureaucracy.

Many government entities make public policy. And since Texas government is so decentralized, even more entities play a part in the public policy process in Texas than other states. The Texas state legislature makes law. The governor can sign directives and propose laws. And the seven statewide elected offices (Lieutenant Governor, Attorney General, Comptroller, Land Commissioner, Agriculture Commissioner, Railroad Commissioner, and members of the board of education) make policy in their designated fields of responsibility.

But this just touches the surface. Hundreds of Texas boards, commissions, and agencies make policy. And on the local level, city councils, county governments, special districts, and school boards make policies. In addition, when judges interpret the law and make judgments, they are making policies. So, many elected and nonelected officials are involved in the public policy process in Texas.

This is why it is inaccurate when somebody says, "*the government* has decided to do this or to ban that." In reality, there is no single entity called "government." In America, with its three branches of government, fifty state governments, and thousands of state and local government entities, government is not one monolithic body but rather a complex array of thousands of decision makers. This is one reason why studying public policy is so complex.

THE PUBLIC POLICY-MAKING CYCLE

Policy-making is a complicated process often shrouded from the public. To help students visualize how this process works, political scientists have developed the Public Policy Model that divides the process into five simple steps: (1) Agenda Setting, (2) Policy Formulation, (3) Policy Adoption, (4) Policy Implementation, and (5) Policy Evaluation. But the reader should know that in reality making public policy is a more intricate and convoluted process than this model suggests.

Public policy

All the laws, regulations, funding, and priorities of government.

Agenda setting

The process by which government decides that a problem exists and that it needs an imminent solution.

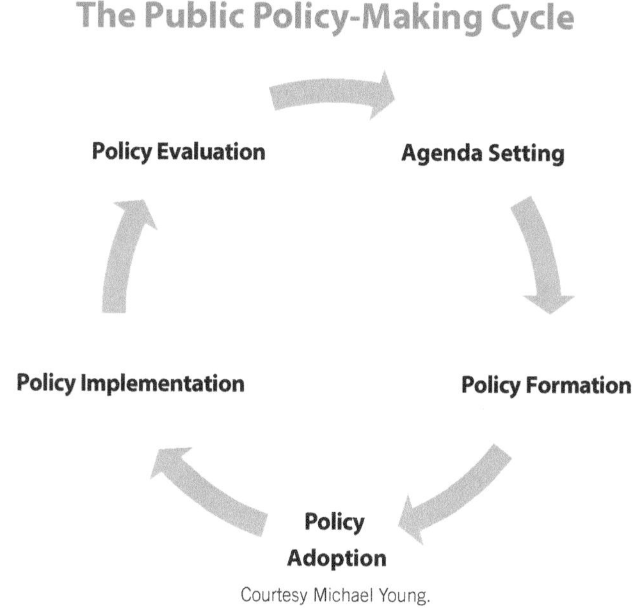

Courtesy Michael Young.

Agenda Setting: *The process by which government decides that a problem exists and that it needs an imminent solution is called* **agenda setting**. Before this can happen, the public needs to feel that a particular issue is a serious problem that needs to be solved now. For example, as the Zika virus spreads from Florida into Texas, people may begin to feel that public officials should devise a plan to deal with this growing health issue. In this way, the media often play a major role in agenda setting by educating the public, creating a sense of urgency, and explaining different policy solutions to the problem.

Policy Formation: As a problem grows, government officials start working on a solution to the problem. This is called *policy formulation*. As legislators craft a bill to address a particular problem, particularly if they are a member of a committee that deals with this issue, they will hold hearings and seek the advice of experts in the field. They may also study how other states or countries dealt with the same problem. An important aspect of formulating a policy is to estimate the cost of the proposed program. Any major government initiative is going to cost money, and that usually means that funds may have to be taken away from another program in order to pay for the new program.

Policy Adoption: When a government entity approves a proposal and makes it legally binding, this is called *policy adoption*. For example, when the legislature passes a bill with a majority vote in both chambers and it is signed by the governor, this is policy adoption. Or when a state agency approves a new policy or regulation, this too is policy adoption. In the case of the legislature, the policy usually needs much public support to get through the difficult process. This is less true of state agencies and commissions. They often make public policy with little media or public awareness.

Policy Implementation: *The process of actually carrying out the reform is called* **policy implementation**. The bureaucracy plays the leading role in this step. Government bureaucrats carry out the detailed and legalistic process of implementing a policy by crafting the rules and regulations that people and businesses must follow. The media often focus much attention on agenda setting and the policy adoption, but the press seldom writes about the important step of the policy implementation. This is a shame because many programs fail when they are not properly implemented.

Policy Evaluation: After a policy or a new agency that was created to implement the policy has been in existence for a number of years, it makes sense to review its performance and see if it is actually working. The process of assessing whether a policy is successfully achieving its intended objective is *policy evaluation*. Many government and non-government entities are involved in evaluating a policy, including legislative committees, governor's task forces, the press, academia, think tanks, and bureaucratic agencies.

Policy implementation

The process of actually carrying out the reform.

In Texas, there are a few agencies that have been created specifically to conduct policy evaluation. The Governor's Office of Budget, Planning, and Policy (GOBPP) and the Comptroller's Office routinely evaluate Texas government agencies, especially on their cost effectiveness. And every twelve years the Sunset Advisory Commission, a ten-member commission, reviews each state agency to evaluate whether it is efficiently doing its job and whether the agency should be abolished.

Before we end this section, students should understand a few things about the policy-making cycle. First of all, there is no beginning and no end. If a government entity or the public decide a policy is not working, then the whole process will start from the beginning with agenda setting and policy formulation. In this way, the Public Policy Model is a never-ending, circular process. Second, policy is seldom made by following each step in an orderly fashion, but may bounce around in a haphazard fashion. Often a law is quickly passed with no policy formation just for political show. The next section will give other examples of how the public policy process can be irrational.

PROBLEMS WITH THE PUBLIC POLICY PROCESS

Making good laws is a very difficult process that takes much study, experience, and prudence. Unfortunately, lawmakers often pass laws in the turbulent political environment with little or no time to properly study the issues. Here is a list of some of the pitfalls policy makers often fail to avoid.

The Law of Unintended Consequences: *Often lawmakers will pass a law to address one issue and then years later realize that they created other, unintended, problems. This is called the* **law of unintended consequences.** One of the most famous examples of this is Prohibition. In 1919, Congress implemented the Eighteenth Amendment, which made alcohol illegal. Contrary to popular belief, it was successful at reducing the consumption of alcohol. However, it also had the unintended consequence of creating a lucrative market for gangsters and bootleggers. A few years later Congress realized its mistake and repealed Prohibition.

Law of unintended consequences

Often lawmakers will pass a law to address one issue and then years later realize that they created other, unintended, problems.

Another example of unintended consequences is the Texas public school testing laws. Every year, high school students must take the State of Texas Assessment of Academic Readiness (STAAR) exams, testing students in

An unintended consequence of Texas's public school testing policy is that teachers teach to the test and ignore the normal curriculum.

English, math, science, and social studies. The legislature said these tests are necessary in order to see if the students are actually learning the core subjects taught in high school. But because poor performance on these tests can adversely affect a school district's reputation and financing, some teachers teach to the test and spend many weeks reviewing test-taking skills instead of actually teaching their subjects. So the unintended consequence of standardized testing is that students may be learning less of their core subjects, not more.

Compassion Trumps Reason: Politicians want to appear to be compassionate and generous, and so they often propose new programs to help the poor or the elderly or some other group even when they know the program won't work or there is no money to pay for it. When politicians run for office, they like to say they will pass a law for the government to provide "free" X, Y, and Z. On the other hand, politicians never run for office by saying they will *cut* programs X, Y, and Z in order to balance this budget. This impulse to be generous (with the taxpayer's money) has led to a national debt of $20 trillion, which is bad public policy.

Another example of how compassion trumps reason is the debate over the $15 minimum wage. Economists agree that a high minimum wage increases unemployment for the young, especially minority groups. Minimum wage jobs, like working at a fast food restaurant or bagging groceries, are entry level jobs designed to give people their first work experience. If the government mandates a high minimum wage, then restaurants will turn to automation and people will bag their own groceries. In April of 2016 Jerry Brown, the governor of California, signed into law a $15 minimum wage mandate. But later he said, "Economically, minimum wage may not make sense, but morally, socially, and politically they make every sense." This statement perfectly describes how in the political arena, laws that look compassionate often win out over laws that are economically sound.

One-Stage Thinking: Related to the above policy-making fallacies is what Thomas Sowell calls "one-stage thinking." As an economist, Sowell, a scholar at Stanford's Hoover Institute, is trained in thinking how a change in one economic variable can result in a multitude of changes down the line. Politicians, however, seldom think past the first stage.

An example of this is the Pell Grant and federal college loans. Today many students use the Pell Grant to help pay for college tuition and textbooks. In the old days, when parents paid for school with their hard earned money, it was very difficult for colleges to raise fees. But when a third party, the federal government, started paying the bills, then it was much easier for colleges to raise their prices. As a result, the price of a college education has skyrocketed over the last thirty years, rising a staggering 1,120 percent, an inflation rate four times higher than medical expenses. Student debt has also skyrocketed. In 2014, U.S. student loan debt exceeded $1.2 trillion, with over 7 million debtors in default.

The Progressive Impulse: Progressivism is characterized by the belief that the positive use of government can be used to fix all social ills. But in reality, many social problems cannot be fixed by government and in some cases non-government entities, like churches or private enterprise, may do some things better than government. But many politicians, Democrats and Republicans, get carried away by the progressive impulse.

A good example of this is Rick Perry's 2007 executive order requiring all Texas girls to receive a HPV vaccine, which protects them against the papilloma virus, a sexually transmitted disease that causes cervical cancer. The public was so upset by this that the legislature passed a law voiding Perry's executive order. The people of Texas felt that it is up to the medical community to decide what vaccines are needed for public safety.

Failure to Win Public Support: The last common fallacy politicians often commit when making public policy is the failure to win public support for a program *before* it is implemented. For big laws that effect a significant portion of the population, politicians need to do the hard work of going out to the public and explaining why a new policy is necessary. This is an essential requirement of step one of the Public Policy Model, agenda setting. The people must believe there is a problem that needs to be fixed and the government has the proper solution, otherwise they will not support a politician's initiative.

Early in Rick Perry's tenure as governor, he learned this valuable lesson. In 2001, Perry proposed the "Trans-Texas Corridor," a $150 billion project to build highways, railroads, and data cables through Texas and into Mexico. And he proposed that it be built and operated by private contractors, who would be paid by tolls. But Perry was never able to convince the public to go along with the plan. Many were angry that such a large public domain project would take away people's farms and homes, property that families held for generations. Others didn't like the idea of creating so many toll roads across Texas. In the end, the project died due to lack of public support.

RED STATES VERSUS BLUE STATES

In recent decades, the country is becoming more polarized, with people separating into two groups: liberals and conservatives. This trend can also been seen on the state level. *Certain states are more liberal and thus always*

Democrats **How USA voted 2016** Republicans

The winning margin in thousands

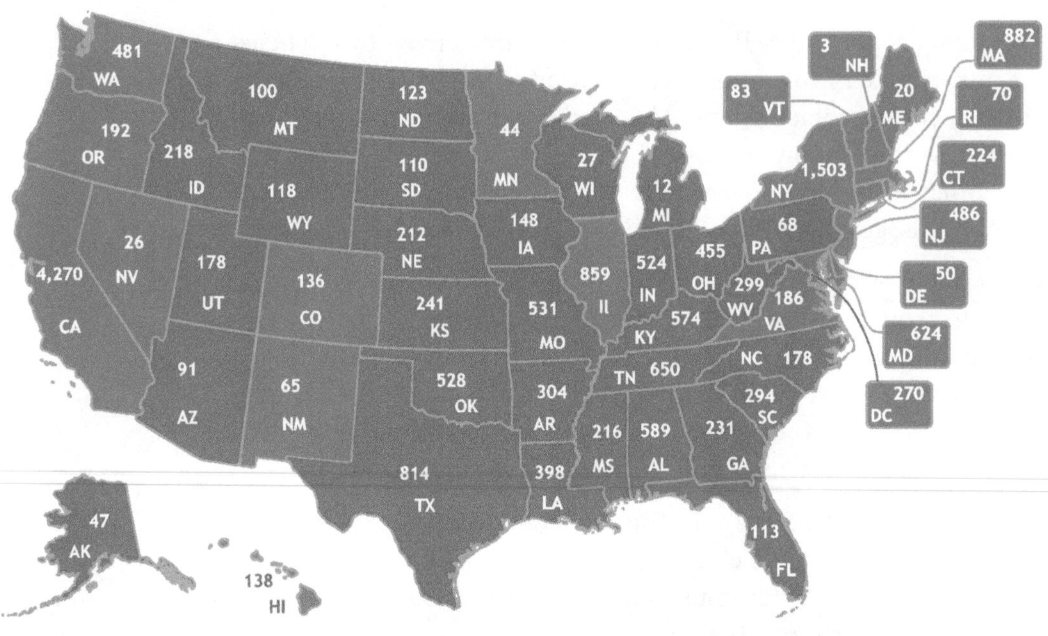

The blue states tend to have liberal public policies, and the red states tend to have conservative public policies.

vote for Democratic candidates. These are called the **blue states**. *And some states are more conservative and always vote for Republican candidates. These are called* **red states**. The blue states have liberal public policies, and the red states have conservative public policies.

Blue states

Certain states are more liberal and thus always vote for Democratic candidates.

According to a 2016 Gallup study, most states are red. Gallup ranks twelve states as "solidly red": Oklahoma, Tennessee, Alabama, South Carolina, Utah, Idaho, Montana, Wyoming, North Dakota, South Dakota, Kansas, and Alaska. And eight states as "leaning red": Texas, Nebraska, Missouri, Arkansas, Indiana, Mississippi, West Virginia, and New Hampshire.

Red states

Some states are more conservative and always vote for Republican candidates.

And Gallup ranks the "solid blue" states as California, New York, Delaware, Maryland, New Jersey, Massachusetts, Rhode Island, Connecticut, New Jersey, Illinois, New Mexico, and Vermont.

Besides political ideology, there are many geographic and socioeconomic differences between the blue and red states. Blue states tend to have large urban centers, less churches, more single people, and are located in the northeast, around the Great Lakes, and on the West Coast. Red states tend to have more rural areas, more married people, more churches, and are located in the South and the Midwest.

Blue State Public Policy: Obviously, since blue states are more liberal than red states, they are going to have more liberal public policies than red states. Most blue states have higher taxes, stricter gun control laws, fewer abortion restrictions, easier access to welfare programs, more business and environmental regulations, looser drug laws, more sanctuary cities (cities that ignore federal immigration laws), more speech codes, more laws protecting unions, less school choice, and no death penalty.

Red State Public Policy: And red states are going to have more conservative policies: lower taxes, more gun rights, fewer business and environmental regulations, stricter drug laws, fewer sanctuary cities, more free speech, more school choice, harder access to welfare, stricter abortion laws, and the death penalty.

Blue and Red State Ranking: Several groups and political scientists keep track of the laws passed by all fifty states and rank them in terms of how liberal or conservative they are. For example, Virginia Gray evaluates all fifty states based on five public policies: gun control laws, abortion

One way to evaluate how liberal or conservative a state is, is to look at the state's gun control laws. Compared to states like Louisiana and Wyoming, Texas actually has moderate gun control laws.

laws, conditions for receiving welfare, taxes, and union laws. Gray determined that the top five most liberal states were California, New York, New Jersey, Vermont, and Connecticut. And the five most conservatives states were Arkansas, Louisiana, Texas, Mississippi, and Florida.

The Cato Institute, a libertarian think tank, ranks the states by how much personal and economic freedom they allow. Cato reviews hundreds of laws of each state, including taxes, land use, labor-market freedoms, lawsuit freedom, incarcerations, free speech, gun control, and gambling. Every year they publish "Freedom of 50 States" on their website (www.freedominthe50states.org/).

In 2016, Cato determined that the states with the least amount of freedom were New York, California, Hawaii, New Jersey, Maryland, Connecticut, Illinois, Rhode Island, and Maine. These are all blue/Democratic states. And the states with the most freedom are New Hampshire, Alaska, Oklahoma, Indiana, South Dakota, Tennessee, Idaho, and Florida. All of these are red/Republican states, except for Florida, which is a swing state. By the way, the Cato Institute ranks Texas twenty-eighth on the freedom index.

INTEREST GROUPS AND PUBLIC POLICY

Interest Groups

Groups of people that get together to form organizations in order to change public policy.

Lobbyist

Somebody who tries to influence public policy on behalf of an interest group.

The activities of interest groups can be divided into two types: electioneering and public policy strategy. In Chapter 16, Political Campaigns, we discussed how interest groups develop an election strategy in order to elect people to office that support their goals. In this section we will discuss how interest groups try to influence the public policy, especially during non-election cycles.

What Are Interest Groups? As you recall from Chapter 16, **interest groups** *are groups of people that get together to change public policy.* They include such groups as the Sierra Club (an environmentalist interest group), The NEA (a teacher's union), The Baptist General Convention of Texas (a religious interest group), the NAACP (an African American interest group), the Texas Restaurant Association (a business interest group), and the Texas Farm Bureau (an agriculture interest group).

In a pluralistic society, all these groups, which represent different ideological and economic interests of people across Texas and America, compete with each other to get their agenda turned into law. Interest groups do this by trying to get lawmakers to implement public policies that they favor, or, conversely, they try to block public policies that they oppose.

Lobbyists: The main way interest groups try to influence public policy is by hiring lobbyists. A **lobbyist** *is somebody who tries to influence public* *policy on behalf of an interest group.* Most often, lobbyists are lawyers or former lawmakers or former staffers. Lawmakers have a special advantage because they have formed a network of friends in the legislature and they know the law-making process. A lobbyist can work for one interest group or several. Sometimes a lobbyist firm will represent dozens of interest groups. In Texas, lobbyists are most active during odd-numbered years when the legislature is in session. Successful lobbyists are paid a handsome salary.

What Do Lobbyists Do? Lobbyists employ several strategies to try to influence lawmakers. In the old days they would wait in the lobby of a capitol building, hoping to see a lawmaker and talk with them—hence the name lobbyist. Today they still sometimes wait in the halls of government buildings and try to accost a lawmaker when they walk by. This is known as "buttonholing."

Whatever method a lobbyist uses to meet a lawmaker or an important government bureaucrat (usually they arrange a meeting), the main thing a lobbyist does is impart information. Lobbyists will *present written information* to a lobbyist about the issue the interest group is concerned with. For a lobbyist to gain the trust of a lawmaker, the information must be accurate and well researched. Lawmakers will rely on the information provided by lobbyist to craft legislation and make public arguments. Or

There are many ways interest groups try to influence public policy, including direct lobbying, media campaigns, and public demonstrations.

sometimes the lobbyist will actually draft a bill or parts of a bill for the lawmaker.

Besides directly providing information to lawmakers, lobbyists engage in several other activities in order to influence public officials. They will testify at committee hearings, talk with lawmakers over the phone, meet with lawmakers at conventions and banquets, inform lawmakers of what bills are working their way through the legislature, and try to convince lawmakers to submit a bill or vote for a bill that the interest group favors. All these activities are called **direct lobbying**: *when a lobbyist contacts a public policy official and provides verbal or written information in order to influence public policy decisions.*

Direct lobbying

When a lobbyist contacts a public policy official and provides verbal or written information in order to influence public policy decisions.

Other Ways Interest Groups Try to Influence Public Policy: In addition to directly providing information to policy makers, lobbyists will also engage in **indirect lobbying**: *they will try to influence public opinion in order to influence public policy.* If an interest group can get the public behind their cause, then this may put pressure on the lawmakers. So lobbyists will launch *media campaigns* and pay for advertisements on TV, radio, magazines, and the Internet, including social media. Interest groups will also *educate the public* about their particular issue. For example, in the 1980s Mothers Against Drunk Driving (MADD) was very successful at

Indirect lobbying

When interest groups try to influence public opinion in order to influence public policy.

Black Lives Matter uses public demonstrations to try to influence public policy with regards to police arrest guidelines and other matters.

educating the public about the dangers of driving while drunk. This led to many states adopting stricter DUI laws.

Besides public relations, interest groups will engage in other things to engage the public. They may call for protests and *public demonstrations.* Black Lives Matters (which has received $100 million from another type of interest group, the Ford Foundation), organizes public demonstrations against police brutality. Interest groups will also work to *grow membership*. The larger the group, the more money and influence they will have. One of the largest, and thus most effective, interest groups in the United States is the American Association of Retired Persons (AARP). And lastly, another way interest groups influence public policy is by *initiating lawsuits*. Over the last few years, gay groups were very effective at getting gay marriage approved on the state and national level.

These are the many ways interest groups try to influence public policy. In our pluralistic society, the tens of thousands of economic, ideological, and social interest groups compete with each other to influence public policy.

NOTES

Jeffrey M. Jones. *Red States Outnumber Blue for First Time in Gallup Tracking*, Gallup, Feb 3, 2016.

Ellen Wexler. "Why is Tuition so High?," *Inside Higher Ed*, Feb 9, 2016.

Cato Institute, "Freedom of 50 States": www.freedominthe50states.org/

These two websites provide information about interest groups: The National Institute on Money in Politics: https://www.followthemoney.org/ & The Center for Responsive Politics: http://www.opensecrets.org/influence/

ESSAY QUESTIONS

1. Describe the steps in the Public Policy Model cycle.
2. List the common flaws public policy officials often make when trying to craft good laws.
3. Describe some of the direct and indirect methods interest groups use to try to influence public policy.

TERMS

Agenda setting: ______________________________

Blue states: ______________________________

Direct lobbying: ______________________________

Indirect lobbying: ______________________________

Interest groups: ______________________________

Law of unintended consequences: ______________________________

Lobbyist: ______________________________

Policy implementation: ______________________________

Public policy: ______________________________

Red states: ______________________________

GLOSSARY

A

Acting governor: The person, usually the Lieutenant Governor, who officially and legally functions as Governor of Texas when the elected governor is travelling out of the state.

Adelsverein Society: An organization that tried to establish a Germany colony in Texas in the mid-1800s.

Agenda setting: The process by which government decides that a problem exists and that it needs an imminent solution.

Amendment Procedure: For an amendment to be added to the Texas Constitution, a proposal must pass both houses of the legislature by a two-thirds vote and be ratified by a majority of the voters in a general or special election.

Anti-Saloon League: A semi-third party/interest group that was successful at turning most counties in Texas dry and supporting Prohibition in 1919.

Appellate Courts: Higher courts consisting of a panel of judges that hear appeals on questions of law from lower courts.

At-large election: In this type of city election, all voters in the city elect the members of the city council.

Attorney General: The chief lawyer for Texas who is constitutionally required to defend the laws and Constitution of Texas, to represent the state in litigation, and to provide legal advice to state officials.

Australian ballot: People vote in private and the government prints the ballot which contained the names of all candidates from both parties.

B

Balanced budget: Lawmakers are forbidden from spending more money than is brought in by tax revenue.

Benefit-based taxes: Taxes on a government service by the people who use that service.

Biannual session: The legislature meets every other year.

Bicameral legislature: A legislature divided into two chambers, the Senate and the House.

Black codes: Laws that denied blacks the right to vote, serve on juries, marry a white person, make their own labor decisions, and many other ordinances that treated Black Americans as second-class citizens.

Block grants: Federal money that is transferred to the states with no strings attached to be used for general purpose.

Blue states: Certain states are more liberal and thus always vote for Democratic candidates.

Boll Weevil Democrats: Conservative southern Democrats who sometimes voted for Republicans.

George W. Bush: The third President of the United States from Texas. He is the son of President H. W. Bush

C

Caddo Indians: The most civilized Texas tribe, which lived in the Piney Woods of East Texas.

Capitalism: The economic system based on competition, property rights, and free commerce without undue government interference. Capitalism fosters progress because it rewards hard work and innovation.

Campaign: Political activity before an election, marked by organized action to influence voters and win an election.

Campaign manager: The person who oversees the campaign staff and heads the campaign.

Candidate appeal: A positive feeling a voter has about a candidate's personality, physical appearance, family, intellect, humor, and way of speaking.

Carpetbagger: A derogatory term for northerners who came to the South during Reconstruction to get jobs.

Categorical grants: Federal monetary grants to the states for specific purposes, which comes with federal rules and regulations.

Central Corridor: This region goes from College Station in the East, to San Antonio in the South, and to Waco in the North, with Austin in the center. This is the governmental and educational core of Texas.

Charter: A document, like a constitution, that defines the governmental structure and rules by which the city operates.

Checks and balances: In order to limit government power and to prevent one branch from becoming too powerful, the Framers created three branches of government, giving each branch some power over the other branches.

Chief of state: The governor is the symbolic leader of Texas and acts as the official representative of the state of Texas.

Citizen lawmaker: An amateur who is not a full-time, professional legislator.

City manager: In a council-manager form of government, the city manager, sometimes called a city administrator, is the head of the city's administration and prepares the budget, appoints and removes agency heads, and manages the daily operations of the city.

Civil law: A system of law concerned with private relations between two individuals.

Classical liberalism: The belief in God-given rights, limited government, the rule of law, and free markets.

Clemency powers: The Governor of Texas has the authority to grant pardons, executive clemency, and parole.

Closed primary: A primary election in which only party members can vote to nominate a candidate for the general election.

Commissioner's Court: The governing body for counties in Texas, it is composed of an elected county judge (at-large) and four elected commissioners (by district).

Competitive federalism: The ideas that states compete with each other to attract businesses and people to their states by offering incentives.

Comptroller: The chief tax collector, accountant, revenue estimator, treasurer, and steward of the state's finances.

Conference committee: A legislative committee consisting of members of the Senate and House that reconcile bills from each chamber.

Constitution: The basic document that provides the structure, powers, and limits of government.

Consumer taxes: Taxes consumers pay when they purchase goods and services.

Cooperative Federalism: The national government and the state governments cooperate and work together to serve the public.

Council–manager Form of Government: A type of city government that consists of an elected city council that makes policy and hires a professional city manager to administer the daily operations of the city.

County judge: This county official serves as the chair of the commissioner's court, analogous to the mayor in a city government.

Court of Criminal Appeals: The final appellate court in all criminal cases in Texas.

Criminal law: A system of law concerned with punishment of those who commit crimes.

Crony capitalism: A system in which business success is enhanced by connections to government officials, knowledge of legal loopholes and tax breaks, and by government favoritism.

D

Decentralized: In decentralized government, power is transferred from a central government to independent agencies and commissions and local bodies.

Delegate role: The idea that a lawmaker should represent the constituents in his or her district and vote in accordance to their views and wishes, even if the lawmaker holds contrary views.

Direct lobbying: When a lobbyist contacts a public policy official and provides verbal or written information in order to influence public policy decisions.

Dual federalism: The national government operated only on its limited enumerated powers while the states retained their sovereign powers, and the two layers of government had separate functions and responsibilities.

E

E Pluribus Unum: This motto of America is Latin for "from many one." It means that individuals of all sorts of backgrounds and ethnicities and religions come together to form one American nation.

Early voting: People can vote between seventeen and four days before the election.

East Texas: Also known as the Piney Woods, a region marked by its thick pine and oak forests, receiving the most rain than any other region of Texas. It can trace its historical roots to the Old South.

Elite theory: The idea that a small group of wealthy and highly educated elites corrupt the political process for their own benefit at the expense of the general public.

Eminent domain: The power of the government to expropriate private property for public purposes, such as to build highways or schools, with fair monetary compensation to the land owner.

Empresario: An agent hired by Spain and then Mexico to recruit and develop a colony in Texas.

Ex officio: Automatically assigned to a board because they hold a particular office.

Excise taxes: Taxes on a particular good, such as gasoline, tobacco, and liquor.

Executive branch: The primary power of the executive branch is to implement and enforce the law written by the legislature.

Extra legislative powers: As part of their office, the Speaker and the Lieutenant Governor are automatically assigned to certain boards outside of the legislature.

F

Federal system: Power and responsibility is divided between the national government and the state governments.

James Ferguson: He was the twenty-sixth Governor of Texas (1915-1917), and served two non-consecutive terms as first gentleman of Texas.

Miriam Ferguson: The first woman Governor of Texas and wife of James Ferguson, the impeached Governor of Texas.

Fiscal policy: The government's policies about taxing and spending, as reflected in the budget.

Filibuster: A long speech made by a Senator as a delay tactic in order to prevent a vote on a bill.

G

James Nance Garner: He was the Speaker of the House of Representatives and the first Vice President of the United States from Texas (1933–1941).

General Law Cities: Cities with fewer than 5,000 citizens that are governed by city charters created by state legislature.

General welfare: Governments provide for the common good of the people.

Gerrymandered district: A legislative district drawn to give one party an advantage, especially if it has an unusual shape.

Grand jury: A body of citizens that decides if the state has enough evidence to proceed to a trial.

Great Society: A federal government program started by Lyndon Johnson, which expanded the welfare state by offering dozens of programs including food stamps, public housing, Head Start, Medicare, and Medicaid.

Greenback Party: In the 1870s, this party represented the small farmer and promoted paper currency in an attempt to inflate farm prices.

H

Habeas corpus: A person cannot be imprisoned without being told what the charges are and must have a trial in a reasonable period of time.

James Stephen Hogg: An East Texas lawyer, Hogg became the twentieth Governor of Texas running as a Populist Democrat.

Home Rule Cities: Cities with over 5,000 citizens that were created by action of local citizens.

Homestead protection: Legal protections that guard somebody from being forced to sell their primary residence in order to pay a debt.

Sam Houston: The hero of the Battle of San Jacinto, he was elected the first and third president of the Republic of Texas. In 1859, he became the seventh Governor of Texas.

Kay Bailey Hutchison: Elected the first woman US Senator representing Texas.

I

Impeachment process: For the Governor of Texas to be impeached, a majority of the members of the House must vote for the articles of impeachment, and two-thirds of the members of the Senate must vote for the governor to be removed from office.

Implied powers: Under the Necessary and Proper Clause of the Constitution, the national government has certain unspecified powers.

Inalienable rights: God-given, inherent rights that were not granted by government, so government cannot take them away.

Income-elastic taxes: When tax revenue fluctuates widely due to economic conditions.

Incumbent: Somebody who is currently holding office.

Independent School District: A unit of local government that provides K–12 education to its residents and that is independent from other local governments.

Indirect lobbying: When interest groups try to influence public opinion in order to influence public policy.

Individualism: The view that government should interfere as little as possible with the private lives of individuals while protecting private property and providing a favorable climate for business.

Interest groups: Groups of people that get together to form organizations in order to change public policy.

Interim committee: A legislative committee that meets when the legislature is out of session to prepare bills, study issues, and conduct business in preparation for the next session.

J

Jacksonian democracy: A political ideology that supported greater voting rights for all white males, trust in the common man, strict adherence to the Constitution, and free markets with no government supported tariffs and monopolies. It promoted national strength, while maintaining state's rights.

Lyndon B. Johnson: Growing up in a small town in central Texas, Johnson rose to become the Majority Leader of the US Senate, Vice President, and President of the United States (1963–1969).

Judicial branch: The primary power of the judicial branch is to interpret the law.

Judicial impeachment: Judges of the supreme court, court of appeals, and district courts can be removed by the governor with a two-thirds vote in each chamber of the legislature.

Judicial review: The power of the Supreme Court to interpret the Constitution and declare a congressional law, a state law, or an executive order null and void if it violates the Constitution.

Juneteenth: A holiday celebrating the abolition of slavery in Texas held on June 19.

K

King Cotton: The era before the Civil War when cotton was the number one crash crop for export. Cotton plantations dominated the Texan economy and formed the epicenter of social and political power.

Ku Klux Klan: During Reconstruction, this white supremacist group used violence to intimidate blacks from voting and participating in politics.

L

Land Commissioner: This official is responsible for the administration and oversight of the state-owned lands of Texas, as well as the management of the Permanent School fund.

Law of unintended consequences: Often lawmakers will pass a law to address one issue and then years later realize that they created other, unintended, problems.

Legislative Budget Board (LBB): A ten-member state agency that is headed by the Speaker and the Lieutenant Governor that writes the budget.

Legislative power: The primary power of the legislature is to make law.

Liberty: An inalienable right central to human existence that allows a person to pursue their own happiness as long as they do not hurt other people.

Lieutenant Governor: The presiding officer of the Texas state Senate who is elected to office by statewide elections.

Limited government: The idea that through such mechanisms as written powers and checks and balances government must be limited in order to protect the liberty of the people.

Line-item veto: The ability of a governor to veto specific provisions of an appropriations bill without vetoing the whole bill.

Lobbyist: Somebody who tries to influence public policy on behalf of an interest group.

M

Majority-minority: When all minority groups combined represent the majority of the state's population, while the white population is in the minority.

Margin tax: A 1 percent tax on corporations and large partnerships.

Media: (plural for medium) refers to all the forms of mass communication, such as television, radio, newspapers, Internet, billboards, and mailings.

Merit system (or Missouri system): The governor chooses a judge from a list compiled by a panel of legal experts. The judge serves a short term, after which the people vote on whether that judge should continue in office.

Metroplex: This region stretches from Dallas to Fort Worth and includes Arlington. Traditionally it has been the banking and commercial center of Texas.

Missions: Outposts in the territory of Texas established by the Spanish Catholic Church to convert Native Indians, but that also served as agricultural, industrial, social, governmental, and religious centers.

Modern liberalism: The belief in the need for a larger central government to ensure greater social justice and equality.

N

Negative ads: Campaign commercials that attack the opponent's character, record, or bring up some sort of scandal or misstep.

Non-partisan elections: In this type of city election, there are no party affiliations (Democrat or Republican) printed on the ballot next to the candidate's name.

O

Open primary: An election by people with any party affiliation to nominate a candidate for the general election.

P

Partisan: One who is devoted to a political party and wants that party to be successful.

Party raiding: When a primary voter crosses over to another party in order to vote for the weaker candidate of the opposition party.

Party realignment: When the majority of the electorate switches over and supports another political party.

Rick Perry: The forty-seventh Governor of Texas, he served from 2000 to 2015, the longest serving governor in Texas history.

Petit jury: A jury of twelve peers that hears criminal or civil cases.

Plural executive: An executive branch in which many powerful state officials are elected by the people and are independent from the governor.

Pluralistic theory: When many interest groups representing a wide variety of economic and ideological interests compete with each other in the political process, power is not concentrated in one group.

Police powers: The traditional powers of the state, which include criminal law, laws effecting public health and safety, and laws regulating public morality.

Policy implementation: The process of actually carrying out the reform.

Political Action Committee (PAC): An organization formed by an interest group to raise and contribute money to a candidate's campaign.

Political culture: The political values, habits, and beliefs of a people, including what they believe is the proper role and scope of government.

Political participation: Engaging in the political process.

Political parties: Organizations consisting of many coalitions that elect officials to government in order to carry out their agenda.

Political platform: A document stating the set of principles of a political party.

Poll tax: An annual fee to register to vote.

Popular sovereignty: The people are the ultimate rulers and the government serves the people.

Populist Movement (1880s to 1896): A political revolt by the farmers against the ruling class, business interests, and intellectual elite.

Populist politician: Often possessing a colorful personality and the ability to communicate with everyday folks, this type of politician runs as a representative of the common man in a fight against the economic and culture elite.

Positive ads: Campaign commercials that depict the candidate in a positive light, highlighting the candidate's ideas and accomplishments while making no reference to the opponent.

Precinct chair: The lowest level party official who organizes and supports the party at the precinct level.

Presidios: Spanish walled fortresses with soldiers in the territory of Texas that were responsible for defending a particular area, including the local missions.

Primary: The voters choose the candidates from each party that they wish to run in the general election.

Progressive Movement (1900–1920): A political movement that sought to use government as a tool to guide the enlightened progress of society, help the common man, and fight business and political corruption.

Progressive taxes: Taxes in which wealthy people pay a higher percentage of their income.

Public policy: All the laws, regulations, funding, and priorities of government.

Q

Qualified veto: The governor can veto any bill passed by legislature, but it can be overridden by a two-thirds vote of both chambers.

R

Railroad Commission: It no longer regulates the railroad industry but instead regulates Texas's vast oil and natural gas industries, making it one of the most powerful state agencies in the nation.

Sam Rayburn: A highly respected member of Congress, he would serve in Congress for forty-nine years, holding the speakership three times: 1911, 1947–49, and 1953–55.

John H. Reagan: He was a postmaster general of the Confederacy, a member of the US House of Representatives, and the first Railroad Commissioner.

Red states: Some states are more conservative and always vote for Republican candidates.

Redistricting: The process of redrawing the boundaries of legislative districts.

Regressive taxes: Taxes in which poor people pay a higher percentage of their income in taxes.

Removal powers: The ability of the governor to fire or remove somebody from office.

Republic: The people vote for representatives to make laws for the common good, not to benefit a privileged class or faction.

Republic of Texas: Texas was an independent nation from 1836–1845.

Ann Richards: The first genuine female Governor of Texas.

Riders: Provisions added to bills, sometimes to bring money to the lawmaker's district, which often have nothing to do with the subject matter of the bill they are attached to.

Runoff election: If no candidate wins a majority of the vote in the primary, then the top two candidates must compete in this election. The winner will run in the general election.

S

Safe seat: A legislative district in which a candidate from either party wins 55 percent or more of the votes.

Scalawag: A derogatory term used during Reconstruction to describe southern Republicans.

Secretary of State: This official oversees Texas state elections and keeps state records.

Separation of powers: The government is divided into three branches: executive, legislative, and judicial.

Seventeenth Amendment: Ratified in 1913, this amendment allows the voters of the state to select the state's two US Senators, rather than the state legislatures as stipulated in the original Constitution.

Allen Shivers. The first man to win three terms as Governor of Texas, in the 1950s Shivers led the conservative wing of the Texas Democrat Party.

Sine die: The Texas legislature has no power to extend its session beyond 140 days.

Single-member district election: In this type of city election, a city is divided into districts, and only the residents of a district can vote for a city council member to represent that district.

Social capital: The sense of shared purpose and values that social connections promote.

Social Conservatism: The belief held by some conservatives that focus on their Christian identity and support conventional families, the right to practice religion in public, and traditional values.

Speaker of the House: The presiding officer of the Texas House who controls the legislative agenda of the chamber.

Special districts: A unit of local government that provides a particular service to residents, such as fire protection, transportation, sewage, or water.

Special session: After the normal session ends, the governor can call a special session of the legislature, lasting thirty days, to complete unfinished business or deal with a special problem.

Spoil system: Government employees are hired and fired after an election based on which political party or candidate they supported.

Standing committees: Permanent legislative committees that convene every session and make most of the legislation.

State of the State Address: At the beginning of each legislative session, the Governor of Texas speaks to both chambers of the legislature, describing the condition of Texas and providing the Governor's plan for the coming year.

State party chair: The head of the state executive committee and the leader of the party for the state.

State sovereignty: In a decentralized federal system, the power of the national government is limited and the states have independent power to take care of many of its own affairs.

Straight party ticket: Voting for Democrats or Republicans for all offices listed on the ballot.

Stump speech: A standard speech used by candidates running for office that is used over and over again with minor alterations depending on who they are speaking to.

Sunset Advisory Commission: A ten-member agency that reviews the purpose and efficiency of each state agency every twelve years and makes recommendations to the legislature concerning whether an agency should be abolished or reformed.

Super PACs: These groups can raise unlimited funds to support a candidate as long as they report their contributions to the FEC and make commercials without coordinating with a campaign.

T

Tax shifting: When businesses pass the tax on to other people.

Tejanos: People of Spanish or Mexican ancestry living in Texas.

Tenth Amendment: It states that "The powers not delegated to the United States by the Constitution, nor prohibited by it to the states, are reserved to the states respectively, or to the people."

Tenure of office of the governor: The Texas governor serves a four-year term with no term limits.

Term limits: Limitations on the number of years a government official can remain in a particular office.

Texas House of Representatives: This chamber of the Texas legislature consists of 150 members who serve two-year terms.

Texas Railroad Commission (RRC): A state agency that regulates the Texas oil and gas industry

Texas Senate: This chamber of the Texas legislature consists of thirty-one members who serve four-year terms.

Texas Supreme Court: The final appellate court in all civil and juvenile cases in Texas.

Ticket splitting: When voters decide to vote for candidates from one party for some offices and candidates from another party for other offices.

Tidelands controversy: After oil was discovered in the Gulf of Mexico in the 1950s, Texas and the US government fought over the extent of Texas's jurisdictional boundary. Texas claimed three leagues from shore (ten miles), but the federal government said Texas can only claim three miles.

Traditionalism: The idea that government should maintain the existing social and political order and should be run by the ruling elites.

Trial courts: Courts that hear cases and juries determine the outcome of the trial.

Trustee model: The idea that a lawmaker represents Texas and uses his or her judgment and experience to do what is best for the long-term interests of the whole state.

Turnout: The percentage of eligible voters that actually cast a ballot.

Turnover: A measure of new membership in a legislative session.

U

Unitary system: All functions and power are controlled by one central government.

W

Welfare state: A government system designed to promote the welfare of the people by enacting laws to alleviate poverty and providing such things as food stamps, healthcare, education, and housing.

Wet: A supporter of the legalization of alcohol.

White primary: The Texas Democratic Party denied Black Americans the right to vote in their primary.

Y

Yellow Dog Democrats: Southern Democrats who remained loyal to the Democrat Party by never voting for Republicans.